Ethical Challenges of AI and Warfare

Pavan Thealla
University of Sunderland in London, UK

Latif Oztosun
https://orcid.org/0000-0003-0475-120X
University of Sunderland in London, UK

Vipin Nadda
https://orcid.org/0009-0002-1041-2941
University of Sunderland in London, UK

IGI Global
Scientific Publishing
Publishing Tomorrow's Research Today

Vice President of Editorial — Melissa Wagner
Director of Acquisitions — Mikaela Felty
Director of Book Development — Jocelynn Hessler
Production Manager — Mike Brehm
Cover Design — Jose Rosado

Published in the United States of America by
IGI Global Scientific Publishing
701 East Chocolate Avenue
Hershey, PA, 17033, USA
Tel: 717-533-8845 | Fax: 717-533-7115
Website: https://www.igi-global.com E-mail: cust@igi-global.com

Library of Congress Cataloging-in-Publication Data

Names: Thealla, Pavan, 1975- editor | Oztosun, Latif, 1989- editor | Nadda, Vipin, DATE- editor
Title: Ethical challenges of AI and warfare / edited by Pavan Thealla, Latif Oztosun, Vipin Nadda.
Description: Hershey, PA : IGI Global Scientific Publishing, 2026. | Includes bibliographical references and index. | Summary: "This book aims to address current ethical dimensions of AI in warfare, focusing on the deployment of autonomous weapons systems, drones, and AI-enhanced cyber capabilities"-- Provided by publisher.
Identifiers: LCCN 2025022200 (print) | LCCN 2025022201 (ebook) | ISBN 9798337336114 hardcover | ISBN 9798337336121 paperback | ISBN 9798337336138 ebook
Subjects: LCSH: Artificial intelligence--Military applications--Moral and ethical aspects
Classification: LCC UG479 .E84 2026 (print) | LCC UG479 (ebook)
LC record available at https://lccn.loc.gov/2025022200
LC ebook record available at https://lccn.loc.gov/2025022201

British Cataloguing in Publication Data
A Cataloguing in Publication record for this book is available from the British Library.

Table of Contents

Detailed Table of Contents

The application of artificial intelligence benefits both offensive and defensive operations by implementing new tactics in cyber warfare. The black hat hackers employ AI to trick users, create deep fakes, and automate tasks. The white hat hackers, however, employ machine learning to detect anomalies, react to intrusions, and predict potential issues. Challenges are encountered in cases where AI systems are in competition since it is difficult to monitor weapon use and demands human oversight. As threats to cyberspace keep increasing, the application of AI is necessary to ensure online safety.

The function of logistics and strategic planning has expanded beyond traditional supply lines as contemporary warfare becomes more complicated. AI is changing military operations by facilitating autonomous logistics systems, real-time data processing, and quicker decision-making. This change is altering how military strategy is developed and implemented, going beyond efficiency improvements. AI provides a level of adaptability never before achievable, from autonomous transport systems and coordinated battlefield support to predictive maintenance of combat vehicles. An intelligent and robust logistics ecosystem is being fostered by the integration of technologies such as swarm robotics, satellite-based monitoring, and quantum-enhanced optimization. But this change also presents operational, ethical, and policy issues. This chapter addresses the hazards of reliance and misalignment while examining the complex effects of AI on military logistics and strategy.

This chapter critically examines the transformative role of artificial intelligence in modern surveillance systems, focusing on the delicate balance between enhancing security and protecting individual rights. It explores how technologies such as facial recognition, behavioral analytics, and predictive policing contribute to crime prevention, national security, and urban management, while also highlighting risks of privacy erosion, algorithmic bias, and democratic suppression. Ethical, legal, and regulatory dimensions are analyzed, emphasizing transparency, accountability, and rights-based governance. The chapter concludes by advocating for responsible, balanced approaches that align AI surveillance with democratic values, ensuring security is pursued without compromising civil liberties.

This chapter explores the evolving landscape of cyber warfare in the age of Artificial Intelligence (AI), examining how AI technologies are both weaponizing and defending digital domains. As AI enables advanced cyber-attacks through automated intrusion, data manipulation, and adaptive malware, it simultaneously empowers robust defense mechanisms including threat detection, real-time response, and predictive analytics. The chapter delves into emerging threats posed by AI-driven cyber operations, the strategic applications of AI in national and global cybersecurity frameworks, and the escalating arms race in cyber capabilities. It also critically analyzes the ethical dilemmas of autonomous cyber weapons, accountability in AI decision-making, and the need for international norms and governance. Through case studies and expert insights, this chapter highlights the dual-use nature of AI in cyberspace, emphasizing the urgent need for balanced strategies that safeguard security while upholding human rights and ethical integrity.

This chapter addresses the effects of ethical leadership to the regulation of artificial intelligence (AI) on cyber-security and the mediating role of Organizational Citizenship Behavior (OCB) as a part of the collaborative governance context in Ethiopia. The results could indicate a significant impact of ethical leadership on the effective control of AI in the field of cyber-security; OCB may also play a mediating role. This implies that leaders with ethics embedded in them facilitate citizenship culture amongst employees, hence creating harmonious relationship in collaborative governance. The shortcomings of these findings are broken down into the discussion of Ethiopia and its changing cyber-security system, whereby ethical leadership is important in the formulation of regulatory policies that maximize AI technologies. The chapter ends with the recommendations that policymakers and leaders in organizations may implement to ensure the facilitation of ethical governance behaviors that may stimulate OCB, which would eventually result in better AI regulation in the cyber-security.

This chapter discusses the emerging nexus of artificial intelligence (AI), military ethics, and security in the future in a prospective model. As AI technologies are taking more independent roles in surveillance, targeting, cyber indicators, and decision-making, it is assailing core concepts of international humanitarian law and the just war theory. In the chapter, new capabilities including autonomous weapons, predictive targeting, and AI-enabled cyberwarfare are critically analyzed, presenting challenges to ideas of accountability, proportionality, and human control in a meaningful and ethical way. It also questions structural imbalances in world AI governance, which exclude Global South views and the concentration of technology in the hands of a few countries and corporations. These ethical and geopolitical dilemmas are answered by the chapter suggesting a normative framework of anticipatory governance that is built on the pivot of responsibility, transparency, inclusivity, precaution, and human dignity.

The conflict between state surveillance and the fundamental right of privacy is apparent even at the conceptual level. The rise of advanced surveillance mechanisms has been another abetting factor to this conflict while on the other hand many theorists have been at work to find a harmonisation between them. Surveillance techniques and mechanisms have indeed been helpful in thwarting the threats to national security and keeping the integrity of a nation. The chapter analyses whether the collective good that upholds state surveillance tends to override the individual interest that advocates the right to privacy. It considers the criteria or procedures followed to arrive at such a decision and whether the authorities could have been advised to find a better solution through harmonization rather than neglecting one in favour of the other. It explores the morality behind surveillance, including the panopticon model by Bentham, which was an example of promoting moral behaviour through surveillance.

This chapter explains the ethical issues that come with using machines to make decisions during war and conflict. Today, machines are used for tasks like finding threats, choosing targets, and sending aid. These were once done by people. While machines work fast and do not get tired, they cannot feel emotions or understand what is right or wrong. This creates serious problems when machines decide who gets help or who might be harmed. If something goes wrong, it is hard to know who is to blame. The chapter also discusses how unfair data can lead machines to treat some groups badly. Legal systems are not fully ready to deal with these problems. To keep people safe, we need clear rules, careful use, and teamwork between countries.

Preface

The accelerating integration of artificial intelligence into military operations and cybersecurity practices represents one of the most consequential transformations in contemporary global security. *Ethical Challenges of AI and Warfare* emerges from a shared concern among the Editors that technological innovation in this domain is advancing far more rapidly than the ethical, legal, and political frameworks required to govern it responsibly. This edited reference volume is conceived as a critical, interdisciplinary intervention into ongoing debates about how AI is reshaping warfare, security, and moral responsibility at both national and global levels.

As AI systems become embedded in the conduct of armed conflict and digital defense, long-standing assumptions about human judgment, accountability, and control are increasingly strained. Autonomous weapons systems, unmanned aerial vehicles, and AI-enhanced decision-support tools promise operational efficiency and strategic advantage, yet they simultaneously raise profound ethical questions—particularly when lethal force may be deployed with limited or indirect human oversight. Issues of proportionality, discrimination between combatants and civilians, and the risk of unintended escalation demand renewed scrutiny in light of these technologies. This volume engages critically with these challenges, situating them within existing international humanitarian law while questioning whether current legal and ethical regimes remain adequate in the age of machine-enabled warfare.

Beyond the kinetic battlefield, the ethical implications of AI are equally acute in the realm of cybersecurity. AI has transformed the scale, speed, and sophistication of cyber operations, affecting how states protect critical infrastructure, conduct surveillance, and engage in offensive cyber activities. The chapters collected here explore ethical tensions surrounding privacy, accountability, and state responsibility in an era of AI-driven cyber defense and cyber conflict. Particular attention is given to the evolving international norms and legal ambiguities that arise when autonomous or semi-autonomous systems play a central role in cyber decision-making.

The volume also addresses broader ethical concerns that cut across both military and cybersecurity contexts, including algorithmic bias, opacity, and regulatory insufficiency. AI systems trained on biased or incomplete data risk reinforcing existing inequalities and producing discriminatory outcomes, especially when deployed in high-stakes security environments. Contributors critically examine the social and ethical consequences of delegating consequential decisions to opaque algorithms, while highlighting the growing gap between rapid technological innovation and the slower development of regulatory and governance frameworks. Throughout the book, the need for international cooperation and shared ethical standards remains a central theme.

Ethical Challenges of AI and Warfare is intended as a comprehensive reference for scholars, policymakers, military strategists, legal experts, and cybersecurity professionals. By bringing together diverse disciplinary perspectives, this volume seeks not only to analyze how AI is transforming global security dynamics, but also to contribute to the development of robust ethical and legal frameworks capable of guiding the responsible use of AI in military, cyber, and socio-political contexts. As Editors, we hope this book will serve as both a critical resource and a catalyst for informed, ethically grounded dialogue on one of the defining challenges of our time.

ORGANIZATION OF THE BOOK

Chapter 1. AI-Powered Cyber Attacks and Automated Defense Systems

This chapter examines the escalating role of AI in cyber warfare, highlighting its dual-use nature in both offensive and defensive contexts. From automated phishing campaigns and deepfake manipulation to AI-driven intrusion detection and predictive defense, the chapter underscores how adversarial AI systems increasingly operate in direct competition with one another. The Editors emphasize the growing difficulty of attribution, oversight, and escalation control in such environments, particularly when autonomous systems interact at machine speed. The chapter reinforces the necessity of human-in-the-loop frameworks and ethical safeguards, positioning AI not as a replacement for human judgment but as a tool that must be carefully governed to preserve stability and security in cyberspace.

Chapter 2. AI-Powered Military Logistics and Strategy: A Paradigm Shift in Modern Warfare

Here, the volume turns to the less visible but strategically decisive domain of military logistics and planning. This chapter explores how AI-driven systems—ranging from autonomous supply chains and predictive maintenance to swarm robotics and satellite-based monitoring—are reshaping strategic decision-making and operational adaptability. The Editors present logistics not merely as an efficiency problem, but as a central pillar of modern warfare transformed by real-time data and algorithmic optimization. At the same time, the chapter critically interrogates the risks of over-reliance, system misalignment, and ethical ambiguity, highlighting the need for policy frameworks that ensure resilience, accountability, and strategic coherence in AI-enabled military ecosystems.

Chapter 3. Balancing Security and Privacy: AI in the Age of Surveillance

This chapter addresses one of the most contested ethical frontiers of AI: surveillance. It critically analyzes how facial recognition, behavioral analytics, and predictive policing are deployed to enhance security, manage urban spaces, and prevent crime, while simultaneously threatening privacy, civil liberties, and democratic participation. The Editors emphasize the structural risks of algorithmic bias, opaque decision-making, and normalization of mass surveillance. By engaging legal, ethical, and regulatory perspectives, the chapter argues for rights-based governance models that embed transparency, accountability, and proportionality into AI surveillance systems, ensuring that security imperatives do not eclipse fundamental freedoms.

Chapter 4. Cyber Warfare and the Role of Artificial Intelligence: Emerging Threats, Strategic Defense, and Ethical Challenges

Expanding on earlier discussions of cyber conflict, this chapter provides a comprehensive examination of AI's role in reshaping digital warfare. It explores how AI enables adaptive malware, automated intrusion, and data manipulation, while also strengthening defensive capabilities through real-time monitoring and predictive analytics. The Editors situate these developments within an intensifying global cyber arms race, raising urgent questions about accountability, autonomous cyber weapons, and international governance. Through strategic analysis and case-based insights, the chapter reinforces the ethical imperative to develop norms and safeguards that recognize AI's dual-use potential while protecting human rights and global stability.

Chapter 5. Ethical Leadership Effect on the Regulation of AI in Cyber-Security by Mediating of OCB by Collaborative Governance in Ethiopia

This chapter offers an important contextual and regional perspective by examining AI regulation in cybersecurity through the lens of ethical leadership and collaborative governance in Ethiopia. The Editors highlight the chapter's contribution in linking ethical leadership practices with Organizational Citizenship Behavior (OCB) as a mediating factor in effective AI governance. By grounding its analysis in an emerging cybersecurity landscape, the chapter demonstrates how values-driven leadership can foster trust, cooperation, and regulatory effectiveness. It concludes with policy-oriented recommendations that underscore the importance of ethical culture in shaping responsible AI governance, particularly within developing and transitional governance systems.

Chapter 6. Future Directions: AI, Ethics, and Global Security

Looking ahead, this chapter engages with the long-term ethical and geopolitical implications of AI in warfare and security. It critically examines emerging capabilities such as autonomous weapons, predictive targeting, and AI-enabled cyber operations, assessing their compatibility with international humanitarian law and just war theory. The Editors draw attention to global asymmetries in AI governance, including the marginalization of Global South perspectives and the concentration of technological power. In response, the chapter proposes an anticipatory governance framework grounded in responsibility, inclusivity, transparency, and human dignity, offering a forward-looking ethical roadmap for global AI security governance.

Chapter 7. Right to Privacy and State Surveillance: Legal and Ethical Challenges

This chapter deepens the ethical inquiry into surveillance by directly confronting the tension between state security and the right to privacy. Through philosophical, legal, and moral analysis, it interrogates whether collective security interests can legitimately override individual rights, and under what conditions. The Editors note the chapter's engagement with classical frameworks such as Bentham's panopticon, alongside contemporary surveillance practices, to question the moral foundations of state monitoring. Rather than endorsing a zero-sum logic, the chapter advocates for harmonization approaches that seek balance, proportionality, and legitimacy in surveillance governance.

Chapter 8. The Ethics of Automated Decision-Making in Conflict

Focusing on one of the most ethically sensitive dimensions of AI in warfare, this chapter examines the delegation of decision-making to machines in conflict settings. The Editors emphasize the profound moral risks associated with automated threat detection, targeting, and humanitarian decision-making, particularly given machines' inability to comprehend context, empathy, or moral reasoning. The chapter highlights challenges of accountability, biased data, and legal inadequacy, arguing forcefully that human judgment and responsibility must remain central. It reinforces a core theme of the volume: AI should augment, not replace, human ethical agency in situations involving life, harm, and care.

Chapter 9. Ethical Dilemmas of AI-Driven Warfare and Its Impact on Civilian Health and Medical Neutrality

The concluding chapter brings the ethical discussion into sharp humanitarian focus by examining the impact of AI-driven warfare on civilians, healthcare systems, and medical neutrality. Drawing on empirical data, case studies, and legal analysis, the chapter exposes the disproportionate toll of autonomous weapons and drone warfare on non-combatants and medical infrastructure. The Editors highlight its contribution in linking ethical theory with real-world consequences, including civilian casualty ratios and attacks on healthcare facilities. By addressing gaps in international humanitarian law and warning of an AI-driven arms race, the chapter underscores the urgent need for global governance mechanisms that protect civilians and uphold ethical norms in increasingly automated conflicts.

CONCLUSION

As the chapters in this volume collectively demonstrate, the integration of artificial intelligence into warfare, cybersecurity, and surveillance is not merely a technical evolution but a profound ethical, legal, and political transformation. AI is reshaping how threats are identified, decisions are made, and force is applied, often at speeds and scales that challenge human comprehension and existing governance structures. Across military operations, cyber conflict, logistics, surveillance, and humanitarian contexts, the contributions to this book reveal a consistent tension between technological capability and ethical responsibility.

From counterterrorism and autonomous defense systems to cyber warfare and automated decision-making, the volume underscores that AI's strategic advantages are inseparable from its risks. The erosion of human oversight, the amplification of bias through data-driven systems, and the ambiguity of accountability in machine-mediated actions pose serious challenges to international humanitarian law, democratic norms, and human rights. Several chapters also highlight how these risks are unevenly distributed, particularly affecting civilians, healthcare systems, and regions with limited regulatory capacity or representation in global AI governance.

A central theme emerging from this book is the inadequacy of existing legal and ethical frameworks to fully address the realities of AI-enabled conflict. While international law and ethical theory provide important foundations, they must evolve to account for autonomous systems, algorithmic decision-making, and AI-driven cyber operations. Equally important is the recognition that ethical governance cannot be achieved through regulation alone. Leadership, institutional culture, international cooperation, and inclusive governance—especially incorporating perspectives from the Global South—are essential to ensuring that AI technologies serve collective security without undermining human dignity.

As Editors, we emphasize that this volume does not argue against the use of AI in security and defense, but rather for its responsible, transparent, and accountable deployment. Human judgment, moral agency, and legal responsibility must remain central, particularly in contexts involving the use of force and the protection of civilians. AI should be understood as a tool that supports human decision-making, not one that replaces ethical reasoning or absolves responsibility.

Ethical Challenges of AI and Warfare is intended to serve as both a reference and a call to action. We hope it will inform scholarship, guide policymakers, and encourage practitioners to engage critically with the ethical dimensions of AI in warfare and cybersecurity. Ultimately, the future of global security will be shaped not only by what AI can do, but by the values, norms, and responsibilities that govern its use. This volume invites readers to participate in shaping that future with care, foresight, and ethical resolve.

Chapter 1

AI-Powered Cyber Attacks and Automated Defense Systems

Sameer Saharan
https://orcid.org/0000-0002-7487-6297
Mody University of Science and Technology, India

Mridu Sharma
Mody University of Science and Technology, India

Baljeet Yadav
https://orcid.org/0000-0003-0624-6784
KR Mangalam University, India

Shailja Singh
Mody University of Science and Technology, India

Rajarshi Chakraborty
https://orcid.org/0009-0007-0353-5923
Mody University of Science and Technology, India

ABSTRACT

The application of artificial intelligence benefits both offensive and defensive operations by implementing new tactics in cyber warfare. The black hat hackers employ AI to trick users, create deep fakes, and automate tasks. The white hat hackers, however, employ machine learning to detect anomalies, react to intrusions, and predict potential issues. Challenges are encountered in cases where AI systems are

DOI: 10.4018/979-8-3373-3611-4.ch001

in competition since it is difficult to monitor weapon use and demands human oversight. As threats to cyberspace keep increasing, the application of AI is necessary to ensure online safety.

1. INTRODUCTION

The integration of AI in the cyber arena is revolutionizing the nature of cyber wars and the methods used to counter them. Cyber war against the networks and computers of other countries now includes strategies other than simple malware and simple hacking methods. Today, artificial intelligence, and its subfields such as machine learning and deep learning, are supporting both sides of cyber war. Recent studies suggest that advances in AI are organically part of the cyber environment and have the power to bring about fundamental changes in it (Ghosh, Chakraborty et al. 2018, Jimmy 2021, Bonfanti 2022, Saharan et al. 2024). The rapid impact of AI on cyber war has triggered rapid actions and repercussions, which have brought about greater engagement by people in research, policy, and cybersecurity.

1.1. Key Concepts and Definitions

i. **Artificial Intelligence (AI):** In the past, tasks were executed through human cognition, however currently, these tasks are carried out by AI. Essentially, AI enables a machine to process language, acquire knowledge from experiences, and make decisions. Artificial intelligence cultivates cognition within a computer. So, AI is defined as concrete ability of non-human machines or artificial entities to execute tasks, solve problems, communicate, interact, and behave logically, similar to biological humans (Gil de Zúñiga, Goyanes et al. 2024).
ii. **Machine Learning (ML):** This is a specialized area within artificial intelligence that enables a machine to independently analyze data to improve its performance over time. Machines powered by machine learning possess the ability to recognize intricate patterns and retain them, enabling them to detect emerging risks and formulate appropriate action plans So, ML involves the exploration of algorithms and techniques aimed at automating solutions to intricate problems that are challenging to address through traditional programming methods (Rebala et al. 2019).
iii. **Deep Learning (DL):** A subset of ML that uses multilayered *neural networks* (inspired by the human brain) to extract higher-level features from data. Deep learning models, such as convolutional neural networks or large transformers, drive many modern AI applications by learning from vast datasets.

iv. **Neural Networks:** Computational models of interconnected nodes ("neurons") organized in layers, which can learn to recognize patterns by adjusting connection weights. Neural networks form the core of deep learning and excel at tasks like speech or image recognition (Aggarwal 2018).
v. **Cyber Warfare:** The strategic use of cyber-attacks (viruses, denial-of-service, hacking) by nation-states or organizations to damage adversary computers or networks. Cyber warfare can target military or civilian infrastructure, seeking espionage, disruption, or influence (Saharan, et al. 2024).
vi. **Autonomous Systems:** Systems (hardware or software) that can sense, decide, and act with minimal human intervention. In cybersecurity, autonomous tools use AI to independently detect threats or execute operations in real time (Sarker 2024). For example, an AI-driven intrusion detection system or a self-driving malware-cleanup agent.

These concepts interlink: machine learning and neural networks are technical methods used to build AI, and AI-powered autonomous systems leverage these methods to act in cyber conflict, whether by attacking or defending. In the sections below, we examine how these technologies are changing cyber-attacks and defenses, with concrete examples of recent incidents and campaigns.

1.2. Evolution of Cyber Attacks with AI

Cyber adversaries have begun to exploit AI to make attacks more effective, automated, and evasive. In the past, many attacks required significant manual effort; today, AI tools can automate reconnaissance, craft attacks, and adapt on the fly. Key emerging offensive trends include:

i. **Hyper-Personalized Phishing:** Attackers use AI and ML (often large language models) to automate and optimize phishing campaigns. By scraping data from social media, company websites, and past communications, AI can generate emails or messages that closely mimic a trusted sender's tone and content. For example, a 2024 case report described a spear-phishing operation against a major bank in India where the attackers trained a language model on executives' public profiles and writing style. The AI-generated emails *perfectly* imitated the company's internal messaging and even the CEO's signature, fooling finance staff into entering credentials on a fake portal. As one security analysis notes, AI-powered cyberattacks can "identify vulnerabilities, deploy campaigns along identified attack vectors, establish backdoors" automatically – and then *evolve* to avoid detection. In practice, this means phishing messages now often contain contextually relevant details and flawless grammar, making them much harder to spot (the FBI warns of "AI-driven phishing attacks" that craft convincing, tailored messages to specific recipients) (Gururaj, et al. 2024, Tanti 2024, Zhang, Wu et al. 2025).

ii. **AI-Driven Deception (Deepfakes):** Generative AI enables attackers to create realistic audio or video forgeries. In cyberwarfare, such deepfakes can be weaponized for fraud and influence. A notable corporate example involved hackers impersonating executives via a deepfake Zoom call: the finance team of a Hong Kong firm witnessed what appeared to be their UK-based CFO and other leaders instructing an employee to transfer funds. In reality, all participants were "scammers" using AI-driven video and audio manipulation, leading to transfers of over $25 million before the fraud was uncovered. On the geopolitical front, AI media fakes have already surfaced in elections. In early 2024, thousands of U.S. voters received a robocall *sounding like* President Biden urging Democrats not to vote in a primary – a message later confirmed to be an AI-generated "deepfake". These incidents underscore how AI-created media (mimicking voices, faces, or digital content) can be deployed in social engineering and influence operations on a massive scale (Apolo and Michael 2024, Tapscott 2024, Lavi and Jabotinsky 2025).

iii. **Autonomous Exploitation and Adaptation:** Beyond social engineering, AI accelerates technical intrusion techniques. Adversaries leverage ML algorithms to automate the discovery of exploitable vulnerabilities and to generate payloads. According to industry reports, AI-enabled attacks can conduct "intelligent reconnaissance" and adapt in real time to bypass defenses. For example, modern malware can use reinforcement learning to improve its ability to propagate or hide based on feedback from the target environment. AI-powered offensive tools can automatically "learn from large data samples" (e.g. public code repositories or leaked data) to craft credible exploit code. As one analyst explains, adversaries increasingly use AI to automate and optimize their campaigns – making attacks faster, more targeted, and able to evade static detection mechanisms. In sum, the integration of AI means that cyber-attacks today can scale up in speed and sophistication well beyond human-controlled limits (Fakhouri, et al. 2024, Arif et al. 2024, Kolluri 2024).

1.3. AI in Cyber Defense

Defenders are likewise harnessing AI and ML to protect networks and systems in automated, intelligent ways. Whereas traditional security relied on fixed rules or signatures, AI-driven defenses can learn from data and adapt. Key defensive mechanisms include:

i. **Anomaly and Threat Detection:** AI-based detection systems analyze vast amounts of telemetry (network traffic, logs, user behavior) to spot unusual patterns. Machine learning models can automatically recognize signs of previously unseen attacks by identifying anomalies. In contrast to signature-based tools, these AI systems "continuously evolve to recognize new attack patterns". For example, ML-driven intrusion detection can flag a novel malware outbreak or lateral movement by learning the normal baseline of activity. As one survey notes, AI/ML offers "a dynamic, adaptive approach to identifying, classifying, and responding to threats," giving defenders the ability to detect zero-day exploits and subtle intrusions before traditional methods would catch them. The capability to autonomously detect anomalies and predict attack vectors in real time allows security teams to see "signals amidst the fog of cyber warfare" that humans might miss (Jeffrey, Tan et al. 2023, Bala and Behal 2024, Inuwa and Das 2024).

ii. **Automated Incident Response:** AI can not only alert on threats but also help contain them without waiting for human action. For instance, an AI-powered system may automatically isolate an infected endpoint, roll out emergency patches, or reroute traffic when an intrusion is detected. This "proactive defense" shortens response times, as AI can act at machine speed. The same AI/ML frameworks used for detection can feed into incident-response playbooks: reinforcement learning agents can learn effective countermeasures (e.g. which firewall rules to apply) in simulated environments before a real attack occurs. In practice, security platforms increasingly incorporate AI-driven automation for tasks like blocking suspicious logins, enforcing quarantine, or orchestrating cross-device defenses. By enabling continuous, adaptive defense mechanisms that operate with minimal human intervention, AI transforms cyber defense from a reactive game into a more resilient, learning-based system (Tanikonda, et al. 2022, Tayyab, et al. 2025).

iii. **Threat Intelligence and Prediction:** Advanced AI tools assist in aggregating and analyzing threat intelligence from diverse sources (public feeds, dark web data, open-source intelligence). Natural language processing and data mining allow defenders to spot emerging attack campaigns or vulnerable trends more quickly (Adewopo 2021, Gioti 2024). For example, AI can process hundreds of vendor advisories and research reports to automatically prioritize patching for critical zero-day vulnerabilities. Over time, machine learning models become better at forecasting likely attack targets based on industry trends. In this way, AI complements human analysts by filtering noise and focusing attention on the most pressing threats, contributing to a tighter defense posture overall.

Overall, the defensive use of AI is a double-edged response to the AI-augmented offense. While AI empowers attackers with automation, it also empowers defenders to handle the massive data flows of modern networks. The result is an accelerating cycle: as one review summarized, “AI is not just a tool for enhancing traditional cybersecurity measures; it is also the driving force behind the development of autonomous systems” for both defense and offense.

1.4. Geopolitical and Strategic Implications

The blending of AI and cyber warfare has profound implications for international security and strategy. AI lowers the barrier to sophisticated cyber operations, changing how nation-states approach cyber conflict and deterrence:

i. **Nation-State Cyber Competition:** Major nations are rapidly enhancing their AI-powered cyber capabilities. In the United States, China, Russia, Iran, and other nations, cyber capabilities are viewed as a critical component of their strategic rivalry (Obioha Val, et al. 2025). A cyber threat assessment for 2025 highlighted those numerous cyber-attacks stem from activities associated with China, alongside the advancement of generative AI. It emphasized how state-supported groups leverage AI to enhance the complexity of their attacks, making them more challenging to mitigate (Gupta et al. 2025). For instance, CISA highlights that malicious actors are highly likely to exploit AI to bypass security measures and initiate harmful large-scale cyber-attacks. In practical terms, AI accelerates the success of threats in cyber warfare by assisting actors in pinpointing network vulnerabilities and crafting convincing deceptive messages. Policymakers engage in the discourse surrounding responsible AI by formulating guidelines, enhancing their cybersecurity measures, and occasionally imposing bans on specific AI-powered weaponry. Each party seeks to obtain a competitive advantage through the implementation of robotic and autonomous technologies in their cybersecurity efforts (Khan et al. 2024).
ii. **Escalation and Stability Risks:** The effect of AI on conflicts is seen in various and sometimes multifaceted ways. One advantage is the ability to stabilize some situations through rapid detection and response; however, one disadvantage is that machine-driven cyber-attacks sometimes spiral out of control. Some analysts suggest that the application of AI to cyber capabilities may compound existing issues and may not necessarily create new ones. Rapid response and covert operations of AI may be able to outmaneuver human decision-making and result in erroneous conclusions. One analysis argues that AI-facilitated cyber-attacks blur the line between espionage and kinetic conflict, increasing the risk of accidental escalation, especially if critical infrastructure or military systems

are targeted. For example, an AI-facilitated cyber intrusion may trigger a rapid counter-action before human decision-makers have detected the intent. This has generated fear that AI shortens the fuse on cyber crises: as one report warns, AI-facilitated attackers may launch attacks which "bypass traditional defense mechanisms" so rapidly that humans cannot intervene. To provide strategic stability in this scenario will require new dialogue and perhaps new doctrines (e.g. rules of engagement for autonomous cyber tools) (Arunthavanathan et al. 2024).

iii. **Dual-Use Challenges:** The same AI technologies empower both sides, making policy responses tricky. For every AI system built to defend a network, there are analogous tools for offense. As one expert puts it, "AI is becoming a critical component in both defense and attack strategies". This dual-use nature implies that commercial AI research (e.g. in natural language or image processing) can be co-opted by malicious actors. It also means that controlling the spread of AI is nearly impossible without also hindering legitimate innovation. Consequently, international efforts are underway to establish norms and best practices. Stakeholders - from governments to tech firms - are discussing frameworks to ensure AI in cybersecurity is used responsibly (Erendor 2024). For instance, analysts emphasize the need for collaborative policy-making so that defensive AI aids do not unintentionally empower attackers, and so that offensive AI use by states is constrained by accountability measures.

iv. **Regulatory and Ethical Dimensions:** Beyond pure strategy, AI in cyber warfare raises questions about law and ethics. Current international law does apply to cyberspace (customs of armed conflict, sovereignty principles, etc.), but AI adds complexity. Who is accountable when an autonomous cyber agent causes damage? How do we define proportional response if an AI-driven cyber-attack blurs attribution? These issues are the subject of ongoing debate in forums like the UN and security conferences. Technologists and policymakers alike are calling for transparent standards. One of the real-world implications is that defense ministries around the world are creating AI cyber strategies; the 2023 U.S. National Cybersecurity Strategy, for example, acknowledges AI's significant role and calls for leadership in secure AI development. NATO and allied organizations are also modeling to understand AI's role in cyber deterrence. The growing consensus is that uncontrolled AI in cyber war could destabilize, so it is essential that governance is prioritized (Lucarelli et al. 2021, Sharma et al. 2025).

The convergence of AI and cyber warfare is producing dramatic changes in strategy and tactics. Offensive cyber strategy is fueled by artificial intelligence using attack automation and optimization, while defense is sped up using information leverage (Saharan and Yadav 2022). Geopolitical changes heighten competition for cyber warfare and bring new management and escalation issues. AI integration into cyber defense and hacking will be a principal force behind cyber warfare. It is critical to direct this trend towards attaining better security results rather than exacerbating issues. Solutions to these issues need to be tackled through cooperation among technology, government, and international diplomacy to ensure AI improves security rather than new threats.

2. AI-POWERED OFFENSIVE CAPABILITIES

The advanced tools and skills are now accessible to malicious actors because of artificial intelligence and machine learning. The use of deep neural networks, generative models, reinforcement learning (RL) and adversarial ML in AI currently supports the automation and improvement of widespread attack techniques. Generative models called GPT-4 and reinforcement agents are examples of illustrations in AI, capable of producing harmful code and emails on their own and also can invent various attacks on computer networks. Adversarial machine learning techniques can be employed by adversaries to manipulate or influence the outcomes of defenders' AI systems. In summary, contemporary AI has the potential to reduce costs (in terms of time, skills, and resources) associated with executing intricate cyberattacks by automating expert tasks. The dismantling of these barriers has enabled less tech-savvy criminals to launch significant and adaptable cyber campaigns (Hossain, Afrin et al. 2024).

2.1. AI-Driven Attack Vectors

Adversaries leverage AI across the cyber kill chain. Key AI-enabled attack types include (Kaloudi and Li 2020, Malatji and Tolah 2024, Waizel 2024, Rodriguez et al. 2025):

i. **AI-Driven Phishing and Social Engineering** – Large language models (LLMs) and generative AI are used to craft highly convincing phishing lures. Tools like ChatGPT can scrape public data on a target (social media profiles, corporate bios, etc.) and write personalized, grammatically flawless emails or SMS messages. For instance, regulators have noted that threat actors use ChatGPT's "GPTs" feature to generate professional-looking phishing emails tailored to a victim's communication style. Investigations confirm this is not hypothetical: one study by SlashNext found a 1,265% increase in malicious phishing emails since ChatGPT's debut, attributing the surge to criminals using generative

AI for Business Email Compromise (BEC) and credential phishing. In a live test, BBC reporters used a custom ChatGPT "Crafty Emails" bot to produce urgent scam messages (e.g. a fake "Hi Mum" money-request text) in multiple languages within seconds. In short, AI can generate vast numbers of targeted social-engineering messages almost instantaneously, greatly amplifying the scale and credibility of phishing campaigns.

ii. **Polymorphic and AI-Generated Malware** – Generative AI can produce novel malware variants and obfuscate payloads on the fly. For example, researchers demonstrated *"BlackMamba"*, a proof-of-concept keylogger that queries a GPT model at runtime to synthesize its malicious functionality and then rewrites its code to evade detection (Shandilya, Prharsha et al. 2023). More broadly, AI can enable automated malware generation: one security framework notes that AI could create new polymorphic or metamorphic malware to evade signature-based defenses. These AI-generated payloads may automatically mutate their code or encryption with each execution, hindering static signature or sandbox detection. GANs (Generative Adversarial Networks) could likewise invent functional exploit code or packers that bypass traditional EDR tools. In essence, machine learning techniques allow malware to be designed and adapted on demand, creating attack variants far faster than human malware authors alone.

iii. **Automated Vulnerability Discovery and Exploitation** – AI can dramatically speed up reconnaissance and exploit development. By analyzing code, network configurations, or historical CVEs, ML models can pinpoint security flaws that human researchers might miss. Recent experiments illustrate this capability: a GPT-4 based "agent" was able to autonomously exploit 87% of tested publicly disclosed ("one-day") vulnerabilities when given their CVE descriptions. In contrast, other LLMs and traditional scanners failed to exploit any. The researchers note this "emergent capability" means once-hard manual processes (months of work by experts) can become automated. Even without full automation, AI tools speed up penetration testing: model-free reinforcement learning agents have been shown to map optimal attack paths through simulated networks, choosing scans and exploits to maximize damage with minimal input. In the wild, such AI may assist nation-state APTs or crime gangs in quickly finding zero-days or misconfigurations, effectively lowering the resource threshold for high-impact breaches.

iv. **AI-Powered Misinformation and Deepfakes** – Beyond conventional hacking, adversaries use AI to create deceptive multimedia for strategic influence and fraud. Deepfake techniques (using GANs or diffusion models) produce realistic but fake audio, video, or images of individuals. Social engineers can exploit this for high-stakes fraud: in one case, fraudsters combined malware and AI to bypass banking authentication by creating a *deepfake video* of a customer's face from stolen mobile phone data. In another well-documented incident (Arup cyber-heist, early 2024), attackers used a deepfake video call impersonating senior executives to trick an employee into wiring $25 million. On the disinformation front, automated AI content generation threatens political processes and public trust. For example, state-linked actors could spam social media with AI-written propaganda tailored to local dialects, or produce convincing fake news segments. Indeed, governments have warned that readily available GenAI tools like "WormGPT" and "FraudGPT" (dark-web LLMs explicitly marketed for crime) are used to craft phishing and malware, highlighting how criminals adapt core AI capabilities for misinformation and fraud (Falade 2023).

v. **Adversarial Attacks on AI Systems** – As organizations increasingly rely on AI defenses (such as ML-based intrusion detectors or face-recognition), adversaries target the AI itself through evasion and poisoning. In evasion attacks, small perturbations to inputs (e.g. slight changes in a malware binary or an image) can fool a machine-learning model. In poisoning attacks, attackers inject malicious data into training sets to backdoor or degrade a model. The U.S. National Institute of Standards and Technology (NIST) emphasizes that adversaries "can deliberately confuse or even 'poison' AI systems to make them malfunction - and there's no foolproof defense" (Tabassi, Burns et al. 2019). For example, an adversary could craft specially modified network traffic that normal-looking but sidesteps anomaly detectors. As another scenario, altering a few pixels on a stop sign can cause a vision AI to misclassify it entirely. These AI-targeted attacks are already practical: research shows vision models and other classifiers can be reliably duped, and methods exist for attackers to extract or reverse-engineer proprietary ML models. In the cyber domain, analogous techniques could let malware slip past AI-driven EDR or allow fake log entries to evade SIEM systems.

2.2. Nation-State and Criminal Exploitation

Both state-sponsored APT groups and cybercriminal organizations are rapidly integrating AI into their operational arsenals, though with different objectives and scales. Recent intelligence reveals that major nation-states are systematically leveraging AI to enhance cyber capabilities.

2.2.1. State-Sponsored Operations

Major powers including China, Russia, Iran, and North Korea are experimenting with large language models to augment hacking operations. OpenAI and Microsoft reported that Chinese APT group "Charcoal Typhoon" used ChatGPT to research target companies, generate exploit scripts, and create phishing content. Similarly, Iran's "Crimson Sandstorm" employed LLM agents to build payloads and craft spear-phishing emails, while other state actors used AI for translation, open-source intelligence gathering, and vulnerability research. These accounts demonstrate that well-resourced APT teams view AI primarily as a force multiplier for routine tasks - coding, language translation, and data gathering - rather than as a source of novel attack strategies.

2.2.2. Criminal Exploitation

Cybercriminal organizations and individual hackers are also flocking to AI tools. Underground forums now advertise custom AI-powered "malware-as-a-service" kits, with LLMs like "WormGPT" and "FraudGPT" explicitly marketed to help criminals with phishing and malware creation. These tools effectively commoditize expertise: low-skilled attackers can access AI agents that write phishing campaigns or generate polymorphic code. A 2023 SlashNext report documented a dramatic surge in AI-linked phishing, noting a "1,000%" rise in targeted business email compromise campaigns concurrent with ChatGPT's release. Independent investigations confirmed that custom-trained GPT bots can produce persuasive scam messages in seconds, bypassing standard AI safeguards. In essence, AI capabilities have permeated all levels of adversary sophistication - from script-kiddie phishers to advanced espionage teams.

2.2.3. Operational Advantage:

The combination of AI-driven automation and anonymity significantly complicates attribution. AI-generated content lacks distinctive creator fingerprints, making attacks appear to originate from anywhere. Machine-learning tools enable mass scanning and reconnaissance at speeds far beyond human capabilities, automatically enumerating targets, vulnerabilities, and network configurations by correlating public data. This rapid, automated research phase means defenders often cannot detect which systems have been probed until AI-powered payloads strike. Large-scale generation of malicious code and content accelerates every stage of the attack lifecycle - reconnaissance, weaponization, delivery, and exploitation - making campaigns broader, faster-moving, and more adaptive.

2.3. Strategic Implications and Evasion

The rise of AI-augmented attacks has profound strategic effects on the offense-defense balance. Crowds of minimally-skilled attackers can leverage AI to mimic sophisticated threats, blurring lines between state and criminal campaigns. Because AI can indefinitely scale operations (producing endless phishing variants or malware mutations), adversaries gain economies of scale: a single AI model can target thousands of victims simultaneously, vastly multiplying an attacker's reach compared to purely manual efforts. Moreover, AI enables *"adaptive"* threats: attacks that learn from feedback (e.g. tweaking a payload until it bypasses a firewall) effectively turn a defense's own signals into a training mechanism for the adversary. NIST cautions there is *"no silver bullet"* defense against such evasion, as attackers continuously evolve their tactics (National Academies of Sciences and Medicine 2024, Science et al. 2025).

From a defense perspective, AI-driven offense undermines traditional security measures. Signature-based antivirus and static rule systems struggle against polymorphic malware or AI-generated content because this change too rapidly for fixed indicators. Behavioral analytics and sandboxing can catch known patterns, but AI-enabled attacks can detect sandbox environments and alter behavior accordingly. For instance, one analysis notes that AI can "mimic benign behavior" to evade sandbox and IDS checks. Even machine-learning security tools themselves are targets: adversaries can craft adversarial examples to mislead AI detectors (e.g. perturbing an input to cause a model to classify malware as benign). In effect, defenders face a growing arms race: as organizations deploy AI for threat hunting and anomaly detection, attackers use adversarial ML to neutralize these advantages. CrowdStrike highlights that AI-powered attacks *"learn and evolve"* over time to defeat static defenses (Kolosnjaji et al. 2024).

The overall result is a tilted balance favoring offense. AI reduces manpower and expertise requirements for attackers, allowing larger or more frequent campaigns for the same effort. Low attribution and rapid automated recon also enable stealthier, more persistent intrusions. Policymakers and defenders must recognize that conventional cybersecurity postures are under strain: proactive measures (such as threat intelligence sharing, AI-driven defense research, and resilient system design) are essential. Organizations will need to harness AI themselves for defense – for example, using ML to detect anomalous patterns that even adaptive attacks slip into – to keep pace with increasingly autonomous threats. Ultimately, the integration of AI into offensive cyber capabilities represents a strategic shift: adversaries now wield tools that scale, adapt, and evade at machine speed, requiring an equally dynamic response (Johnson 2020).

2.4. Key Characteristics of AI-Driven Attacks (adapted from CrowdStrike):

- **Automation:** AI automates the attack chain from reconnaissance to exploitation, reducing manual effort and human oversight.
- **Rapid Reconnaissance:** ML models can scan networks, codebases, and open sources almost instantaneously, identifying vulnerabilities far quicker than human teams.
- **Customization:** AI excels at parsing public data (e.g. social media profiles) to tailor phishing lures or malware to specific victims.
- **Adaptation:** Attacks using AI can learn from failed attempts and change tactics or payloads in real time, thereby evading static defenses.
- **Stealth:** AI-assisted malware often employs novel obfuscation (polymorphism) and behavioral mimicry, making detection by traditional signature- or heuristic-based tools much harder (Bhambri and Bajdor, 2024).

AI and other trends in cybersecurity make it harder for defenders because offenses can be quick, flexible and use data-driven tools. To improve security, organizations should integrate AI into their systems for early detection, constant surveillance and quick handling of dangers. Being aware of how AI helps attackers is important for experts and officials to build better defenses as threats advance in this field.

3. AI-ENHANCED DEFENSIVE SYSTEMS

3.1. Strengths and Limitations

The integration of AI significantly enhances the capabilities of cyber defense. It can analyze significantly larger data sets in real time, surpassing human capabilities. AI tools are normally better than ordinary tools at finding hidden and hard-to-detect issues. They can keep adjusting their expectations based on the changing network which helps them find any new security risks. With AI, computers are able to act swiftly by, for example, blocking, quarantining or patching, so they can block quick threats before they are noticed by anyone else. With AI, information from endpoint, email, cloud and network threats is incorporated, so that any coordinated attack from different areas can be detected. By using AI, predictive analytics enables security experts to find threats by studying what has happened before and gives ideas about future threats (Sanjeewani, Neuber et al. 2024).

Still, there are obstacles that must be dealt with during the use of AI systems. Because there are flaws in models, anti-terrorism systems may occasionally identify innocent people as suspicious and label them as false positives. Occasionally, these notifications must be checked by staff which creates a condition called alert fatigue. When a business engages in a proper file transfer that is not common, it might be seen as unusual by the system. It is still hard to achieve a good balance between sensitivity and specificity. It is possible for people to manipulate information given to AI to trick it intentionally. Reckless users can generate bogus data or use the training method to take advantage of machine learning algorithms. So, vendors use methods such as creating fake data to improve the security of their models, but the war against cyberattacks is not over. Environmental changes can lead to a shift in the model's understanding of what constitutes the ordinary, ultimately diminishing its accuracy. It is crucial to update and re-train the system. Experts recommend the regular monitoring of AI performance and the retraining with new data to prevent drift. In the absence of this, an AI connected to last year's data may swiftly lose its relevance.

The integration of AI into operations brings forth challenges concerning its management and oversight. AI analytics can require substantial computing resources and rely heavily on high-quality training data. As models analyze user behavior, it is crucial to address privacy concerns and ensure data quality, necessitating careful handling of data. At its core, AI does not absolve humans of their responsibility to take control. In line with established guidelines, AI is designed to assist analysts rather than replace them. Observations indicate that individuals ought to scrutinize AI notifications, modify AI models based on their insights, and comprehend the outcomes produced by AI. An effective SOC leverages AI to automate the majority of tasks, while ensuring that analysts remain engaged for critical decision-making processes (Yaseen 2022). In summary, the acceleration of incident detection and response through AI is evident, yet the importance of monitoring and engaging with individuals is crucial for its reliability.

3.2. National Cyber Defense Strategies

Governments worldwide are embracing AI as a force multiplier in national cyber defense. The U.S. National Cybersecurity Strategy and agency roadmaps highlight AI/ML for threat intelligence, resilience, and early warning. For example, the Department of Homeland Security's Science & Technology Directorate notes that AI/ML "can provide the homeland unprecedented opportunity to enhance its cybersecurity posture" by processing vast data and deploying models to "detect threats, increase resilience and provide more supply chain oversight" (Montasari 2024). CISA (the U.S. Cybersecurity and Infrastructure Security Agency) explicitly uses AI to "automatically detect and analyze potential threats, flag unusual network activity, and identify patterns in vast amounts of data" related to critical infrastructure. In practice,

CISA has prototyped an "AI Use Case Inventory" including unsupervised learning for network anomaly detection in critical infrastructure (the CyberSentry program uses ML to surface anomalies for analysts) (Prieto and Blakely 2023).

Policymakers are also calling for AI-enabled early warning systems. In 2024, analysts urged Congress to establish an "early warning system" for novel AI-powered threats, where private developers report emerging AI attack capabilities to a central clearinghouse and share defensive AI insights. The aim is to give defenders maximal lead time against AI-amplified cyber weapons. Similarly, U.S. cyber strategies emphasize a "network of networks" where machine-to-machine threat-sharing augments human collaboration. In allied nations and multinational bodies (NATO, EU), AI features in cybersecurity modernization plans as well – whether through improved threat hunting platforms or automated incident response in national CERTs (Kim 2022).

On the offensive side, national security agencies are researching how to use AI for cyber operations, underscoring the dual-use nature of the technology. But strategically, defense organizations see AI as indispensable for strategic defense: to monitor election infrastructure, critical communications, financial systems and defense networks continuously, and to hunt adversary campaigns at internet scale. For instance, novel AI tools are being integrated into the DoD's cyber missions and Navy/Air Force cyber units to sift through signals intelligence or network telemetry rapidly (McGowan 2025).

In sum, AI is rapidly evolving from a niche tool to a cornerstone of cyber defense strategy. At the national level, AI-driven threat hunting, automated interdiction, and predictive intelligence are being institutionalized. Agencies like CISA and DHS explicitly invest in AI prototypes, and new policies encourage public–private collaboration on AI threat-sharing. As one DHS article put it, advances in AI enable "more advanced machine-to-machine sharing of data" and actionable intelligence to drive threat response at machine speed. Governments recognize that in the era of AI-augmented adversaries, early-warning and resilient defense must also be AI-enabled.

4. THE ARMS RACE DYNAMICS: AI VS. AI

4.1. Offensive AI Capabilities

Offensive cyber actors are employing AI to automate and amplify traditional attack chains. Examples include:

i. **Automated reconnaissance and exploit generation:** Reinforcement-learning (RL) agents can be trained to map network topology and find vulnerabilities.

In experiments, "red" RL agents learned to explore network graphs and exploit nodes, achieving higher long-term rewards than random attackers. For instance, researchers trained an RL defender against two APT-like RL attacker agents and found the defender could reliably counter continual automated attacks. Conversely, one can imagine specialized RL "attack" agents that continuously probe and compromise systems once known defenses change. Unlike static automated tools, such AI-driven attackers can adapt their strategy based on feedback, improving over time (Lin 2025).

ii. **AI-crafted payloads and malware:** Generative models are used to produce novel attack vectors. Notably, GANs (Generative Adversarial Networks) have been used offensively to morph malware or generate zero-day payloads. Research prototypes like "MalGAN" have shown that GAN-generated malware samples can evade ML-based detectors with near-total effectiveness – one study reports reducing detection from 92% to ~0.19% by training on GAN-crafted samples. In other words, GAN-powered attackers can produce polymorphic or adversarial malware that escapes signature and ML defenses (Arifin et al. 2024, Gebrehans, Ilyas et al. 2025). State actors with large compute can potentially exploit these techniques to rapidly create custom exploit code or honeypots aimed at defenders.

iii. **Adaptive data poisoning and evasion:** Attackers may manipulate defender ML training data (poisoning) or craft adversarial examples to blind detectors. For example, researchers demonstrated how an LLM-powered red-team agent could be "tricked" by adversarial techniques that recognized it as AI and altered responses to make it fail. More broadly, any AI-based intrusion detection or antivirus system can be deceived by carefully perturbed inputs. Academic surveys note that adversaries can perturb malware just enough to evade ML detectors (e.g. inserting benign code segments or reordering instructions) without changing functionality. These tactics allow AI attackers to hide their activities under the radar of static and learned defenses. Overall, attackers leveraging adversarial ML techniques can significantly complicate detection and response (Hutchens 2023).

iv. **AI-driven social engineering and deepfakes:** Beyond code, AI enables highly convincing phishing, business-email-compromise, and deepfake attacks. LLMs can craft personalized phishing emails or generate spoken deepfakes of executives, vastly increasing the scale and believability of social-engineering campaigns. An enterprise study noted that 70% of malicious emails now use AI-generated content indistinguishable from legitimate messages. State hackers can use these tools to impersonate officials or manipulate targets at scale (Falade 2023, Yu, Yu et al. 2024). Similarly, GANs used for image and voice synthesis allow fabrication of realistic fake videos or biometric spoofing, which can be weaponized for fraud or political disinformation.

v. **Continuous adaptation and co-evolution:** Modern attackers can embed AI "agents" that continuously monitor defensive measures and adjust tactics in real-time. In a simulated co-evolution experiment, researchers showed that iteratively retraining red and blue agents enabled each side to learn from the other's improvements. In effect, an AI attacker observing a deployed defensive model could automatically generate new exploits to bypass it. This mirrors an arms race – each AI updates to overcome the other's latest capability. State actors with access to such technology could deploy fleets of AI agents that probe networks, retreat when detected, learn from outcomes, and adapt their exploits dynamically (Saniuk et al. 2024, Singh 2024).

4.2. Defensive AI Strategies

Defenders likewise employ AI and ML extensively to detect, mitigate, and neutralize threats – effectively "fighting AI with AI." Key defensive strategies include:

i. **AI-based anomaly and threat detection:** Self-learning AI models are used to scan logs, network flows and user behavior for subtle anomalies beyond static signature-based rules. For example, enterprise SOCs report that "self-learning AI pinpoints subtle signals humans overlook, enabling proactive defense". In practice, this means algorithms trained on normal network traffic can flag suspicious deviations (like unusual data flows or login patterns) far faster than human teams. Early detection models and UEBA (user/entity behavior analytics) tools use unsupervised learning to spot previously unseen attacks. Gartner calls these "preemptive cybersecurity" solutions critical to keep pace with AI attackers. Successful deployments have detected zero-day exploits by recognizing outliers in telemetry that rule-based systems would miss (Zhang et al., 2025, Ahmed, Nazir et al. 2025).

ii. **Automated response and remediation:** Many defenders automate response actions via AI. Reinforcement-learning "blue" agents can be trained to take corrective actions (e.g. reimage servers, isolate hosts, deploy honeypots) to thwart detected intrusions. In a network simulation, an RL-based defense agent was able to reliably defend against continuous APT-style attacks by proactively evicting threats and shuffling network assets. In the real world, concepts like Microsoft's Security Copilot envision LLMs that suggest or even execute containment steps (guided by analysts). Autonomous patch management, dynamic firewall reconfiguration, and deception technologies (auto-deploying decoys) are examples of how AI can rapidly respond to emerging incidents. Such automated response systems aim to reduce the "mean time to detect/contain" which CISOs now measure as key performance indicators (Rahman et al. 2025).

iii. **Training on adversarial samples:** Paradoxically, the same GAN technology can be turned defensively. Researchers have used GANs to produce adversarial examples of malware or exploits to harden detectors. One study found that augmenting intrusion-detection training data with GAN-generated "unseen" malware increased zero-day detection accuracy from very low to about 98%. In practice, security teams can use adversarial-ML tools to "stress test" their models: feeding synthesized attack samples to find blind spots. By iteratively training on such adversarial data, defenders can harden classifiers against AI-crafted threats. This co-training approach is akin to vaccine development: exposing the system to variants so it learns to recognize novel attacks (Di Nucci 2020, West et al. 2023).
iv. **Threat intelligence augmented by AI:** On the intelligence side, commercial and government tools use AI to process massive threat feeds and reports. For example, Microsoft's Security Copilot combines GPT-4 with real-time threat data to summarize attack details and recommend actions. Similarly, network monitoring platforms (e.g. CrowdStrike, Darktrace, Palo Alto XDR) integrate machine learning to correlate indicators of compromise across clients worldwide. These systems can automatically propagate knowledge of new malware hashes or phishing sites at machine speed. In effect, defenders harness LLMs and data science to scan unstructured threat reports and generate automated alerts, easing analyst workloads (Garza et al. 2020).
v. **Deception and active defense:** Some modern defense strategies leverage AI-driven "active defense". For instance, honeypots and deceptive assets can be dynamically deployed by AI to attract and trap attackers. By analyzing attacker behavior in decoys, AI algorithms can refine detection rules. While mostly in research/prototype stages, DARPA and private cyber ranges are experimenting with autonomous blue/red teams that play offense and defense against each other. These simulation environments (e.g. CyberBattleSim, CybORG) allow testing of AI defense agents in realistic scenarios (Esteban 2022, Drašar et al. 2023).

Overall, defensive AI strategies focus on extending human capabilities: automating routine tasks, surfacing hidden threats, and reacting in seconds. As one practitioner put it, "Leveraging AI is the best defense against AI-powered attacks". Notably, many industry leaders emphasize that as attackers adopt AI (polymorphic malware, AI phishing, etc.), legacy rule-based defenses fail, and only adaptive, learning-based defenses can keep up. The defensive side, however, is not unchallenged: detectors themselves can be attacked via adversarial ML, and reliance on AI raises issues of robustness and false positives. The consensus is that defenders must constantly update and validate their AI models, ideally by co-evolving them against simulated attacker AIs.

4.3. Model-vs-Model Dynamics

The core of the AI arms race lies in real-time model-versus-model engagements, where offensive and defensive AI systems adapt and counter each other at machine speed. In simulations, co-evolutionary training - iteratively updating red and blue AI agents against each other - demonstrates how both sides can rapidly escalate capabilities. Experiments show that after each training iteration, new attacker models can overcome previous defenders, forcing defenders to retrain, creating a continuous feedback loop. This automated duel mirrors traditional arms races, but operates at computational speeds far beyond human decision-making timelines.

4.3.1. Current State and Future Scenarios

While fully autonomous cyber duels remain largely in research stages, the foundation is being actively built. DARPA's 2016 Cyber Grand Challenge, which pitted automated systems against each other to find and patch vulnerabilities, foreshadowed this AI competition. Today, governments and firms are developing testbeds for autonomous engagement. Researchers at Oak Ridge envision hierarchical "Cyber Agents" - specialized units for binary analysis, network traversal, and exploit deployment - that coordinate like tactical teams. If deployed operationally, such systems could perform on-the-fly attacks and counterattacks at speeds that compress human OODA loops from hours to seconds.

4.3.2. Implications

A compelling future scenario involves networks under continuous AI siege: attacker agents probe defenses while defender AIs dynamically reconfigure networks and patch vulnerabilities in real-time. Each side adapts within seconds, with machine-speed decision cycles. Forecasts predict that by the mid-2020s, cybercriminals will deploy "AI-powered malware and automated vulnerability discovery as standard tools," creating virtual "AI-factories" that autonomously exploit zero-days at scale. Symmetrically, defenders will require "zero-day data security"- AI systems capable of detecting novel threats instantly - to avoid catastrophic breaches. In this environment, human analysts become supervisors of fast-moving AI battles rather than direct operators. The critical technical challenge is ensuring robustness: even small machine-learning model errors can be exploited by adversarial AI, making model reliability paramount for both sides.

4.4. Ethical and Strategic Challenges

Autonomous AI-on-AI cyber conflict raises profound issues:

i. **Escalation risks:** Taddeo and Floridi highlight that unchecked AI warfare has the potential to trigger a cyber escalation, which could ultimately lead to conventional warfare. The automation of retaliation may lead to escalated attacks from both parties following each attempt by the opposing side. They believe that a lack of clear rules could potentially lead to someone resorting to physical violence. This situation parallels the Cold War era, where nuclear deterrence proved effective; an unexpected or misinterpreted assault by AI could result in significant consequences. Due to their ability to operate continuously, autonomous AIs may accelerate the escalation of conflicts beyond the response capabilities of humans (Taddeo and Floridi 2021, Taddeo 2024).
ii. **Loss of human control:** UN officials have highlighted that the rapid development of AI is outpacing the establishment of regulations and frameworks for its safe military application, posing a risk to human oversight of weapon systems. A cyberspace AI may behave in ways that were not anticipated, regardless of its role. When there is not enough oversight of an AI agent, errors may occur in selecting key targets and planning how to protect them. Those present in Security Council debates stress that proper rules are needed and that individuals should be included to keep these actions from being harmful. For this reason, it is important to add fail-safes and give individuals a role in shaping the decisions of AI cyber tools (Gilbert and Gilbert 2024, Jafariandehkordi 2024).
iii. **Attribution complexity:** AI-driven attacks can be deliberately obfuscated to conceal origin. As one analysis notes, an AI attacker can mimic other groups' tactics, "masking the true origin of an attack" and confusing forensic efforts. This undermines a core pillar of cyber deterrence: knowing who attacked. For example, if a Russian APT uses an AI that replicates Chinese hacking patterns, defenders may misdirect retaliation. The study cites recent cases where Russian and Iranian actors used such obfuscation to hinder investigations. As automation increases volume and scale of attacks, the classic attribution problem worsens: even if a signature is detected, tying it to a state or actor becomes harder. This ambiguity may embolden attackers (they escape blame) and paralyze defenders (who hesitate to respond without clear attribution) (Minhaj 2023, Waizel 2024).
iv. **Legal and policy frameworks:** There is currently no international agreement specific to autonomous cyber weapons. Traditional laws of armed conflict apply in theory, but their extension to non-physical AI attacks is unresolved. Taddeo/Floridi argue states "need regulations that establish legitimate uses of AI for national defence" and define "proportional responses, clear thresholds, or 'red

lines'" for cyber conflict. However, multilateral discussions have stalled. In 2017, the UN Group of Governmental Experts failed to agree even basic norms for cyber engagement. The recent UN Security Council debate reiterated the urgency of AI governance, warning that "deep fakes" and autonomous systems could trigger crises without proper guard-rails. In absence of agreed rules, nations may act unilaterally, raising risks of miscalculation. On the corporate side, questions of liability and ethics arise: e.g. if a vendor's defensive AI mistakenly shuts down critical infrastructure, who is accountable? Regulatory frameworks (e.g. standards for testing AI cyber tools, transparency requirements) will be needed to manage these concerns (Mačák 2017, Meyer 2020).

v. **Ethical concerns:** In addition to strategy, the significance of ethics cannot be overlooked. Should computers or robots play a role in decisions that can significantly impact human life online, particularly in cyberspace? When attacks using AI lead to the spread of disinformation that brings about unrest, it is often difficult to determine the person or group that initiated the problem. When AI chooses to delete data from targeted sources, it can sometimes cause problems for uninvolved users. Over time, ensuring civilian safety was a priority in ethical cyber work, but self-learning AI may not follow this unless it is trained to do so (Hosmer 1994).

According to experts, only with both technical improvements and new laws can these issues be handled. The use of RAS-style modeling to spot problems ahead of time, set up defenses for automated tools and organize conferences with other nations to set cyber-AI standards. The UN Secretary-General has proposed the establishment of global platforms, such as an AI Security Council, to ensure the safe implementation of AI in military operations. The focus of NATO and the EU is currently directed towards the examination of AI in the realm of cyber defense. Additionally, organizations are enhancing the security of their AI systems by implementing robust auditing and validation processes (Medvidovic and Edwards 2010).

For researchers and security professionals, the key takeaways are:

i. **Innovation in offensive AI is accelerating.** Stay alert to new adversarial techniques (GAN-morphed malware, poisoned data, LLM-generated social attacks) and test defenses accordingly (McGinnis 2018).
ii. **Defensive AI must be robust and continuously updated.** Incorporate adversarial training and anomaly detection, and assume attackers will use AI (Alotaibi and Rassam 2023).
iii. **Policy and governance need catch-up.** Advocate for standards on AI tool deployment, validation, and international norms to avoid uncontrolled escalation (Cihon 2019).

iv. **Attribution will be harder.** Invest in diverse intelligence sources (beyond technical traces) and collaborate internationally to reduce misidentification (el Rahwan 2022).
v. **Maintain human oversight.** Even as systems automate, preserve human-in-the-loop checks for critical actions (Pöhler et al. 2025).

By examining both technical strategies and high-level implications, we see that "AI vs. AI" is not just science fiction: it is an emerging reality in cyber conflict. Proactive research, vigilant deployment, and thoughtful policy-making will be essential to navigate this new era of autonomous cyber warfare safely and effectively.

5. STRATEGIC IMPLICATIONS AND NATIONAL SECURITY CONSIDERATIONS

AI-enhanced cyber warfare is rapidly reshaping deterrence, escalation dynamics, and strategic stability. Machine-learning tools can dramatically increase the scale, speed and stealth of cyber operations – for example automating spear-phishing or hacking campaigns – while reducing the cost and human effort required. This raises the risk of inadvertent escalation: leaders may have only seconds or minutes to interpret fast-moving cyber events and avoid triggering broader conflict. As one analyst observes, the new generation of AI-augmented cyber capabilities "will likely exacerbate the military escalation risks associated with emerging technology, especially inadvertent and accidental escalation" – a concern particularly acute where nuclear systems or other strategic assets are targetedwarontherocks.comdoras.dcu.ie. In effect, AI does not create entirely new escalation pathways, but *amplifies existing ones*: faster decision loops and deeper convergence of cyber, conventional, and nuclear domains make miscalculation more likely than in the pastdoras.dcu.iedoras.dcu.ie.

At the same time, AI also offers new avenues for cyber defense and deterrence. Automated threat-detection, anomaly monitoring, and predictive analytics can bolster denial-based defenses, making networks more resilient. AI-driven forensic tools and pattern analysis can improve post-attack attribution (identifying the perpetrators) and thus support "deterrence by punishment". NATO leaders note that "the expanding use of artificial intelligence (AI) is enhancing cyberattacks and cyber deterrence alike," suggesting a kind of symbiosis: both attackers and defenders are arming themselves with AI. In practice, however, credible deterrence in cyberspace has always been fragile – it relies on clear signaling and proportional retaliation, which are complicated by AI's ambiguity. Experts warn that human cognition and decision-making will remain central: new AI tools "will augment but not fundamentally change strategy" of states in crisis. Nevertheless, the criteria for responding to attacks are shifting. As one recent study found, even if AI balance does not by itself raise the perceived escalation risk, commanders may increasingly "target adversary's battle networks" when planning in the shadow of potential nuclear war (Roy 2024, Saharan et al. 2025, Sharma et al. 2025).

i. **Lowered thresholds and surprise:** AI can automate Advanced Persistent Threat (APT) operations and exploit zero-day flaws more quickly, enabling even low-skilled actors to penetrate critical systems (for example, using generative models to rewrite malware on the fly). This broadens the attack surface and can compress surprise timetables.
ii. **Speed and scale:** Rapid AI-driven scanning of networks or automating large-scale social engineering (e.g. mass-customized phishing) can overwhelm defenders before human operators have time to react. By contrast, defensive AI tools run continuously without fatigue, but this requires constant updating to keep pace with attackers' evolving AI techniques.
iii. **Escalation reflex:** In a crisis, uncertainty about whether a breach or disruptive incident was an automated malfunction or a hostile cyber strike could trigger worst-case assumptions. If an AI-enabled attack (say, a "deepfake" order or spoofed sensor data) creates the appearance of an imminent threat, a receiver state may feel pressured to escalate first – especially when national security systems (like NC3 or early-warning) are involvedwarontherocks.comdoras.dcu.ie. Thus AI raises "the possibility of unpredictable and potentially undetectable errors, malfunctions and behavioral manipulation" of critical systems.

Taken together, these effects mean that traditional deterrence models are under strain. In classical terms, cyber deterrence mixes denial (hardening networks) with punishment (credible retribution). But AI affects both sides. On denial: while AI tools can harden cyber defenses, the very ease of launching attacks makes "denial" challenging – it may be cheaper to attack with AI than to defend against it. On punishment: attribution becomes more vexed. Attackers can use AI to disguise signatures or mimic other actors (for example by constantly rewriting malware code via generative models), making it harder to pin blame. Conversely, defenders are applying AI to piece together attacker "fingerprints" from subtle patterns. Experts caution that while AI can improve attribution in theory, the technological race will be one step ahead of legal and political processes. As one policy brief notes: "Effective cyber deterrence requires coupling resilience and attribution with credible punishments," but the international legal framework is still evolving in how it applies to cyber operations (Nye Jr 2016, Digmelashvili and Lagvilava 2023, Sharma et al. 2025).

5.1. Attribution, Proportional Response, and Strategic Ambiguity

The challenges of attribution and response are magnified in an AI-driven battlespace. Attackers may deliberately inject ambiguity using AI tools. For instance, AI "deepfakes" or sophisticated social-engineering can create false trails or impersonate trusted sources to mask origins. Generative models can rewrite code to evade signature-based detection. Such techniques can turn any cyber incident into a puzzle: was it a probing espionage run, a staged raid by non-state proxies, or a direct attack by a rival government? When attribution is unclear, decision-makers face strategic ambiguity: they may hesitate to retaliate for fear of hitting an innocent party, or conversely may overreact out of caution (Dsouza et al. 2024).

Calibrating a proportional response is similarly fraught. Cyber norms and international law on "use of force" remain unsettled, especially as cyber effects may range from nuisance to near-physical. It is often unclear *a priori* how damaging an AI-enhanced cyberattack must be to justify kinetic retaliation. Scholars suggest using an "effects-based" threshold: defining red-lines by the real-world impact of the attack (economic loss, casualties, crippling of infrastructure). For example, states might agree that a crippling power-grid blackout equates to an armed attack, whereas minor data theft does not. However, drawing such lines is itself contentious. If a covert AI cyber operation (so-called "prepositioning" or implanting malware) is discovered, its intent can be ambiguous: is it espionage or the first stage of a destructive strike? This ambiguity "raises questions about whether they qualify as threats of aggression under international law" (Dsouza et al. 2024).

Analysts argue that any cyber retaliation must be carefully "calibrated and communicated" to signal credibility without spurring uncontrollable escalation. Possible responses could range from diplomatic protests and sanctions to counter-cyber operations or, in extreme cases, limited military strikes – but only if the legal and political context is clearly established. Punishment must be credible yet proportional: one briefing notes that "punishments will be most credible and effective if they are proportional and reserved for the most destructive behavior in cyberspace". Overly aggressive reprisals risk spiraling into a larger conflict or normalizing cyber violence, while under-reaction can embolden further attacks. The Stuxnet incident (an Israeli cyberattack on Iran's nuclear program) is often cited as a caution: it arguably set a precedent for kinetic-style cyber strikes, but also "pre-empted a potential norm against cyberattacks on nuclear facilities" by changing the accepted boundaries of cyberspace aggression (Drucker and Gumpert 2000, Nye Jr 2016).

Key challenges and paradoxes include:

i. **Attribution ambiguity:** AI tools can both conceal attackers' identities and improve attribution. Attackers constantly alter malware signatures (e.g. ChatGPT-generated code variants) to evade detection, while defenders deploy AI forensic analysis to reconstruct attack chains. The balance is dynamic, but accurate attribution (state or proxy) is harder and more politicized in the age of AI (Charfeddine, Kammoun et al. 2024).
ii. **Proportional response:** International law (UN Charter, IHL) applies to cyberspace, but defining what level of cyber damage justifies armed self-defense is unsettled. Experts propose using objective impact metrics and clear red-lines, but achieving consensus is difficult when AI can create novel forms of harm (e.g. AI-caused industrial accidents) (Focarelli 2021).
iii. **Strategic ambiguity:** When AI reduces clarity, decision-makers may adopt "worst-case assumptions." For example, an AI-driven disinformation campaign (deepfakes targeting leadership) could be misconstrued as an act of war, forcing a hasty response. Conversely, attackers may exploit ambiguity by conducting "grey-zone" cyber operations, hoping retaliation will be unclear or muted (Focarelli 2021).
iv. **Communication and signaling:** Keeping deterrence credible will require states to communicate their cyber "thresholds" clearly. As one analysis notes, deterrence requires not just abstract threats, but "calibrating and communicating which punishments - ranging from diplomatic denouncements, to sanctions, to kinetic military strikes, to retaliation in the cyber realm - are plausible in response to which forms of cyber aggression". This demands both strategic ambiguity (to avoid locking into one response) and enough clarity to deter aggression (Nye Jr 2016, Longabaugh 2020).

In sum, AI in cyber operations tightens the tension between the desire for ambiguity (to allow political flexibility) and the need for clarity (to deter adversaries). Navigating this requires new doctrines and likely new cyber-specific confidence-building measures among major powers.

5.2. Cyber Norms, Responsible State Behavior, and International Law

AI is also driving a reexamination of cyber norms and international law. Traditional cyber norms (such as the UN GGE's 2015 guidelines) are non-binding and broad: e.g. not to attack civilian infrastructure, to protect critical institutions, to assist other states under threat. These still apply, but AI introduces fresh wrinkles. For instance, if an AI-agent inadvertently causes civilian harm, does it break a norm? If a deepfake video incites violence, is that aggression? The proliferation of dual-use

AI (civilian/military) also raises sovereignty debates: some states argue that private AI tools used by citizens could count as "involvement" in cyber conflict.

International actors are debating how to update norms in this context. The UN has spotlighted AI's implications for warfare: at a Security Council meeting in December 2024, Secretary-General Guterres warned that AI "without human oversight would leave the world blind - and perhaps nowhere more recklessly than in global peace and security," and urged nations to build "international guard-rails" for AI. He highlighted specific threats such as deepfakes that could trigger crises and cautioned that integration of AI into nuclear command-and-control "must be avoided at all costs". However, views on norms are divided. Russia (echoing China's stance) explicitly warned against Western-led rules in cyberspace and AI, reflecting a desire for its own agenda. Meanwhile, Western powers (the US, EU and NATO members) are pushing for stronger collective rules: for example, recent NATO documents emphasize that allies must apply international law to AI usage and uphold responsible AI principles in defense applications (Gill 2020).

Specific legal issues under discussion include extension of existing law, new norms for AI weapons, transparency and confidence-building, responsible behavior and civilian protection [Figure 1].

Figure 1. Establishing AI Cyber Norms

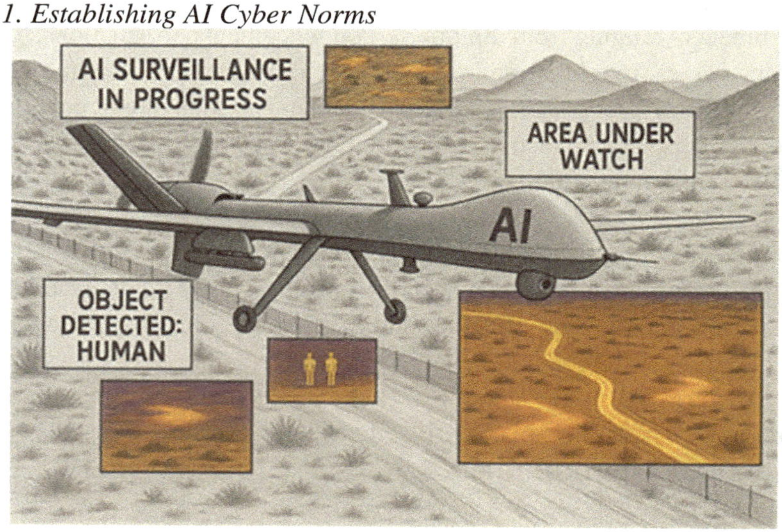

In summary, AI is motivating policymakers to revisit cyber norms. The existing paradigm – voluntary standards supplemented by national law – is being stress-tested. Many analysts call for either new international agreements or at least common guidelines on AI in cyber conflict. The risk is that without consensus, each great power may define "responsibility" differently, raising the prospect of a fragmented ruleset and lower crisis stability.

5.3. Great-Power Competition: US, China, Russia, and the EU

AI cyber tools have become a critical axis of great-power rivalry, with major nations racing to develop superior capabilities while the EU strives to maintain strategic autonomy through regulation and investment.

5.3.1. United States

The US government views AI as essential to both cyber defense and offense. Recent national security directives emphasize securing the AI supply chain and developing robust testing frameworks through NIST's AI Safety Institute. The Biden Administration's 2023 National Cybersecurity Strategy underscores investments in advanced technologies and public-private partnerships to deter adversaries, while the 2024 National Security Memorandum on AI mandates safety measures for critical infrastructure. US agencies and military commands - including the Pentagon's JAIC and Cyber Command - are incorporating AI/ML for threat hunting and network defense. Politically, the US seeks to maintain technological superiority through initiatives like the proposed Five Eyes AI collaboration while imposing export controls to protect strategic capabilities.

5.3.2. China

Beijing has made AI a strategic priority through its 2017 "New Generation Artificial Intelligence Development Plan" and subsequent national security frameworks. Through ambitious military-civil fusion programs, the PLA is rapidly integrating AI across all domains under the doctrine of "intelligentized warfare." Chinese strategic writings emphasize "systems confrontation"- using AI to paralyze adversary command, control, and communications systems rather than attriting forces. Beijing equips its cyber forces with AI tools for surveillance, signals intelligence, and cyber-attack development, while funding large-scale data collection domestically and abroad. China promotes its sovereignty-focused cyber norms in international forums, preferring frameworks that justify its operational approaches.

5.3.3. Russia

While lagging in pure AI research, Russia leverages available AI tools to sharpen its cyberwarfare capabilities. Recent reports from Ukraine's cyberdefense services indicate Russian hackers increasingly use AI to process stolen data and refine espionage campaigns. At the Munich Security Conference, Western officials warned that "Russia is increasingly leveraging artificial intelligence to refine its cyber espionage and enhance attack precision." Russian GRU and affiliated groups employ AI for automated vulnerability scanning and social media manipulation. Russia's strategy relies on ambiguity and offensive freedom, reflected in its resistance to Western AI rules during UN debates.

5.3.4. European Union and NATO

The EU and member states are working to catch up through large funding programs, including a €1.3 billion cybersecurity initiative, while tightening rules via the AI Act and critical tech supply chain regulations. The April 2025 ProtectEU strategy aims to bolster resilience against hybrid threats. NATO's 2021 AI strategy commits to "standards of responsible use of AI technologies, in accordance with international law and NATO's values," while its 2025 Data Strategy envisions secure sharing of AI models among allies. The transatlantic approach emphasizes ethical and legal guardrails - ensuring AI systems are interpretable and secure - while investing heavily in AI-enabled cybersecurity to counterbalance Chinese and Russian narratives.

5.4. Alliances and Collective Cyber Defense

Major alliances are integrating AI into collective defense strategies, recognizing that no single country can manage AI-augmented cyber threats alone. NATO, Five Eyes, and regional coalitions are developing frameworks for shared capabilities and coordinated responses.

5.4.1. NATO

The Alliance has made AI a formal priority through its 2021 AI Strategy, which establishes ethical principles for member states and covers both offensive and defensive applications. NATO's 2025 Data Strategy pledges to build a secure ecosystem for sharing AI/ML models and data among allies, ensuring interoperability of AI tools for joint situational awareness and strengthening collective deterrence. The Vilnius Summit (2023) and subsequent meetings have stressed the need for "a blend of technologies including AI" to harden critical infrastructure and accelerate threat response. Practically, NATO is incorporating AI into its Cooperative Cyber Defence Centre of Excellence and Defence Innovation Accelerator for the North Atlantic (DIANA) programs to foster collaborative research and rapid deployment.

5.4.2. Five Eyes

The intelligence alliance of the US, UK, Canada, Australia, and New Zealand is expanding its long history of signals intelligence sharing into AI collaboration. In 2023, U.S. lawmakers proposed a Five Eyes working group on AI to "advance and accelerate the interoperability of AI systems used for intelligence sharing" and joint command-and-control. The AUKUS pact includes tracks for advanced technology collaboration, including AI. Five Eyes partners have already conducted joint cyber attributions, collectively identifying Russian and Chinese malware campaigns. Building shared AI tools for rapid cyber forensics and countering disinformation is now a priority, with defense experts noting that to "fight as a system, you have to start sharing technology now."

5.4.3. Challenges and Limitations

Alliance integration of AI faces significant hurdles. Export controls on AI software and chips can slow cooperation, and trust barriers exist before sharing sensitive data. The proposed Five Eyes AI bill explicitly states that each country retains control under its export laws, reflecting these constraints. Nevertheless, the imperative is clear: collective AI development for cyber defense serves as both a force multiplier and a united front. NATO's Enhanced Cyber Defence Pledge (2022) now includes AI research commitments, and many allies contribute to NATO Cyber Ranges to test AI defenses collaboratively.

6. ETHICAL, LEGAL, AND REGULATORY CHALLENGES IN AI CYBER WARFARE

6.1. The Accountability Gap in Autonomous Cyber Operations

The integration of AI into cyber warfare significantly complicates attribution of responsibility in digital conflicts. A 2024 Oxford Internet Institute study indicates that international laws are inadequately equipped to address scenarios where autonomous AI independently executes cyber-attacks. Analysis of AI-related cyber incidents reveals that conventional attribution methods were ineffective in 73% of cases involving machine-learning tools.

Accountability challenges intensify when examining meaningful human oversight in cyber operations. Berkman Klein Center experts found that AI-enabled attackers can act faster than humans, potentially violating international humanitarian law requirements for human presence in wartime decisions. Traditional principles - distinction, proportionality, and precaution - struggle to apply to AI cyber operations due to unprecedented operational speeds.

Evidence from the Center for Strategic and International Studies shows that AI's ability to generate convincing digital tracks, mimic threat actors, and self-modify makes attribution 3.4 times more difficult than conventional cyber-attacks. This attribution crisis undermines deterrence frameworks that depend on identifying perpetrators.

6.2. Legal Framework Inadequacies

Significant gaps exist in applying international law to AI cyber warfare. The Tallinn Manual 2.0, developed as a guide for international law in cyberspace, predates AI's prominent role in cybersecurity. According to NATO's Cooperative Cyber Defence Centre of Excellence (2024), uncertainty remains regarding how Tallinn Manual principles translate to AI-driven operations.

Three critical legal ambiguities emerge. First, AI systems can execute attacks faster than traditional self-defense doctrines accommodate, complicating timely defensive responses. Second, because autonomous systems operate at machine speed, the temporal element of "imminent threat" becomes difficult to assess. Third, AI's ability to simultaneously target military and civilian infrastructure with precision makes intent challenging to determine prospectively.

A Georgetown University Law Center study (2024) examined how national laws are evolving to address AI cyber warfare, identifying significant cross-country variations. The United States relies on the Computer Fraud and Abuse Act, while the EU advances comprehensive regulation through the AI Act targeting dual-use technologies. China emphasizes state control of cyber technologies, though specifics of offensive operations remain opaque.

Current legal frameworks face particular difficulty with AI attacks transcending borders. Most mutual legal assistance treaties and extradition frameworks target individual perpetrators, proving insufficient when AI autonomously conducts attacks across jurisdictions. The study documented 34 cases where legal proceedings involving AI-assisted cyber-crimes were complicated by jurisdictional uncertainties and technical attribution challenges.

6.3. Regulatory Approaches and Policy Frameworks

Nation-states and international organizations are formulating legislation for AI-driven cyber-attacks, though comprehensiveness and efficacy vary significantly. A 2024 RAND report revealed that 18 nations have established regulations differing substantially in strength, compliance mechanisms, and international coordination.

6.3.1. European Union

The EU AI Act aims to establish comprehensive regulations for dual-use AI systems. Analysis by the Centre for European Policy Studies indicates the Act addresses high-risk AI aspects but allows significant national security exemptions, potentially undermining effectiveness in preventing cyber warfare applications.

6.3.2. United States

The American approach utilizes executive orders and agency regulations. The 2024 Brookings report indicates that NIST's AI Risk Management Framework offers strategies for addressing AI risks in cybersecurity, though lacking enforceable regulations. Reviews reveal inadequate implementation of AI principles within federal cybersecurity initiatives.

6.3.3. China

Regulations analyzed by the Australia Strategic Policy Institute (2024) focus on centralizing state power and utilizing advanced cyber technology for strategic objectives. The framework prioritizes national security applications while maintaining strict controls over private sector AI development affecting cyber operations.

6.3.4. International Efforts

Research by the United Nations Institute for Disarmament Research (2024) analyzed UN Group of Governmental Experts discussions on Lethal Autonomous Weapons Systems, finding states divided on whether AI cyber capabilities warrant similar restrictions. Analysis of 47 countries identified three approaches: comprehensive regulation advocates (primarily European states), limited regulation supporters (including the US and Russia), and status quo maintainers (various developing nations).

6.4. Privacy Rights and Civil Liberties

AI-powered cyber defense systems raise significant privacy concerns, particularly when monitoring civilian communications. Research examining 15 major AI cybersecurity deployments found 87% involved collection and analysis of personal data without explicit individual consent.

Threat detection using machine learning typically requires access to extensive network traffic, including private communications, browsing history, and personal files. National security justifications have enabled routine online activity monitoring, creating "surveillance creep" in cybersecurity operations.

The Stanford Human-Centered AI Institute (2024) examined whether invasive data collection significantly improves security effectiveness, discovering that less intrusive approaches achieved comparable results. This suggests stronger privacy standards could maintain both security and individual freedoms.

Research also documented potential bias in AI-based cyber defense algorithms. Scientists studying 23 commercial AI cybersecurity products found threat analysis techniques often disproportionately target particular groups, raising discrimination concerns in AI system deployment.

6.5. Corporate Responsibility and Dual-Use Technology Governance

Private companies developing AI technologies face questions about responsibility when their tools enable cyber warfare. Research analyzing major technology companies found most lack comprehensive safeguards to prevent AI misuse in conflict. Only a minority have established complete measures managing risks of dual-use AI applications.

A Carnegie Mellon Software Engineering Institute investigation (2024) examined AI export controls, finding that traditional restrictions on physical shipping inadequately address AI technology spread through cloud computing and open-source platforms. This presents unique challenges for controlling dual-use AI capabilities.

6.6. Emerging Ethical Frameworks and Future Directions

The 2024 Future of Humanity Institute at Oxford University provided ethical principles for examining AI cyber-attacks, drawing on consequentialist, deontological, and virtue ethics. The framework addresses AI use in military actions, distribution of advantages and risks linked to AI cyber capabilities, and impacts of autonomous online battles.

A Princeton University Center for Information Technology Policy study (2024) surveyed 340 experts, policymakers, and AI practitioners, revealing substantial disagreement on fundamental issues regarding AI in cyber operations, indicating need for enhanced collaboration toward unified perspectives.

Future ethical frameworks require guidance on human oversight of AI cyber systems, rules for protecting civilian infrastructure, and standards for handling vulnerabilities in AI systems. Addressing these challenges successfully demands collaborative strategies among technology specialists, ethicists, policymakers, and civil society organizations, creating frameworks that evolve with technological advancement while adhering to accountability, proportionality, and human rights principles.

7. FUTURE TRAJECTORIES AND EMERGING TRENDS IN AI CYBER WARFARE

7.1. Quantum-AI Convergence and Cryptographic Disruption

A new threat to existing cybersecurity is created by the link between quantum computing and artificial intelligence. Studies reveal that in the next 10-15 years, quantum-aided AI technology may crack RSA-2048 encryption, putting the most important security features used in digital environments at risk (Marrow 2025). Using machine learning in quantum-AI hybrid systems is useful for dealing with errors in quantum computers and creating better algorithms which may help increase their practical use in cryptography.

It affects more features than merely the skill of reading codes. It is very hard to identify patterns and enhance processes in cyber operations, but quantum machine learning can help a lot. The research on quantum computing shows that using quantum AI could detect new ways for attacks, process network data fast in the present moment and improve the attacks themselves. Likewise, with such abilities, quantum-AI is able to offer stronger security, discover and address many threats much more quickly than standard computers could (Brooks 2024).

When switching to quantum-resistant cryptography, unique security threats occur. There are now several complete and early versions of candidate algorithms for post-quantum cryptography thanks to the standardization process by the National Institute of Standards and Technology. Even so, successfully using these algorithms worldwide will take a considerable period of time. In the later stages, uniting these kinds of systems might lead to new risks when classical AI and quantum algorithms are merged in AI.

7.2. Artificial General Intelligence and Autonomous Cyber Warfare

Cyber warfare could be significantly affected by the rise of artificial general intelligence (AGI) in the next two decades. AI systems can handle just a few tasks well, but they do not have the general reasoning ability found in humans. AGI systems are designed to think, solve problems and make decisions like humans in all aspects which could greatly change how cyber operations are conducted.

OpenAI, DeepMind and Anthropic have found that AGI systems can carry out entire cyber campaigns on their own, from gathering information, picking targets, to attacking and achieving their objectives. Unlike current artificial intelligence, AGI systems would have the ability to come up with fresh attack methods, adjust to unexpected defenses and decide how and when to respond strategically in conflicts.

The threat of using AI in cyber attacks increases concerns about how much control people have and how stable strategies can be. Experts from RAND Corporation and the Center for Strategic and International Studies believe that there is the possibility that AGI systems might be able to launch cyber attacks at such high speeds and scales that humans can barely comprehend, possibly causing rapid escalation or mistakes. Having AGI cyber capabilities improve in various countries might result in a type of competition where decisions are made at high speed and conflicts are autonomous (Burdette et al. 2025).

8. CONCLUSION

Artificial intelligence is having a major impact on the nature of cyber warfare. Tools that involve AI such as models for custom phishing and malware or agents that scan networks by themselves, have simplified the process for attackers and shortened how much time each attack requires. Therefore, defenders have used automated systems that catch anomalies, use artificial intelligence for predictions and respond in real time to threats with SOAR tools to contain them.

The competition that arises from AI agents mimicking and learning from each other causes unusual changes in cybersecurity. As a result of this, technical games are matched with changes in strategic forces, so accidents could result in higher stakes, increased confusion about who did what and difficulties in preventing conflict. More efficient, secret and widespread attacks of this kind mean that those responsible for national security need to respond quickly and cope with significant uncertainties.

Governments around the world and in alliances are trying to adopt AI into their cyber security policies, spending on research and defense systems. Even though the US, China, Russia and EU countries have their own ways of dealing with AI and cybersecurity, NATO, Five Eyes and other groups try to share threats and work together. Policies and laws are still behind the progress in technology, so no clear rules exist for regulating autonomous cyber actions.

The main challenge now will be ensuring that this merging energy benefits society instead of causing new challenges. It is important for defenders to strengthen their AI models, make sure they work as intended, use adversarial training and preserve safeguards involving humans. Policymakers should negotiate new guidelines for cyber-AI that state when someone can use these tools, how these things are identified and include principles for ethical usage. It is possible to take advantage of AI in cyber defense only by involving technology, having strict guidelines and collaborating with others on an international scale.

REFERENCES

Adewopo, V. (2021). *Exploring open source intelligence for cyber threat prediction*. University of Cincinnati.

Aggarwal, C. C. (2018). *Neural networks and deep learning*. Springer. DOI: 10.1007/978-3-319-94463-0

Ahmed, U., Nazir, M., Sarwar, A., Ali, T., Aggoune, E.-H. M., Shahzad, T., & Khan, M. A. (2025). Signature-based intrusion detection using machine learning and deep learning approaches empowered with fuzzy clustering. *Scientific Reports*, *15*(1), 1726. DOI: 10.1038/s41598-025-85866-7

Alotaibi, A., & Rassam, M. A. (2023). Adversarial machine learning attacks against intrusion detection systems: A survey on strategies and defense. *Future Internet*, *15*(2), 62. DOI: 10.3390/fi15020062

Apolo, Y., & Michael, K. (2024). Beyond a reasonable doubt? Audiovisual evidence, AI manipulation, deepfakes, and the law. *IEEE Transactions on Technology and Society*, *5*(2), 156–168. DOI: 10.1109/TTS.2024.3427816

Arif, A. (2024). An overview of cyber threats generated by AI. *International Journal of Multidisciplinary Sciences and Arts*, *3*(4), 67–76. DOI: 10.47709/ijmdsa.v3i4.4753

Arifin, M. M. (2024). A survey on the application of generative adversarial networks in cybersecurity: prospective, direction and open research scopes. arXiv preprint arXiv:2407.08839.

Arunthavanathan, R., Sajid, Z., Khan, F., & Pistikopoulos, E. (2024). Artificial intelligence–Human intelligence conflict and its impact on process system safety. *Digital Chemical Engineering*, *11*, 100151. DOI: 10.1016/j.dche.2024.100151

Bala, B., & Behal, S. (2024). AI techniques for IoT-based DDoS attack detection: Taxonomies, comprehensive review and research challenges. *Computer Science Review*, *52*, 100631. DOI: 10.1016/j.cosrev.2024.100631

Bhambri & Bajdor (2024). AI-Powered Predictive Analysis for Proactive Cyber Defense. Handbook of AI-Driven Threat Detection and Prevention. CRC Press.

Bonfanti, M. E. (2022). Artificial intelligence and the offence-defence balance in cyber security. In *Cyber Security: Socio-Technological Uncertainty and Political Fragmentation* (pp. 64–79). Routledge. DOI: 10.4324/9781003110224-6

Brooks, C. (2024). *Inside Cyber: How AI, 5G, IoT, and Quantum Computing Will Transform Privacy and Our Security*. John Wiley & Sons. DOI: 10.1002/9781394310562

Burdette, Z. (2025). *The Risks of Preventive Attack in the Race for Advanced Artificial Intelligence*. Center for Open Science.

Charfeddine, M., Kammoun, H. M., Hamdaoui, B., & Guizani, M. (2024). Chatgpt's security risks and benefits: Offensive and defensive use-cases, mitigation measures, and future implications. *IEEE Access : Practical Innovations, Open Solutions*, *12*, 30263–30310. DOI: 10.1109/ACCESS.2024.3367792

Cihon, P. (2019). Standards for AI governance: International standards to enable global coordination in AI research & development. *Future of Humanity Institute. University of Oxford*, *40*(3), 340–342.

Di Nucci, E. (2020). *The control paradox: From AI to populism*. Rowman & Littlefield. DOI: 10.5040/9798881816193

Digmelashvili & Lagvilava. (2023). Cyber Deterrence Strategies in the 21st Century. Future Human Image, 20.

Drašar, M. (2023). The Road Towards Autonomous Cybersecurity Agents: Remedies for Simulation Environments. *European Symposium on Research in Computer Security*, Springer.

Drucker, S. J., & Gumpert, G. (2000). CyberCrime and punishment. *Critical Studies in Media Communication*, *17*(2), 133–158. DOI: 10.1080/15295030009388387

Dsouza, D. S. (2024). Deepfakes in Social Engineering Attacks. Space Law Principles and Sustainable Measures. Springer. DOI: 10.1007/978-3-031-64045-2_8

el Rahwan, A. (2022). Artificial Intelligence and Interoperability for Solving Challenges of OSINT and Cross-Border Investigations. Eur. L. Enf't Rsch. Bull., 6(179).

Erendor, M. E. (2024). *Cyber Security in the Age of Artificial Intelligence and Autonomous Weapons*. CRC Press. DOI: 10.1201/9781003441700

Esteban, J. (2022). *Simulating Network Lateral Movements through the CyberBattleSim Web Platform*. Massachusetts Institute of Technology.

Fakhouri, H. N. (2024). Ai-driven solutions for social engineering attacks: Detection, prevention, and response. 2024 2nd International Conference on Cyber Resilience (ICCR), IEEE.

Falade, P. V. (2023). Decoding the threat landscape: Chatgpt, fraudgpt, and wormgpt in social engineering attacks. arXiv preprint arXiv:2310.05595.

Focarelli, C. (2021). Self-defence in cyberspace. Research handbook on international law and cyberspace. Edward Elgar Publishing. DOI: 10.4337/9781789904253.00026

Garza, V. R., (2020). Machine Learning Techniques for Identifying Anomalous Network Traffic. Academic Press.

Gebrehans, G., Ilyas, N., Eledlebi, K., Lunardi, W. T., Andreoni, M., Yeun, C. Y., & Damiani, E. (2025). Generative Adversarial Networks for Dynamic Malware Behavior: A Comprehensive Review, Categorization, and Analysis. *IEEE Transactions on Artificial Intelligence*, *6*(8), 1955–1976. DOI: 10.1109/TAI.2025.3537966

Ghosh, A., Chakraborty, D., & Law, A. (2018). Artificial intelligence in Internet of things. *CAAI Transactions on Intelligence Technology*, *3*(4), 208–218. DOI: 10.1049/trit.2018.1008

Gil de Zúñiga, H., Goyanes, M., & Durotoye, T. (2024). A scholarly definition of artificial intelligence (AI): Advancing AI as a conceptual framework in communication research. *Political Communication*, *41*(2), 317–334. DOI: 10.1080/10584609.2023.2290497

Gilbert, C., & Gilbert, M. A. (2024). The security implications of artificial intelligence (AI)-powered autonomous weapons: Policy recommendations for international regulation. *International Research Journal of Advanced Engineering and Science*, *9*(4), 205–219.

Gill, A. S. (2020). The changing role of multilateral forums in regulating armed conflict in the digital age. *International Review of the Red Cross*, *102*(913), 261–285. DOI: 10.1017/S1816383121000059

Gioti, A. (2024). *Advancements in Open Source Intelligence (OSINT) Techniques and the role of artificial intelligence in Cyber Threat Intelligence (CTI)*. Πανεπιστήμιο Πειραιώς.

Gururaj, H. (2024). *Social Engineering in Cybersecurity: Threats and Defenses*. CRC Press.

Hosmer, L. T. (1994). Strategic planning as if ethics mattered. *Strategic Management Journal*, *15*(S2), 17–34. DOI: 10.1002/smj.4250151003

Hossain, M. T., Afrin, R., & Biswas, M. A.-A. (2024). A Review on Attacks against Artificial Intelligence (AI) and Their Defence Image Recognition and Generation Machine Learning, Artificial Intelligence. *Control Systems and Optimization Letters*, *2*(1), 52–59. DOI: 10.59247/csol.v2i1.73

Hutchens, J. (2023). *The Language of Deception: Weaponizing Next Generation AI*. John Wiley & Sons.

Inuwa, M. M., & Das, R. (2024). A comparative analysis of various machine learning methods for anomaly detection in cyber attacks on IoT networks. *Internet of Things : Engineering Cyber Physical Human Systems*, *26*, 101162. DOI: 10.1016/j.iot.2024.101162

Jafariandehkordi, M. (2024). The AI Battlefield: Legal Challenges of Autonomous Weapon Systems under International Humanitarian Law. Academic Press.

Jeffrey, N., Tan, Q., & Villar, J. R. (2023). A review of anomaly detection strategies to detect threats to cyber-physical systems. *Electronics (Basel)*, *12*(15), 3283. DOI: 10.3390/electronics12153283

Jimmy, F. (2021). Emerging threats: The latest cybersecurity risks and the role of artificial intelligence in enhancing cybersecurity defenses. *Valley International Journal Digital Library*, *1*(2), 564–574. DOI: 10.18535/ijsrm/v9i2.ec01

Johnson, A. F. (2020). Communications, Cyber Resilience, and the Future of the US Electric Power System: *Proceedings of a Workshop*, National Academies Press.

Kaloudi, N., & Li, J. (2020). The ai-based cyber threat landscape: A survey. *ACM Computing Surveys*, *53*(1), 1–34. DOI: 10.1145/3372823

Khan, A. (2025). Future Trends and Challenges in Cybersecurity and Generative AI. Reshaping CyberSecurity With Generative AI Techniques, 491-522.

Khan, M. I. (2024). AI's Revolutionary Role in Cyber Defense and Social Engineering. *International Journal of Multidisciplinary Sciences and Arts*, *3*(4), 57–66. DOI: 10.47709/ijmdsa.v3i4.4752

Kim, S. (2022). The Inter-network Politics of Cyber Security and Middle Power Diplomacy: A Korean Perspective. Korea's Middle Power Diplomacy: Between Power and Network. Springer.

Kolluri, V. (2024). Revolutionary research on the ai sentry: An approach to overcome social engineering attacks using machine intelligence. *International Journal of Advanced Research and Interdisciplinary Scientific Endeavours*, *1*(1), 53–60.

Kolosnjaji, B. (2024). *Artificial Intelligence for Cybersecurity: Develop AI approaches to solve cybersecurity problems in your organization*. Packt Publishing Ltd.

Lavi & Jabotinsky (2025). Seeing is Believing? Deepfakes in Financial Markets. Deepfakes in Financial Markets, 44.

Lin, Z. (2025). Adaptive Cyber Defense Against APT28: A Comparative Evaluation of Reinforcement Learning-Based Policies in an Emulated Network Environment.

Longabaugh, E. E. (2020). *Signaling for coercion in cyberspace*. Naval Postgraduate School.

Lucarelli, S. (2021). *NATO decision-making in the age of big data and artificial intelligence*. NATO.

Mačák, K. (2017). From cyber norms to cyber rules: Re-engaging states as law-makers. *Leiden Journal of International Law*, *30*(4), 877–899. DOI: 10.1017/S0922156517000358

Malatji, M., & Tolah, A. (2024). Artificial intelligence (AI) cybersecurity dimensions: A comprehensive framework for understanding adversarial and offensive AI. *AI and Ethics*, 1–28.

Marrow, A. A. (2025). *Quantum Computing: Evaluating the Threat Landscape and Risk Management Strategies*. Capitol Technology University.

McGinnis, J. O. (2018). Accelerating AI. Research handbook on the law of artificial intelligence. Edward Elgar Publishing.

McGowan, J. (2025). How Thiel, Musk & Omidyar Turned UFO Hype Into A Security Risk. *SSRN*. DOI: 10.2139/ssrn.5261806

Medvidovic, N., & Edwards, G. (2010). Software architecture and mobility: A roadmap. *Journal of Systems and Software*, *83*(6), 885–898. DOI: 10.1016/j.jss.2009.11.004

Meyer, P. (2020). Norms of responsible state behaviour in cyberspace. The ethics of cybersecurity, 347-360.

Minhaj, S. M. U. H. (2023). Study of artificial intelligence in cyber security and the emerging threat of AI-driven cyber attacks and challenge. Available at *SSRN* 4652028.

Montasari, R. (2024). *National security in the Artificial Intelligence era: Challenges and implications of advanced technologies*. Cardiff Metropolitan University.

National Academies of Sciences. (2024). AI for Scientific Discovery. *Proceedings of a Workshop*.

Nye, J. S.Jr. (2016). Deterrence and dissuasion in cyberspace. *International Security*, *41*(3), 44–71. DOI: 10.1162/ISEC_a_00266

Obioha Val, O. (2025). Cyber Espionage in the Age of Artificial Intelligence: A Comparative Study of State-Sponsored Campaign. Cyber Espionage in the Age of Artificial Intelligence: A Comparative Study of State-Sponsored Campaign.

Pöhler, J. (2025). Keeping the human in the loop: are autonomous decisions inevitable? i-com, 24(1), 9-25.

Por, L. Y. (2024). A systematic literature review on the methods and challenges in detecting zero-day attacks: Insights from the recent crowdstrike incident. *IEEE Access : Practical Innovations, Open Solutions.*

Prieto, I., & Blakely, B. (2023). Proposed uses of generative AI in a cybersecurity-focused soar agent. *Proceedings of the AAAI Symposium Series.*

Rahman, A. (2025). *Reinforcement Learning for Cyber Operations: Applications of Artificial Intelligence for Penetration Testing*. John Wiley & Sons. DOI: 10.1002/9781394206483

Rebala, G. (2019). Machine learning definition and basics. An introduction to machine learning, 1-17.

Rodriguez, M. (2025). A framework for evaluating emerging cyberattack capabilities of ai. arXiv preprint arXiv:2503.11917.

Roy, K. (2024). *Artificial intelligence, ethics and the future of warfare: Global perspectives.* Taylor & Francis. DOI: 10.4324/9781003421849

Saharan, S. (2024). The future of Cyber-Crimes and cyber war in the metaverse. Forecasting cyber crimes in the age of the metaverse. IGI Global Scientific Publishing.

Saharan, S. (2024). Cyber Forensics: A Boon to Cybersecurity. Digital Technologies in Modeling and Management: Insights in Education and Industry. IGI Global.

Saharan, S. (2025). Role of Drones in Climate Change Mitigation and Adaptation. Artificial General Intelligence-Based Drones for Climate Change. IGI Global Scientific Publishing. DOI: 10.4018/979-8-3693-6457-4.ch003

Saharan, S. (2025). Human-AI Collaboration in Moderating AI-Generated Harmful Content. Content Moderation in the Age of AI. IGI Global Scientific Publishing.

Saharan, S., & Yadav, B. (2022). Digital and cyber forensics: A contemporary evolution in forensic sciences. Crime Scene Management within Forensic Science: Forensic Techniques for Criminal Investigations. Springer.

Saniuk, S. (2024). *Smart Organizations in Industry 5.0: A Human-centric Approach.* Taylor & Francis.

Sanjeewani, P., Neuber, G., Fitzgerald, J., Chandrasena, N., Potums, S., Alavi, A., & Lane, C. (2024). Real-time personal protective equipment non-compliance recognition on AI edge cameras. *Electronics (Basel)*, *13*(15), 2990. DOI: 10.3390/electronics13152990

Sarker, I. H. (2024). *AI-driven cybersecurity and threat intelligence: cyber automation, intelligent decision-making and explainability*. Springer Nature. DOI: 10.1007/978-3-031-54497-2

Science, C. (2025). The Age of AI in the Life Sciences: Benefits and Biosecurity Considerations. Academic Press.

Shandilya, S. K. (2023). GPT Based Malware: Unveiling Vulnerabilities and Creating a Way Forward in Digital Space. *2023 International Conference on Data Security and Privacy Protection (DSPP)*, IEEE. DOI: 10.1109/DSPP58763.2023.10404552

Sharma, D. (2025). *Artificial Intelligence for Cyber Security and Industry 4.0*. CRC Press. DOI: 10.1201/9781032657264

Singh, T. (2024). *Artificial Intelligence and Ethics: A Field Guide for Stakeholders*. CRC Press. DOI: 10.1201/9781003502708

Tabassi, E., Burns, K. J., Hadjimichael, M., Molina-Markham, A. D., & Sexton, J. T. (2019). A taxonomy and terminology of adversarial machine learning. *NIST IR*, *2019*, 1–29. DOI: 10.6028/NIST.IR.8269-draft

Taddeo, M. (2024). *The Ethics of Artificial Intelligence in Defence*. Oxford University Press. DOI: 10.1093/oso/9780197745441.001.0001

Taddeo, M., & Floridi, L. (2021). Regulate artificial intelligence to avert cyber arms race. Ethics, Governance, and Policies in Artificial Intelligence. Springer. DOI: 10.1007/978-3-030-81907-1_14

Tanikonda, A. (2022). Advanced AI-Driven Cybersecurity Solutions for Proactive Threat Detection and Response in Complex Ecosystems. *Journal of Science and Technology*, *3*(1).

Tanti, R. (2024). Study of Phishing Attack and their Prevention Techniques. International journal of scientific research in engineering and management, 10(8), 1-8.

Tapscott, B. (2024). *Trivergence: Accelerating Innovation with AI, Blockchain, and the Internet of Things*. John Wiley & Sons.

Tayyab, M. (2025). AI-Powered Threat Detection in Business Environments: Strategies and Best Practices. Generative AI for Web Engineering Models. IGI Global.

Waizel, G. (2024). Bridging the AI divide: The evolving arms race between AI-driven cyber attacks and AI-powered cybersecurity defenses. International Conference on Machine Intelligence & Security for Smart Cities (TRUST) Proceedings.

West, P. (2023). "The Generative AI paradox": What it can create, it may not understand. arXiv preprint arXiv:2311.00059.

Yaseen, A. (2022). Accelerating the SOC: Achieve greater efficiency with AI-driven automation. *International Journal of Responsible Artificial Intelligence*, *12*(1), 1–19.

Yu, J. (2024). The Shadow of Fraud: The Emerging Danger of AI-powered Social Engineering and its Possible Cure. arXiv preprint arXiv:2407.15912.

Zhang, J., Wu, P., London, J., & Tenney, D. (2025). Benchmarking and Evaluating Large Language Models in Phishing Detection for Small and Midsize Enterprises: A Comprehensive Analysis. *IEEE Access : Practical Innovations, Open Solutions*, *13*, 28335–28352. DOI: 10.1109/ACCESS.2025.3540075

Chapter 2
AI-Powered Military Logistics and Strategy:
A Paradigm Shift in Modern Warfare

Ananya Pandey
https://orcid.org/0000-0002-2419-6314
Christ University, Bangalore, India

ABSTRACT

The function of logistics and strategic planning has expanded beyond traditional supply lines as contemporary warfare becomes more complicated. AI is changing military operations by facilitating autonomous logistics systems, real-time data processing, and quicker decision-making. This change is altering how military strategy is developed and implemented, going beyond efficiency improvements. AI provides a level of adaptability never before achievable, from autonomous transport systems and coordinated battlefield support to predictive maintenance of combat vehicles. An intelligent and robust logistics ecosystem is being fostered by the integration of technologies such as swarm robotics, satellite-based monitoring, and quantum-enhanced optimization. But this change also presents operational, ethical, and policy issues. This chapter addresses the hazards of reliance and misalignment while examining the complex effects of AI on military logistics and strategy.

INTRODUCTION

Logistics is the invisible but essential backbone of the complex apparatus that is military operations. War is rarely won without strong logistical frameworks, even though battlefield tactics and combat maneuvers sometimes take center stage in

DOI: 10.4018/979-8-3373-3611-4.ch002

public discussions. The viability of entire military campaigns is determined by the capacity to transport troops, maintain equipment, supply weapons, and distribute food, water, and medical aid—sometimes over large and difficult terrains. "The sinews of war are infinite money," as Carl von Clausewitz once said, and a large portion of that expenditure goes toward logistics, the unseen facilitator of combat endurance and force projection. The science and art of organizing and carrying out the movement, upkeep, and support of military forces can be summed up as military logistics. It covers the acquisition, allocation, and storage of facilities, staff, and equipment. Logistics, which includes everything from fuel supply chains to casualty evacuation, guarantees that military capabilities are transferable into ongoing operations rather than being restricted to the drawing board. Supply, transportation, maintenance, support for health services, and infrastructure are some of the essential components of the traditional logistics chain, and each is essential to maintaining mission success and operational continuity. The intricacy, unpredictability, and severity of military logistics' operating conditions set it apart from civilian supply chain management. Under the strain of time and potentially fatal consequences, logistics in a battlefield must adjust to quickly changing tactical needs, hazardous conditions, and enemy intervention. The logistical lifeline needs to be both robust and responsive in conflict areas where communication channels are brittle and the landscape is uninhabitable.

The Significance of Logistics in Contemporary Warfare and National Defense

History is filled with instances where the outcome of wars was dictated by logistics. A sobering reminder of the vital role logistics play is provided by Napoleon's catastrophic Russian campaign in 1812, which was characterized by overcrowded supply lines and insufficient provisioning. Similar to this, logistical expertise—including the capacity to create temporary ports, move resources across oceans, and oversee supply lines for millions of troops—was a key component of the Allied victory in World War II. Logistics has changed from being a support function to a strategic instrument in contemporary conflicts. Accuracy and agility in logistics have become critical as military doctrines have changed to emphasize multi-domain operations, asymmetric warfare, and quick deployment. In addition to storing war material, 21st-century defense readiness today requires the ability to quickly mobilize and modify resources, frequently across transnational or expeditionary areas. Globally, national security policies are beginning to see logistics as a deterrent in peacetime as well as a need in times of conflict. Projecting logistical supremacy increases alliance dependability, discourages aggressiveness, and communicates preparedness.

Logistics is at the vanguard of a shift in military operations brought about by the emergence of artificial intelligence (AI). AI offers a cognitive augmentation—the capacity to evaluate, forecast, adjust, and learn from data at previously unheard-of speeds—in contrast to other technology revolutions that were largely concentrated on firepower or surveillance.

AI is already being used in military settings in areas like cyber defense, battlefield intelligence, autonomous weapon systems, and strategic simulations. However, AI has the potential to cause the biggest structural change in the field of logistics, which is perhaps the most data-rich and decision-intensive. Predictive analytics for equipment maintenance, real-time supply chain optimization, robotic smart warehousing, and automated convoy management with unmanned vehicles are all made possible by the integration of AI into logistics. In addition to decreasing human error, these capabilities improve operating tempo, lower risks in hazardous environments, and guarantee quicker decision-making in the face of uncertainty. Crucially, artificial intelligence enables logistics to shift from a reactive to a proactive field. AI systems may anticipate dangers, reroute supplies, and dynamically balance resource distribution based on battlefield realities, rather than reacting to logistical failures or shortages after they happen. This development represents a paradigm change: logistics is now an intelligent, flexible part of mission execution rather than a static backend procedure. In order to fully explore how artificial intelligence is revolutionizing military logistics, this chapter provides a thorough analysis of how developments in AI are changing supply chains, operational planning, and decision-making in defense-related settings. The goal is to critically examine the strategic consequences of technical advancements, not just to list them. This includes how AI is changing the nature of warfare, pushing the limits of logistical viability, and forcing a reevaluation of human roles, structures, and doctrines.

To set the tone for comprehending the scope of the change taking place, the conversation will start with a conceptual and historical review of military logistics. After delving into the fundamental technologies that underpin AI applications in logistics, it will examine real-world applications in supply chain management, maintenance, transportation, and medical assistance. The chapter will demonstrate the promise and difficulties of integrating AI through real-world case studies from top military nations and defense corporations.

It will also cover the more general moral, legal, and practical conundrums that AI-enabled logistics present. These include the risk of becoming overly reliant on machine-driven judgments, cybersecurity flaws in networks controlled by AI, and accountability concerns in autonomous systems. By doing thus, the chapter seeks to offer a critical and impartial perspective of AI's dual nature as a tool with both potential and drawbacks. In the end, this chapter makes the argument that AI-powered logistics is a strategic enabler that has the ability to completely alter the nature and conduct of combat, rather than just being a tool for contemporary armies. The capacity to use intelligent logistics could be the deciding factor between success and failure on the battlefield of the future as tensions around the world increase and military operations become more complicated.

HISTORICAL OVERVIEW OF MILITARY LOGISTICS

Even before military logistics was officially recognized as a field of study, it was a persistent feature of battle. Logistics was essentially about survival in the pre-industrial era, when armies relied on crude supply routes, lengthy baggage trains, or local foraging. The capacity to organize, maintain, and supply sizable unit formations over wide geographic distances influenced ancient military operations, such as those commanded by Alexander the Great or Roman legions. Despite being unwritten, logistics dictated the scope and length of campaigns (Luttwak, 2001). Logistics underwent a dramatic change throughout the Industrial Revolution. New levels of efficiency and scale were brought about by mechanized transportation, such as steamships and railroads. The American Civil War (1861–1865) and the Crimean War (1853–1856) both brought to light the growing difficulty of supporting contemporary armies. The advent of telegraph systems made it easier for frontlines and supply centers to coordinate in real time (Van Creveld, 1977). As a result of these technological developments, military logistics was formalized as a strategic discipline, expanding beyond the simple transportation of cargo to include procurement, warehousing, and medical evacuation.

World Wars I and II introduced previously unheard-of levels of technology integration and scale into military logistics as conflict entered the 20th century. Coordinated multi-theater operations were made possible by rail networks, motorized vehicles, and marine convoys. The effective logistical support offered by initiatives like the Red Ball Express, which delivered more than 400,000 tons of material to the advancing armies after D-Day, was a major factor in the Allied victory in Europe during World War II (Huston, 1966). From being a support role, logistics evolved into a strategic instrument that could make the difference between success and loss. Logistics systems began to be digitalized in the latter half of the 20th century (Pandey & Joseph, 2025). The foundation for today's digital logistics environment was laid during the Gulf War (1990–1991), which brought barcoding, automated logistics systems, and satellite-based tracking. The advent of integrated digital supply chains in defense was signaled by information systems like the Defense Logistics Agency's Standard Automated Materiel Management System (SAMMS) (Eriksen, 2005).

From Traditional to Modern Military Logistics

Bulk provisioning, manual coordination, and linear supply lines were the hallmarks of traditional military logistics. Because logistics officials relied so much on established supply lines, any interruption, whether man-made or natural, may halt operations. Demand was manually and reactively forecasted using static planning techniques, historical data, and intuition. Modern military logistics, on the other hand, are data-driven, dynamic, and becoming more automated (Pandey& Joseph, 2025a). In order to provide predictive supply insights, modern systems combine real-time data from sensors, satellites, and business resource platforms. Modern armies use automated warehousing, artificial intelligence, and just-in-time (JIT) logistics to maintain lean, flexible supply chains rather than indiscriminately stockpiling (Gunzinger & Dougherty, 2020). Furthermore, supplying the appropriate equipment to the appropriate location at the appropriate time has become more important than bulk. Mobility and reach represent yet another significant distinction. Modern air transportation, driverless cars, and aerial drones have redefined operating boundaries, but traditional logistics frequently failed in inhospitable terrain. Unlike the heavy logistics tails of previous conflicts, modern logistics facilitates expeditionary warfare through fast deployment, minimum footprint, and decentralized sustainment.

Insights from Past Logistic Experience

Important insights into the development of logistics can be gained from the international conflicts of the 20th and 21st centuries. The importance of logistical planning in multi-theater operations was brought to light during World War II. It took coordinated naval convoys, inland transportation, and air resupply missions to convey that many soldiers and supplies across the Atlantic and Pacific (Huston, 1966). Operation Overlord's logistical prowess established a standard for resource sharing, integrated planning, and real-time flexibility. Digital logistics were introduced during the Gulf War. The effectiveness of prepositioned stocks and centralized logistics coordination was proved by the U.S. Department of Defense's capacity to deploy nearly 500,000 troops together with their support infrastructure in a matter of months. Barcodes, satellite communications, and GPS enabled precise supply tracking and decreased waste (Eriksen, 2005). But it also exposed flaws: reliance on massed logistical centers posed security problems, and centralized systems were prone to overload.

The war in Afghanistan made it clear how crucial adaptable and durable logistics are. Traditional supply channels were unworkable due to harsh terrain, insurgency threats, and inadequate infrastructure. Consequently, U.S. and NATO forces depended more on local procurement, modular logistics packages, and air-dropped supplies

(McKinsey & Company, 2017). The necessity of sustainability was also highlighted by the experience; logistical planning now had to take operational theaters' effects on energy, water, and the environment into account.

The Logistical Difficulties of Contemporary Hybrid Combat

Complex logistical needs are presented by modern hybrid warfare, which combines conventional, irregular, cyber, and information warfare. Hybrid battles are not limited to certain battlefields like regular fighting is. They frequently entail the deployment of proxy forces, supply chain cyberattacks, and urban warfare. This calls for resilient, decentralized, and real-time logistics systems that can adjust to changing threats. Maintaining cybersecurity in logistics networks is one difficulty. The increasing interconnectedness of logistical systems makes them appealing targets for enemies. Operational efficacy can be paralyzed by GPS disruption or attacks on supply chain management software. Working in surroundings that are rejected or contested presents a second difficulty (Pandey, 2026). Aerial drones, mobile micro-warehousing, and autonomous systems are necessary in these places because traditional convoys or depots may be attacked (Gunzinger & Dougherty, 2020). Moreover, hybrid warfare entails ongoing operations in which military and civilian personnel are mixed together. Ensuring civilian access to logistics infrastructure while protecting security presents ethical and practical issues. Furthermore, logistics now have to support data centers, electronic warfare instruments, and psychological operations—needs that weren't present in earlier conflicts. The role of logistics must change as military doctrines advance to include multidomain operations—land, sea, air, space, and cyber. It now involves the comprehensive integration of data, energy, materials, and persons in a dynamic threat environment rather than only the transportation of tangible commodities.

EMERGING TECHNOLOGIES IN TRANSFORMING MILITARY LOGISTICS

The incorporation of Artificial Intelligence (AI) into military logistics has brought about a paradigm change in the changing terrain of contemporary combat, altering the way defense forces handle infrastructure, resources, and operational readiness. A variety of AI technologies are being used more and more to optimize traditional supply chains and logistics networks, which are frequently hindered by inefficiencies and lag times. They all contribute differently to increasing productivity, accuracy, and flexibility. These include digital twins, robotics, computer vision, natural language processing, machine learning, and the Internet of Military Things (IoMT).

Machine Learning: Predictive maintenance and demand forecasting

Machine learning-based demand forecasting is among the most revolutionary uses of AI in military logistics. ML algorithms can precisely forecast future logistical needs by examining both historical data and real-time inputs, such as troop movements, mission parameters, and weather trends. By minimizing shortages and overstocking, this forecasting ability eases logistical strains and gives decision-makers more confidence when allocating resources (Miller & Frazier, 2021). Predictive maintenance also benefits greatly from machine learning. Machine learning algorithms analyze sensor data from military vehicles and equipment to find patterns that point to wear or malfunction before a failure happens. The transition from reactive to predictive maintenance guarantees the best possible deployment of vital assets and improves operational continuity (Lele & Goswami, 2020).

Computer Vision: Monitoring and Stock Control

In military applications, computer vision technologies have transformed surveillance and inventory operations by allowing systems to analyze and act upon visual data. Autonomous systems with computer vision capabilities can reduce the need for manual checks and human error in logistics warehouses by monitoring inventory levels, identifying lost products, and detecting anomalies in stock conditions (Chen et al., 2020). Computer vision technologies enable automated reconnaissance and surveillance on the battlefield. Unmanned vehicles and drones improve situational awareness and command effectiveness by using visual inputs to detect threats, navigate terrain, and relay actionable intelligence in real-time.

Natural Language Processing (NLP): Multilingual Coordination and Real-Time Communication

Particularly in multilingual and multi-national settings, Natural Language Processing (NLP) greatly improves cooperation across military logistical units. Effective communication between allied soldiers with disparate linguistic origins is frequently necessary for military operations. Real-time translation of logistics instructions and documents using NLP-powered systems can improve interoperability and minimize misunderstandings (Poria et al., 2021). Furthermore, frontline staff may use natural speech to submit supply requests, consult manuals, and connect with logistics databases with the use of voice-based AI assistants driven by natural language processing (NLP), which streamlines processes in high-stress situations.

Autonomous Systems and Robots

Both operational effectiveness and human safety have increased as a result of the use of robotics and autonomous technologies in military logistics. Ammunition, medical supplies, and meals are currently transported across difficult terrains without posing a threat to human life using autonomous ground vehicles and drones (Zhao et al., 2022). These systems are frequently directed by AI algorithms that evaluate dangers, examine environmental data, and choose the best pathways. Additionally, loading and unloading procedures are automated by robotic arms and manipulators in logistics hubs, which cuts down on labor costs and processing times. These technologies are especially important in remote or high-risk locations where conventional supply lines can be jeopardized.

Internet of Military Things (IoMT) with AI Support

The Internet of Military Things is a networked environment in which artificial intelligence (AI) is used to integrate and connect different military assets, such as wearable soldier technology and vehicles. Logistics systems can make decentralized, real-time judgments thanks to this network's smooth data flow. An IoMT-enabled system, for example, can autonomously coordinate a refueling procedure without human interaction by detecting a vehicle's fuel status, environmental circumstances, and the presence of nearby resupply drones (Tan et al., 2019). In order to analyze this vast amount of data, find trends, and proactively meet logistical demands, artificial intelligence (AI) is essential. The flexibility of combat logistics is greatly increased by IoMT systems' dynamic and self-healing characteristics.

TRENDS UNDER AI-POWERED LOGISTICS

The integration of AI into logistical frameworks has become a key enabler of combat superiority in the quickly changing terrain of contemporary military operations. Logistics' transformation from a reactive to a proactive, data-driven field highlights a dramatic change in military doctrines across the globe. The application of AI technologies in military logistics is examined in this part, with a focus on how they are influencing supply chain management, mobility, maintenance, medical assistance, and cyber-infrastructure.

Supply Chain Management

Management of the Supply Chain

Supply chain management stands to gain the most from the incorporation of AI in defense logistics. Manual forecasting, stockpiling mistakes, and logistical bottlenecks during quick deployments are some of the reasons why traditional military supply chains frequently suffer from inefficiency. AI-powered smart inventory systems are assisting the military in making the shift to more predictive and responsive models. To precisely track supplies, smart inventory systems use real-time data from sensors, RFID tags, and satellite surveillance. Artificial intelligence (AI) algorithms automatically modify stock levels across geographically scattered bases, assess consumption patterns, and forecast resupply needs. By doing this, operational continuity is ensured by lowering both overstocking and understocking (Boyson, 2019). Furthermore, machine learning-powered predictive analytics provides improved insight into supply and demand cycles. In order to predict logistical needs, AI algorithms mimic a variety of scenarios based on weather, geopolitical changes, and battlefield dynamics. When logistical flexibility becomes a mission-critical feature, such as in humanitarian crises, peacekeeping missions, and hybrid warfare, this level of readiness is very beneficial (Gansler & Lucyshyn, 2020).

Mobility and Transportation

Since they dictate how quickly and safely materials are transported across difficult and frequently hostile terrains, mobility and transport are essential to military logistics. With the introduction of intelligent route planning and autonomous convoy systems, AI is making major strides in this area. By employing driverless trucks and ground vehicles, autonomous convoy operations lessen the danger to human drivers in conflict areas. Real-time AI navigation systems that include GPS, LIDAR, and terrain recognition algorithms are essential to these convoys. Using little assistance from humans, military convoys using autonomous systems can detect threats, maintain formations, and adjust to changing situations. This capability is demonstrated by the U.S. Army's Expedient Leader-Follower program, which aims to develop resupply missions that are safer and more effective (Defense Innovation Board, 2021). Additionally, AI helps with route optimization by evaluating battlefield data, including enemy movement, weather, and obstacles in the landscape, to determine the most effective and safe paths for transport troops. Particularly important in disputed logistics situations, these dynamic routing decisions improve agility and lower fuel usage (Sharma et al., 2021).

Operations for Maintenance and Repair (MRO)

AI is also proving to be essential in maintaining the operational readiness of military weapons. Military forces now manage the lifecycle of their vehicles, planes, and weapon systems in a completely new way thanks to predictive maintenance. AI systems can identify abnormalities in equipment performance and anticipate component failures before they happen by using machine learning algorithms that have been trained on previous failure data. AI platforms that track temperature, vibration, and utilization levels get performance data continuously from sensors integrated into vital equipment. Logistics teams can prevent unexpected malfunctions during missions by using these insights to plan repair in advance (Chien et al., 2020). Predictive maintenance is enhanced by automated diagnostics, which cut down on the time and labor needed to find problems. AI-powered inspection drones, for instance, are able to visually scan armored vehicles or airplanes and identify wear or damage that human technicians might not see right away. In addition to saving time, these technologies improve mission reliability and decrease logistical downtime (Tranter & Earley, 2022).

Logistics for Medical and Humanitarian Support

Effective delivery of medical help is essential in disaster relief efforts and high-intensity conflict situations. AI is being used more and more to enhance the efficiency, precision, and coordination of emergency response logistics and combat medical treatment. By predicting demand for medications, surgical instruments, and emergency supplies based on mission data and injury trends, artificial intelligence systems help manage medical resources on the battlefield. Medical logistics teams can more efficiently pre-position resources by using AI-based planning technologies that can also model casualty rates in various war scenarios (Yao et al., 2023). AI also helps optimize emergency medical responses during evacuations during natural catastrophes or combat. Real-time artificial intelligence (AI) systems, for example, use field reports and satellite data to prioritize assistance distribution, find accessible escape routes, and plan the delivery of vital medical supplies via unmanned aerial vehicle (UAV) to besieged or inaccessible areas. When dangerous conditions cause human logistics teams to be delayed, these capabilities are essential for providing relief quickly (Zhou & Miao, 2021).

Logistics via Cyberspace

Logistics in the digital theater of contemporary warfare involves not just the safe transfer of data but also the provision of tangible goods. By protecting supply chains from digital disruption and improving traceability, AI is essential to strengthening cyber-logistics. AI is being used for automated incident response, anomaly identification, and real-time cyber threat monitoring in order to secure AI-driven logistics networks. For instance, AI systems can start automated lockdown procedures or divert communications to secure channels when they identify odd patterns, such illicit access or irregular data transfers. This is particularly important when adversaries use information warfare to target logistics infrastructure (Gordon et al., 2021). When combined with AI, blockchain technology ensures the safe provenance and traceability of military supplies, adding an additional layer of resilience. When combined with AI, blockchain technology ensures the safe provenance and traceability of military supplies, adding an additional layer of resilience (Joseph & Pandey, 2025). Blockchain keeps an unchangeable record of transactions, and artificial intelligence makes sure that these records are regularly checked for inconsistencies. In addition to preventing fraud and manipulation, this collaboration gives commanders complete information regarding the movement and state of assets from the depot to the deployment zone (Tapscott & Tapscott, 2016).

STRATEGIC AND OPERATIONAL ADVANTAGES OF AI-POWERED MILITARY LOGISTICS

Modern defense operations are now designed and carried out in a completely different way as a result of the development of artificial intelligence (AI) in military logistics. Defense forces throughout the world are experiencing a range of strategic and tactical advantages by using AI into logistical operations, radically altering how war is fought and the support networks behind the front lines. These advantages go beyond simple technical ease and tackle important problems like operational tiredness, inefficiency, and unpredictability. Enhanced speed, accuracy, and adaptability; decreased human error and resource waste; real-time situational awareness and decision-making; improved force projection and readiness; and cost-effectiveness with sustainability are the five main benefits of integrating AI that are covered in this section.

Enhanced Flexibility, Speed, and Precision

In logistics operations, speed and accuracy are now essential for gaining a competitive edge. Military logistics units can significantly cut down on decision-making time thanks to AI's ability to process large, complicated datasets more quickly. For instance, whereas it used to take hours or days to establish the best delivery routes, machine learning algorithms can now assess terrain data and satellite photos in a matter of seconds. The U.S. Department of Defense (2021) claims that in simulation situations, including AI into logistics systems has shortened operational planning times by as much as 60%. In addition to speed, AI systems provide a degree of accuracy and adaptability that human operators can find difficult to attain under pressure. Real-time supply chain logistics recalibration by adaptive algorithms can react to changing combat conditions, such as shifting weather patterns, enemy movement, or equipment breakdown. This responsiveness guarantees that troops and assets receive the appropriate support at the appropriate moment by giving commanders the freedom to change plans without compromising operational effectiveness.

Decrease in Human Error and Waste of Resources

Conventional military logistics mainly rely on human judgment, which is useful but prone to mistakes, particularly when information is lacking or under pressure. AI systems can greatly lessen these vulnerabilities through automation and predictive modeling. Predictive maintenance, a procedure where AI detects possible equipment breakdowns before they happen, is one prominent example. AI can forecast wear and tear and recommend prompt fixes by evaluating sensor data from automobiles, airplanes, and other equipment, averting malfunctions while on a mission (Gonzalez & Shukla, 2022). Furthermore, by predicting consumption trends using real-time data, AI-enhanced inventory systems reduce overstocking and understocking. This accuracy lowers the risk exposure of supply lines by reducing the logistical footprint in battle zones and reducing resource waste. Up to 30% more resources were used during joint military exercises when AI-driven logistics models were used, according to a 2020 study by NATO's Science and Technology Organization.

Situational Awareness and Decision-Making in Real Time

AI's ability to improve situational awareness is among its most compelling benefits for military logistics. AI systems combine sensors, drones, satellite imagery, and real-time data feeds to combine diverse data into a coherent operational picture. Previously impossible, commanders can now keep an eye on supply movements, foresee risks, and make well-informed decisions with more clarity and speed. For example, using pattern recognition and anomaly detection, AI platforms can track convoys and predict hazards like ambushes or topographical impediments. AI functions as an intelligent advisor when paired with real-time communication technologies, continuously monitoring the logistics ecosystem for interruptions and recommending the best course of action. By reducing delays and bottlenecks, this ongoing feedback loop guarantees that decisions are made more quickly and accurately (Allen & Chan, 2017).

Improved Force Readiness and Projection

The ability to deploy and maintain military power over long distances, or force projection, is largely dependent on logistical proficiency. This procedure is streamlined by AI-enhanced logistics solutions, which shorten lead times and automate vital supply chain operations. By transporting supplies without direct human interference, autonomous vehicles—such as unmanned ground or aerial delivery systems—can increase armed forces' operational reach while protecting humans. AI also maximizes preparedness through sophisticated simulation and planning. For instance, digital twin technologies enable planners to model different scenarios and results by simulating logistics networks. By anticipating weaknesses and improving logistical plans, this predictive capability enhances mission readiness (Wang et al., 2023). As a result, militaries can guarantee that troops are not only adequately equipped but also able to adjust to tactical needs that change quickly.

Sustainability and Economic Efficiency

Military activities always include costs, especially when there are long-term conflicts or financial constraints. AI creates efficiencies that have a direct impact on cost reduction. While effective supply chain management decreases waste, redundancy, and fuel consumption, automation reduces labor-intensive activities. A 2020 study by the RAND Corporation estimates that the U.S. The Army may save up to 15% a year in operating expenses by implementing AI in logistics. AI helps with environmental sustainability, which is becoming a concern for military operations, in addition to economic efficiency. The environmental impact of logistics operations is decreased through more efficient use of energy, waste minimization, and route optimization. This is consistent with the growing emphasis on climate resilience and environmental accountability in international military plans (NATO, 2023).

ETHICAL, LEGAL AND SECURITY CONCERNS

One significant technological advancement is the incorporation of AI into military logistics. It promises improved operational readiness, resilience, and efficiency. However, a number of moral, legal, and security-related issues have surfaced as countries adopt AI-driven logistics. To make sure that the advantages of AI do not come at the expense of accountability, human rights, or international stability, these issues require serious consideration.

Dual-Use Issues and Abuse Risk

The dual-use nature of AI technologies is one of the most important ethical issues. Autonomous transport systems and predictive maintenance algorithms are examples of tools created for military logistics that can be used for civilian surveillance or offensive military actions. The possibility that AI-driven logistics platforms will be used for unauthorized or illegal activities is increased by this dual-use feature. The issue is not only hypothetical; instances like the US project Project Maven, which was first created for video object detection, sparked intense discussion regarding the application of AI to deadly autonomous weapon systems (Kania, 2018). The possible spread of these technologies calls into question export regulations and global governance, particularly if they end up in the hands of authoritarian governments or non-state entities.

Cybersecurity and Data Privacy Risks

Massive datasets, including personnel data, geospatial data, and real-time combat analytics, are crucial to logistics AI systems. There are several privacy and cybersecurity issues associated with the gathering, storing, and processing of such sensitive data. These data platforms could reveal army movements, strategic vulnerabilities, or the whereabouts of vital infrastructure if they are compromised. Furthermore, AI platforms are becoming increasingly and more interconnected through the Internet of Military Things (IoMT), which makes them appealing targets for cyberattacks. Supply chains could be destroyed by a well-planned attack on a military logistics AI network, which could result in mission failure or casualties. According to reports, military supply chains are still vulnerable to supply chain cyber threats, especially in wealthy countries (Boulanin et al., 2020). When enemies employ AI-enhanced cyber weapons themselves, it is frequently insufficient to ensure strong encryption, network segmentation, and resilient backup systems.

Reliance on Self-Sustained Systems

The increasing reliance on autonomous technologies for vital logistics tasks is another urgent problem. AI techniques are becoming essential for everything from automated inventory systems at forward operating bases to unmanned aerial vehicles (UAVs) transporting supplies. However, there are serious concerns associated with over-reliance on such systems. Catastrophic errors may result from AI misinterpreting sensor data, adversarial manipulation, or system breakdowns. An AI logistics routing algorithm's misclassification, for example, can cause vital medical supplies to be diverted from a conflict area, which would have catastrophic humanitarian repercussions. Additionally, over time, this reliance may weaken human knowledge, making it harder for military people to make wise decisions in the event that AI systems malfunction. Researchers like Sharkey (2019) have cautioned that placing too much faith in AI in vital systems could lead to "automation bias," which is the tendency to ignore human error even when the algorithm is bad.

International Humanitarian Law Adherence

The use of logistical systems driven by AI also calls into question adherence to International Humanitarian Law (IHL), which regulates behavior during armed conflict. The results of logistical systems can have a big impact on mission sustainability, supply prioritization, and targeting even when they are not directly involved in combat. Lines of legality become hazy if AI systems inadvertently assist military actions that contravene IHL, such as permitting disproportionate force or assisting occupation logistics without due process. At its core, AI systems lack the moral and legal reasoning abilities to determine whether their results align with the Geneva Conventions' requirements for necessity, distinction, and proportionality of outcomes. In order to guarantee human oversight and legal compliance at all operational levels, the application of AI in logistics must be closely examined within a legal framework (Schmitt, 2020).

Problems with Decision Liability and Accountability

Possibly the most intricate legal issue is accountability. Who is morally and legally liable if an AI-powered logistics system has a major malfunction, like sending the incorrect payload to the wrong place? Is it the manufacturer who constructed the hardware, the developers who taught the algorithm, or the commander who authorized the technology? Justice and restitution for impacted parties may be impeded when accountability is diluted by the division of responsibilities among several players. Furthermore, the majority of international laws and military legal concepts have not yet been modified to take non-human actors into consideration when making decisions. Joint operations involving several allied nations, where culpability norms and legal jurisdictions may clash, make the issue much more acute. Though this is only a theoretical framework with little practical implementation, legal experts like Pagallo (2017) argue for the formation of a new legal category—"electronic agents"—to assign limited liability.

CHALLENGES AND LIMITATIONS

Artificial intelligence has the potential to revolutionize military logistics, but there are significant obstacles that prevent its smooth deployment. The compatibility of AI-based platforms with legacy systems is one of the main issues. The legacy infrastructure used by many defense agencies was built decades ago and lacks the compute power, communication protocols, and adaptability needed to support contemporary AI solutions (Kott & Perconti, 2018). AI integration in these settings presents operational and technological challenges and requires expensive retrofitting or total redesigns. The gap in infrastructure and technology, particularly between countries with different degrees of defense preparation, is another major obstacle. While some nations have created digital logistics ecosystems, others are still limited by inadequate cybersecurity measures, unreliable communication networks, or underdeveloped digital infrastructure (O'Meara & Kania, 2020). For data interchange and autonomous decision-making, AI systems require reliable and secure networks; any infrastructure compromise jeopardizes their dependability in emergency situations or during combat.

The gap in infrastructure and technology, particularly between countries with different degrees of defense preparation, is another major obstacle. While some nations have created digital logistics ecosystems, others are still limited by inadequate cybersecurity measures, unreliable communication networks, or underdeveloped digital infrastructure (O'Meara & Kania, 2020). For data interchange and autonomous decision-making, AI systems require reliable and secure networks; any infrastructure compromise jeopardizes their dependability in emergency situations or during combat. The problem of trust and integration between humans and machines is equally urgent. Military personnel need to gain trust in AI systems so they can rely on their results, particularly in high-stakes situations. However, system openness, interpretability, and prior performance all influence trust in AI, which is not a given (Gustetic et al., 2021). Operator resistance or skepticism may arise from an over-reliance on opaque "black box" algorithms, while under-reliance may lead to an underutilization of AI's potential. Iterative training methods and human-centric AI design are essential to closing this trust gap.

Lastly, procurement complexity and financial limitations serve as structural obstacles. Defense procurement processes are frequently risk-averse and bureaucratic, making them unsuitable for the rapid, iterative development cycles that characterize AI innovation. Furthermore, the high expenses of AI research, such as R&D, testing, cybersecurity, and hiring expertise, might put a burden on defense resources, particularly in economies with lower incomes (Boulanin & Verbruggen, 2017). It's still difficult to strike a balance between the need for innovation and financial sustainability. In conclusion, even though AI has the capacity to completely transform military logistics, institutional, sociocultural, and technical barriers are preventing its widespread deployment. In addition to technological solutions, overcoming these obstacles calls for strategic planning, global collaboration, and ethical consideration.

CONCLUSION

Artificial intelligence's incorporation into military logistics represents a major change in the way contemporary combat is conceptualized, organized, and carried out, not just a technical advancement. AI turns logistics into a strategic force multiplier by automating supply chains and facilitating real-time decision-making and predictive maintenance. In addition to improving responsiveness and efficiency, it also changes the speed and agility of military operations. But as the military rapidly advances toward an AI-driven future, a careful balance needs to be struck. Innovation holds great promise, but it must be balanced with responsibility. There are serious concerns with operational control, legal limits, and ethical accountability as logistics systems become more autonomous. The creation of thorough governance structures that direct the development, application, and supervision of AI in a manner consistent with humanitarian ideals and international standards is imperative. Investing in strong and secure infrastructure, encouraging civil-military cooperation for responsible AI research, and creating standards that stop abuse or escalation should be the three main focuses of policy efforts. To maintain operational dependability and trust, human staff must be trained and upskilled to collaborate with intelligent technology. AI has the potential to become an integral part of military doctrine in the future. It will have an impact on strategy, tactics, and long-term military planning in addition to logistics. Similar to how new weapons and strategies characterized earlier war revolutions, the degree to which AI is assiduously—and morally—integrated into military ecosystems will determine the current evolution. AI adoption in logistics is therefore no longer discretionary but rather necessary, requiring forethought, caution, and a steadfast dedication to both moral responsibility and technological excellence.

Future of AI in Military Logistics

(AI) has the potential to completely transform military logistics in the future by making decentralized, robust, and autonomous systems possible. Swarm intelligence, which refers to collective behavior among decentralized, AI-driven platforms—like self-governing drones or cars—is one noteworthy advancement that enables co-operatively carrying out intricate logistical tasks without centralized management (Brambilla et al., 2013). This paradigm lessens susceptibility to single-point failures and improves adaptability in contested contexts. The operational frontier of AI is being expanded concurrently by integration with satellite and space-based logistics. With the help of AI algorithms, satellites can foresee weather disruptions, reroute assets dynamically, and continuously monitor supply chain conditions (Crespo-Pereira et al., 2021). This capacity is particularly important for international military operations that ask for accuracy and flexibility across geographically separated troops. Furthermore, logistical decision-making could be significantly accelerated by quantum computing. Quantum-enhanced AI has the potential to transform combat supply chain resilience, inventory distribution, and route planning by resolving optimization problems at hitherto unachievable speeds (Kais, 2021). Green logistics powered by AI is also becoming a strategic necessity. Without sacrificing preparedness, advanced algorithms can optimize energy use, minimize fuel use, and facilitate predictive maintenance, all of which support environmentally friendly defense operations (Gonzalez-Feliu & Morana, 2014). Lastly, interoperable AI systems that can harmonize various data standards and communication protocols are becoming more and more important for cross-border coalition logistics. AI promotes logistical efficiency in joint missions while maintaining operational sovereignty by facilitating smooth coordination between ally forces (Defense Science Board, 2019). Collectively, these developments represent a move away from reactive supply tactics and toward proactive, intelligent logistics ecosystems that can function independently, morally, and sustainably across domains.

REFERENCES

Allen, G., & Chan, T. (2017). *Artificial Intelligence and National Security*. Belfer Center for Science and International Affairs, Harvard Kennedy School. https://www.belfercenter.org/publication/artificial-intelligence-and-national-security

Boulanin, V., Goussac, N., & Wareham, M. (2020). *Limits on autonomous weapon systems: Identifying practical elements of human control*. Stockholm International Peace Research Institute (SIPRI). https://www.sipri.org

Boulanin, V., & Verbruggen, M. (2017). *Mapping the development of autonomy in weapon systems*. Stockholm International Peace Research Institute (SIPRI). https://www.sipri.org/sites/default/files/2017-11/siprireport_mapping_the_development_of_autonomy_in_weapon_systems_1117_1.pdf

Boyson, S. (2019). AI and the end-to-end supply chain: A new era of digital logistics. *Supply Chain Management Review*, *23*(5), 26–33.

Brambilla, M., Ferrante, E., Birattari, M., & Dorigo, M. (2013). Swarm robotics: A review from the swarm engineering perspective. *Swarm Intelligence*, *7*(1), 1–41. DOI: 10.1007/s11721-012-0075-2

Chen, Y., Du, Z., & Yang, G. (2020). Computer vision-based logistics warehouse monitoring. *Journal of Intelligent Manufacturing*, *31*(2), 285–296. DOI: 10.1007/s10845-019-01468-5

Chien, S., Tran, D., Rabideau, G., & Davies, A. (2020). *Predictive maintenance in military systems using AI: Reducing mission downtime*. *IEEE Aerospace Conference Proceedings*, 1–12. DOI: 10.1109/AERO47225.2020.9172301

Crespo-Pereira, D., López-Cedrún, J., García-Álvarez, M. T., & López-Carreiro, I. (2021). AI and satellite-based logistics: A vision for global operations. *Journal of Space Policy and Logistics*, *3*(2), 45–58.

Defense Innovation Board. (2021). *AI principles: Recommendations on the ethical use of AI by the Department of Defense*. U.S. Department of Defense. https://innovation.defense.gov

Defense Science Board. (2019). *AI and the Future of Defense Logistics*. U.S. Department of Defense.

Eriksen, R. (2005). Transforming military logistics: A necessary revolution. *Joint Forces Quarterly*, (39), 57–65.

Gansler, J. S., & Lucyshyn, W. (2020). Transforming logistics through AI: Enabling agile defense support. *Journal of Defense Analytics and Logistics*, *4*(1), 45–58.

Glaessgen, E. H., & Stargel, D. S. (2012). The digital twin paradigm for future NASA and U.S. Air Force vehicles. *53rd AIAA/ASME/ASCE/AHS/ASC Structures, Structural Dynamics and Materials Conference*, 1–14. DOI: 10.2514/6.2012-1818

Gonzalez, M., & Shukla, R. (2022). Predictive maintenance using AI in military equipment logistics. *Defence Science Journal*, *72*(1), 34–42. DOI: 10.14429/dsj.72.17042

Gonzalez-Feliu, J., & Morana, J. (2014). *Sustainable urban logistics: Concepts, methods and information systems*. Springer. DOI: 10.1007/978-3-642-31788-0

Gordon, C., Coleman, S., & Tavassoli, A. (2021). Cybersecurity in military logistics: The growing role of AI and blockchain. *Military Cyber Affairs*, *6*(1), 1–17.

Gunzinger, M., & Dougherty, C. (2020). *Resilient logistics: The key to winning future high-end wars*. Center for Strategic and Budgetary Assessments (CSBA). https://csbaonline.org/research/publications/resilient-logistics

Gustetic, J., Rose, D., & Linick, J. (2021). Trust in human-machine teams: A multi-dimensional perspective. *Journal of Cognitive Engineering and Decision Making*, *15*(1), 3–17. DOI: 10.1177/1555343420959863

Huston, J. A. (1966). *The Sinews of War: Army Logistics, 1775–1953*. U.S. Army Center of Military History.

Joseph, J., & Pandey, A. (2025). Human-AI Collaborative Intelligence: Ethical and Legal Considerations. In *Humans and Generative AI Tools for Collaborative Intelligence* (pp. 403-422). IGI Global Scientific Publishing.

Kais, S. (2021). *Quantum Information and Computation for Chemistry*. Wiley.

Kania, E. B. (2018). *Battlefield singularity: Artificial intelligence, military revolution, and China's future military power*. Center for a New American Security. https://www.cnas.org

Kott, A., & Perconti, P. (2018). Long-term challenges for autonomous systems. *Computer*, *51*(5), 70–75. DOI: 10.1109/MC.2018.2381130

Lele, A., & Goswami, P. (2020). Predictive maintenance using AI for military vehicles. *Defence Science Journal*, *70*(3), 256–263. DOI: 10.14429/dsj.70.15367

Luttwak, E. N. (2001). *The Grand Strategy of the Roman Empire: From the First Century A.D. to the Third*. Johns Hopkins University Press.

McKinsey & Company. (2017). *The future of military logistics: Rethinking supply chain agility and resilience*. https://www.mckinsey.com/industries/public-and-social-sector/our-insights/the-future-of-military-logistics

Miller, B. W., & Frazier, A. W. (2021). Machine learning for logistics demand forecasting in military operations. *Military Operations Research*, *26*(1), 19–35. DOI: 10.5711/1082598326115

NATO. (2020). *Science & Technology Trends 2020–2040*. NATO Science and Technology Organization. https://www.nato.int/science/reports/2020-trends

NATO. (2023). *Climate Change and Security Impact Assessment*. NATO Headquarters. https://www.nato.int/cps/en/natohq/topics_91048.htm

O'Meara, A., & Kania, E. (2020). AI and future warfare: Implications for international security. *The Journal of Strategic Studies*, *43*(2), 145–170. DOI: 10.1080/01402390.2020.1773524

Pagallo, U. (2017). *The laws of robots: Crimes, contracts, and torts*. Springer.

Pandey, A. (2026). Harnessing Artificial Intelligence for Sustainable Innovation and Policy: The Eco-Intelligence. In *Leveraging AI for Inclusive and Equitable Development* (pp. 159-178). IGI Global Scientific Publishing.

Pandey, A., & Joseph, J. (2025). Sustainable Service Marketing: The Ethics of Corporate Social Responsibility. In *Strategic Workforce Reskilling in Service Marketing* (pp. 295-314). IGI Global Scientific Publishing.

Pandey, A., & Joseph, J. (2025a). Emerging Trends in Usage of Drone Technology: Exploring the Ethico-Legal Frontiers. *Innovations and Developments in Unmanned Aerial Vehicles*, 171-196.

Poria, S., Cambria, E., Hazarika, D., & Vij, P. (2021). Natural language processing in military communications: Advances and challenges. *IEEE Intelligent Systems*, *36*(2), 72–80. DOI: 10.1109/MIS.2021.3054259

Raji, I. D., Smart, A., White, R., Mitchell, M., Gebru, T., Hutchinson, B., & Barnes, P. (2020). Closing the AI accountability gap: Defining an end-to-end framework for internal algorithmic auditing. *Conference on Fairness, Accountability, and Transparency (FAT)*. DOI: 10.1145/3351095.3372873

RAND Corporation. (2020). *Leveraging Artificial Intelligence to Improve Army Sustainment*. https://www.rand.org/pubs/research_reports/RR4292.html

Schmitt, M. N. (2020). Autonomous weapon systems and international humanitarian law: A reply to the critics. *Harvard National Security Journal*, *4*(1), 1–37.

Sharkey, N. (2019). Autonomous weapons systems, killer robots and human dignity. *Ethics and Information Technology*, *21*(2), 75–87. DOI: 10.1007/s10676-018-9494-0

Sharma, A., Kumar, P., & Singh, M. (2021). AI-based route optimization in dynamic logistics environments: Military applications and challenges. *Defense Transportation Journal*, *77*(3), 22–31.

Tan, K. H., Lim, C. P., & Platts, K. (2019). Real-time logistics systems and the Internet of Military Things: Towards autonomous battlefield resupply. *International Journal of Production Research*, *57*(9), 2760–2773. DOI: 10.1080/00207543.2018.1511535

Tapscott, D., & Tapscott, A. (2016). *Blockchain revolution: How the technology behind bitcoin is changing money, business, and the world*. Penguin.

Tranter, R., & Earley, B. (2022). Automated diagnostics in combat zones: The role of AI in technical maintenance. *Defense Technology Review*, *9*(2), 30–39.

U.S. Department of Defense. (2021). *Artificial Intelligence and Military Modernization Report*. https://media.defense.gov/2021/Mar/01/AI-logistics-report

Van Creveld, M. (1977). *Supplying War: Logistics from Wallenstein to Patton*. Cambridge University Press.

Wang, H., Li, J., & Zhang, Y. (2023). Digital twin-based logistics optimization in military operations. *Journal of Defense Modeling and Simulation*, *20*(2), 118–131. DOI: 10.1177/15485129221110932

Yao, M., Yang, L., & Shen, H. (2023). AI in battlefield healthcare logistics: Trends, technologies, and ethics. *Military Medicine*, *188*(3-4), e701–e710. DOI: 10.1093/milmed/usac255

Zhao, Y., Meng, M. Q. H., & Hu, X. (2022). Autonomous systems for military transport logistics. *Robotics and Autonomous Systems*, *147*, 103903. DOI: 10.1016/j.robot.2021.103903

Zhou, R., & Miao, X. (2021). Emergency logistics coordination in complex terrains using AI and UAVs. *Journal of Humanitarian Logistics and Supply Chain Management*, *11*(2), 145–160.

Chapter 3
Balancing Security and Privacy AI in the Age of Surveillance

Fakhriddin Bekchanov
Mamun University, Uzbekistan

Barno Matchanova
Urgench State Pedagogical Institute, Uzbekistan

Temur Eshchanov
Urgench State University, Uzbekistan

Munir Ahmad
https://orcid.org/0000-0003-4836-6151
Survey of Pakistan, Pakistan

ABSTRACT

This chapter critically examines the transformative role of artificial intelligence in modern surveillance systems, focusing on the delicate balance between enhancing security and protecting individual rights. It explores how technologies such as facial recognition, behavioral analytics, and predictive policing contribute to crime prevention, national security, and urban management, while also highlighting risks of privacy erosion, algorithmic bias, and democratic suppression. Ethical, legal, and regulatory dimensions are analyzed, emphasizing transparency, accountability, and rights-based governance. The chapter concludes by advocating for responsible, balanced approaches that align AI surveillance with democratic values, ensuring security is pursued without compromising civil liberties.

DOI: 10.4018/979-8-3373-3611-4.ch003

INTRODUCTION

Artificial intelligence (AI) has presently played a major role in transforming the face of surveillance in recent years (Fontes et al., 2022). AI-enhanced systems are becoming more and more popular with governments, law enforcement agencies, and other private organizations, helping them to pay attention to individuals, analyze their actions, and anticipate possible risks (Goel et al., 2023; Mahor et al., 2022). The use of technologies like facial recognition, behavioral analytics, and predictive policing is an example of this transformation; they have allowed for to detection of risks more efficiently and enhanced security and governance mechanisms. These systems do not exist within a classic law enforcement setting anymore, but they are integrated into the streets, offices, and even online, which is indicative of an increasingly dependent society on AI as a means to preserve safety and order (Berk, 2021; Hall et al., 2022; Mishra et al., 2024).

Nevertheless, this growth causes a serious question or dilemma as to the trade-off between increased security and loss of individual privacy. Although there are considerable benefits of having an AI surveillance system involved in crime prevention, counterterrorism, and maintaining the safety of the population, it also creates a significant threat to civil liberties. Opaque algorithmic decision-making, constant surveillance, and the risk of misusing personal data extend to the primary rights to freedom of movement, association, and expression. How to reconcile the collective security and ensure the safeguarding of individual rights has thus become one of the most burning questions of the digital era.

The chapter takes a critical look at the role of AI in surveillance that evolves, and unloads its promises and perils. It discusses the technologies that support AI-based surveillance systems and the security benefits offered by them, along with the legal, ethical, and social risks these pose. With a balanced discussion, the argument is expected to lead policymakers, technologists, and civil society into frameworks that can support security without undermining basic rights. The chapter also underlines the importance of the rights-respecting strategies that would protect democratic values in the era of ubiquitous AI spying.

AI TECHNOLOGIES IN MODERN SURVEILLANCE

Artificial intelligence has significantly changed the quality and the extent of surveillance by bringing advanced processing devices that can process large data volumes on the fly. With the advent of AI-based surveillance, unlike conventional systems that either depended on manual monitoring or rudimentary rule-based systems, machine learning, computer vision, and predictive modeling can all be combined to provide dynamic, adaptive, and highly scalable monitoring solutions. This part discusses the technologies that lie at the heart of contemporary surveillance, how they interconnect with the larger digital networks, applications in real life, and new tendencies that define the future of security and privacy.

Facial Recognition Technologies

Facial recognition is one of the most evident and disputable uses of AI in surveillance. These systems are developed on the basis of deep learning algorithms and computer vision methods aimed at capturing, analyzing, and comparing facial features with huge databases in real-time (Kostka et al., 2021; Meddeb et al., 2023). Facial recognition has been adopted by governments and law enforcement agencies to cover a broad spectrum of purposes, including suspect tracking and the investigation of missing persons, as well as border security and identity theft. The use of AI-based face-matching technology in biometric screening has become the new standard in airports all over the world, as a method to streamline passenger traffic, at the same time enhancing security measures.

The uses are also varied in the private sector. Facial recognition is used by the retail sector to learn more about customers, track their buying patterns, and prevent shoplifting, and by banks and financial institutions to enhance a higher level of authentication of online transactions (Moriuchi, 2021; Zhong et al., 2021). Nevertheless, in spite of these benefits, there are still important challenges. Research has always indicated that facial recognition systems are less accurate when used on women, children, and ethnic minorities, leading to more misidentification and false targeting. Such weaknesses bring up ethical and legal issues of fairness, accountability, and possible discrimination. To this end, the controversies are still going on as to whether facial recognition should be limited, suspended, or under stringent regulations in democratic societies. Table 1 shows the summery of applications of facial recognition.

Table 1. Applications of Facial Recognition Across Sectors

Sector	Applications	Benefits	Challenges
Government & Law Enforcement	Tracking suspects, locating missing persons, enhancing border security	Faster identification, improved safety	Misidentification risks, bias against minorities
Airports	Biometric screening, automated passenger verification	Streamlined flows, heightened security	Privacy concerns, data misuse
Retail	Studying demographics, monitoring shopping behavior, theft prevention	Customer insights, reduced losses	Ethical issues, surveillance fatigue
Banking & Finance	Authentication for digital transactions	Stronger fraud prevention	Data protection, potential discrimination

Behavioral Analytics and Activity Recognition

AI surveillance is no longer just about recognizing a person but now examines the manner in which they behave and communicate, both in real and virtual worlds. Behavioral analytics are based on progressive computer vision and pattern recognition in the process of tracking gestures, postures, and movements, consequently, allowing the establishment of suspicious or abnormal behavior (Hussain et al., 2024; Yun et al., 2022). As an example, CCTV cameras in transportation centers, which can be automatically controlled by means of an artificial intelligence algorithm, are capable of identifying unattended bags, a crowd crowding at an instance, or the signs of aggression in real-time. Activity recognition, as used in traffic management, is used to track the movements of vehicles, detect a traffic violation, and forecast a possible collision, thus minimizing accidents and enhancing citizen safety.

The systems have gained popularity in big societal places like airports, stadiums, and urban centers to facilitate the management of disasters and emergencies. They can deliver important minutes to the authorities by giving proactive alerts that might help prevent a violent attack or reduce crises. Nevertheless, predictive systems cannot be one hundred percent accurate. False positives may lead to unwarranted interventions, false arrest, or even a worsening of conflict in a sensitive setting. Besides, the constant surveillance of behaviour poses the danger of naturalising the culture of surveillance in which regular actions are perceived as a possible danger. This relationship poses serious doubts about the dimensions of collective security and the value of individual liberty in democratic states.

Predictive Policing and Risk Assessment

Predictive policing is a major change in the approach to law enforcement, which involves machine learning algorithms to analyze crime trends in the past to predict the future. Predictive systems are expected to optimize the deployment of police and prevent crime before it happens, because they can identify the geographic hotspots, high-risk people, and likely criminal patterns (Hamilton, 2021; Strikwerda, 2021). Cities (like Los Angeles, Chicago, and London) have experimented with tools like PredPol (Benbouzid, 2019) and other applications that give police an opportunity to create risk maps so that patrols can be organized more effectively and decrease response time. The systems also purport to enhance management of resources, whereby emphasis is placed on the areas that are prone to crime.

However, predictive policing is not without controversy as well. Critics say that these tools are dependent on historic crime data, making them vulnerable to perpetuating and propagating biases. When some areas have in the past been over-policed, the algorithm can falsely determine that these areas are of constant high risk, continuing loops of surveillance and structural inequality. Ethical concerns of justice, fairness, and accountability have been put into question because of the risk of profiling marginalized communities, especially on racial or socio-economic grounds. Moreover, proprietary algorithms remain opaque to the public, and citizens are not sure how their lives are determined. Therefore, although predictive policing can transform the way people do law enforcement is conducted, it is a two-edged sword and the implications it has on society need to be monitored. Table 2 provides the overview of predictive policing.

Table 2. Predictive Policing – Benefits vs. Controversies

Claimed Benefits	Controversies
Identifies crime hotspots for efficient patrolling	Bias amplification from historical crime data
Improves resource allocation and reduces response times	Risk of profiling marginalized communities
Enables proactive crime deterrence	Lack of algorithmic transparency and accountability
Optimizes law enforcement strategy	Reinforces structural inequalities

Integration with Biometrics, IoT, and Big Data

Combined with other digital ecosystems, the surveillance capabilities of AI are substantially enhanced. The use of biometric systems has gone well beyond facial recognition to fingerprint, iris scans, voice recognition, and even gait analysis. These modalities, when stacked together, form strong, multi-factor identification systems able to pinpoint individuals with a high degree of accuracy. As an example, agencies in charge of border control and airports tend to merge facial recognition with a fingerprint or iris scan to make sure that the passengers can be screened more accurately (Bacalu, 2021; Montasari, 2023; Pinney et al., 2024).

In the meantime, the Internet of Things (IoT) enables surveillance to penetrate the innermost depths of city life. Traffic lights, vehicles, and other types of utilities have smart sensors and can be used to generate streams of real-time data, which can be processed by the AI systems to track mobility, consumption, and social interactions. Such systems, when paired with big data analytics, can provide patterns of population movement, consumer actions, and even health patterns, and are potent for governance and commerce. But the new risks are also brought about by this interdependence. Constant cross- and multi-environment tracking also adds to the risk of mass surveillance, unauthorized profiling, and personal information being used commercially. Absent robust controls, the combination of AI with biometrics, IoT, and big data may result in the establishment of a surveillance network that is ubiquitous and hard to control. Figure 1 illustrates how AI surveillance systems interact with biometric identification, IoT devices, and big data analytics to create interconnected monitoring ecosystems.

Figure 1. Integration of AI with Biometrics, IoT, and Big Data

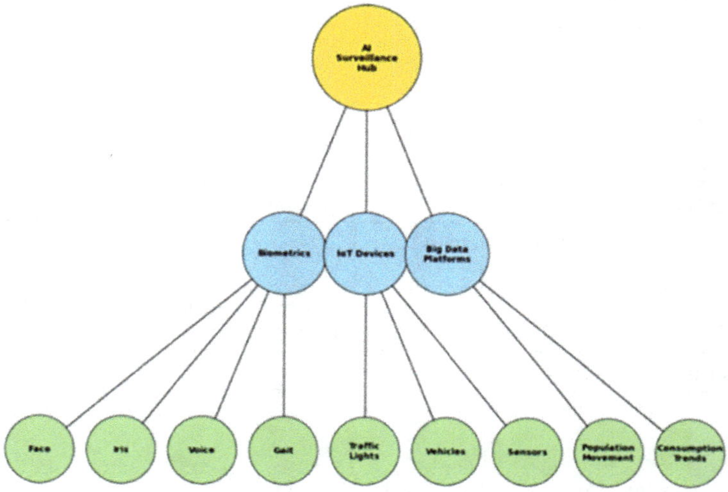

Examples of Deployment

The internationalization of AI surveillance is subject to a variety of case studies at the political and economic levels. In China, artificial intelligence-driven surveillance has been a part of the giant programs known as smart cities, with facial recognition and tracking behavioral patterns aiding in the maintenance of city security, as well as aiding the social credit system, which is widely criticized. These are used to track compliance, control the movement of populations, and implement social control by combining them with enormous networks of data. Predictive policing devices like PredPol (Benbouzid, 2019) are already tested in several cities in the United States, and airports are more and more likely to use AI-enhanced biometric screening to make sure passengers are verified effectively.

In Europe, real-time video analytics has been employed during mass events to control crowds, anomalies, and prevent violence (Mugari & Obioha, 2021). The role of private corporations also plays a key role: retail chains use AI to recognize theft and optimize the operations of stores, and technology companies use biometric surveillance to authorize users and monitor them in the workplace. These cases demonstrate how many areas AI surveillance can be applicable, yet they also indicate its contentious character. Democracies are under pressure to reconcile innovation and civil liberties, unlike authoritarian regimes, where such technologies can be used to consolidate power, and thus, there exist different global trajectories on governance of surveillance. Table 3 shows some examples of AI surveillance.

Table 3. Examples of AI Surveillance

Country/ Region	Technology Deployed	Sector/Context	Key Characteristics / Outcomes
China	Facial recognition, behavioral monitoring	Smart cities, social credit	Integrated with vast databases for compliance and social control
United States	Predictive policing (e.g., PredPol), biometric screening	Law enforcement, airports	Risk maps for deployment; faster passenger verification
Europe	Real-time video analytics	Public events, transport hubs	Crowd management, anomaly detection

Trends in Surveillance Technology

Moving forward, AI surveillance is also taking a new turn of innovation that will guarantee to make it even more powerful, efficient, and ubiquitous. The development of deep learning and edge computing has now made it possible to perform real-time analytics on devices (like cameras and drones) without having to rely on centralized data centers, and the ability to make decisions faster than before in the field. It is also developing emotion recognition to speculate about a stress condition, an angry mood, or a deceiver, but with a degree of scientific reliability that is widely disputed and an ethical concern that is deep.

Another field of fast growth is drone-based surveillance, which allows the authorities to patrol large-scale events, disaster scenes, and borderlines in new ways with mobility and flexibility. Drones, when integrated with thermal and AI analytics, are able to offer real-time situational awareness and thus can serve as useful security and humanitarian assets. Moreover, the deployment of 5G networks will radically speed up the process of data transmission, providing the ability to connect millions of devices with a surveillance infrastructure on a seamless basis. Such a meeting of AI, IoT, and high-speed connectivity is an indicator of the future where surveillance will not only become ubiquitous but also smarter, automated, and harder to control. These new technologies will lead to the further entrenchment of the same security and privacy issues that characterize the era of AI surveillance unless active control is implemented.

SECURITY GAINS AND SOCIETAL BENEFITS

The implementation of artificial intelligence in the surveillance area is frequently explained by its measurable contribution to security and governance. AI-enhanced surveillance systems can automatically monitor, identify risks, and foresee threats, which human operators could not do in the past. From crime prevention to urban management, these technologies have given societies better tools to protect citizens, national interests, and a complex environment. There are always the questions of ethics and privacy, but one must acknowledge the security increase and benefits to society that lie behind their successful growth.

Enhancements in Crime Detection, Prevention, and Response

The adoption of AI-based surveillance has radically altered how law enforcement agencies fight crime: in terms of detection, prevention, and response. Compared to old traditional surveillance systems, where a substantial human factor is necessary to watch over video data, AI-driven platforms can process large volumes of video and audio data through real-time analysis and highlight anomalies that could represent possible threats (Khoei & Singh, 2024; Monika & Kumar, 2024). As an example, high-tech video analytics makes it now possible to observe any unusual or suspicious actions, like a long stay in places of high security, a sudden dispersal of a crowd, or a person with threatening gestures. Likewise, the use of weapon detection algorithms is able to identify firearms, knives, or any other dangerous object even in complicated conditions of a large train station or a shopping mall, preventing the possibility of a delayed response.

Machine learning algorithms are also good at filtering historical surveillance archives, which could previously be done in thousands of investigative man-hours. Such systems can search through a series of camera feeds faster for suspects, the timeline of criminal activity, and patterns that can connect a case that may seem unrelated. This not only speeds up investigations but makes them far more accurate and comprehensive. In addition to retrospective analysis, predictive policing models are based on the past, including crime history, socio-economic aspects, and geographical features, to predict the possible hotspot of criminality. Police departments can use gathering time or an area with a higher risk to be more strategic in their use of patrol, preventing crime with proactive presence and narrow intervention.

A collective outcome of these innovations is a more sensitive, data-driven mode of law enforcement. An earlier identification results in expedited deployment of officers, whereas more analytical insights would help in closing cases with better rates of success. AI-fueled monitoring is set up not as an after-the-occurrence solution but as a preemptive mechanism, making crime control a more proactive process rather than an after-the-occurrence one. Table 4 summarizes key AI applications in crime detection and prevention, highlighting the mechanisms, benefits, and challenges associated with each.

Table 4. AI in Crime Detection, Prevention, and Response

Application	Mechanism (AI Capability)	Benefits	Challenges
Behavior analysis (loitering, aggression)	Video analytics & pattern recognition	Real-time threat alerts, faster response	False positives, privacy issues
Weapon detection	Object recognition algorithms	Early detection of armed threats	Complexity in crowded environments
Historical archive search	Machine learning pattern matching	Faster suspect identification, timeline reconstruction	Data overload, accuracy variations
Predictive policing	Crime data + socio-economic/geospatial modeling	Proactive deployment, deterrence	Bias reinforcement, over-policing

Applications in National Security and Counterterrorism

Terrorism, organized crime, and cyber-facilitated extremism represent an ever-growing threat to national security agencies, and AI surveillance technologies have become invaluable means of solving these problems. AI systems are able to use advanced pattern recognition to scan through massive volumes of data, such as communication metadata, financial transactions, and travel itineraries, and determine individuals or groups engaging in suspicious activities. As an example, unusual transfer of funds that is associated with extremist groups or cross-border activities in unstable areas can cause red flags that trigger further exploration (Khan et al., 2023; Syllaidopoulos et al., 2025).

In the most vital levels of infrastructure like airports, seaports, and border crossings, the enhanced AI-based facial recognition and biometric verification systems have significantly made detecting high-risk individuals more precisely and fast. One can cross-reference travelers with global watchlists in seconds, made possible by these technologies, which means fewer dangerous actors can get away unnoticed. Moreover, AI object recognition, together with drone-based surveillance, allows real-time situational awareness in conflict regions, allowing security organizations to follow the movements of insurgent groups, follow smuggling pathways, and secure the borders without directly endangering personnel.

The other important use is in the setup of open-source intelligence (OSINT) monitoring. It is possible to analyze online forums, social media posts, and blogs at scale with AI algorithms, where signs of extremist propaganda, recruitment efforts, or a coordinated disinformation campaign can be identified. The tools of natural language processing enable multilingual tracking, which means that trends in many regions can be captured at once. The ability to map digital communication networks can also help find hidden links between suspected groups or individuals, which helps improve counterterrorism strategies with the help of AI.

Such abilities place AI as not just a defensive instrument but an active one in national security protection. A helping hand in securing citizens through boosting the ability of governments to ensure their security, by allowing states to detect potential danger before it arises, AI-based surveillance enhances the chance of governments avert disastrous incidents. These advantages, however, have to be put against overreach, especially where the scope of monitoring moves into individual rights or political dissension.

Figure 2 illustrates the layered application of AI surveillance in counterterrorism, from border control to cyber monitoring, showing how multiple data streams converge into actionable intelligence.

Figure 2. AI Applications in National Security and Counterterrorism

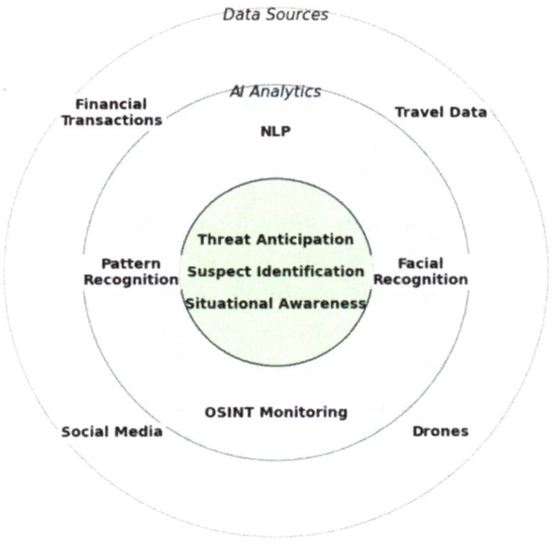

Role in Urban Management, Smart Cities, and Public Safety

In addition to policing and counterterrorism, the use of AI surveillance systems has become the core of any urban management and the development of smart cities. Traffic jams, overcrowding, and insecurity are some of the challenges that are encountered in contemporary cities and require frequent observation and urgent action. Traffic management designed with the help of AI can use real-time video and sensor data to optimize traffic and dynamically change the duration of signals, as well as to re-route vehicles during accidents or road closures. These systems not only enhance mobility but also less fuel consumption and emissions of greenhouse gases, and urban governance is consistent with the aspirations of sustainability in general (Fan et al., 2025; Koormala et al., 2025; Thakur et al., 2021).

AI-enhanced crowd management has also helped in the safety of people in large crowds at concerts, sporting events, or political rallies. Algorithms will be able to keep track of the number of people present, abnormal flows like stampedes or panic dispersals, and alert the authorities to control the situation before it begins to spiral into a crisis. AI-based thermal imaging can also help to identify those in need during emergencies to provide faster aid. In times of natural disasters, such as floods, earthquakes, or wildfires, drones with an AI vision and geospatial analyses can send real-time situational maps, directing the rescue teams to the areas where the people are trapped or the infrastructure has been most impaired.

Environmental monitoring is also a part of urban resilience. The surveillance systems that are incorporated with AI can monitor the quality of the air, the dangerous waste that is dumped illegally, or the building code violations that are likely to make the cities healthier and safer. Moreover, AI sensors installed in the infrastructure in the most dangerous areas, bridges, tunnels, and utility systems, can sense when they are about to fail or be tampered with, stopping accidents and sabotage.

AI surveillance is revolutionizing the way cities are run and developed by integrating safety, efficiency, and sustainability. It allows the local governments not only to protect citizens but also to create adaptive, resource-efficient, crisis-resistant urban environments. Such enlargement of the scope of use of AI in the context of non-standard surveillance reflects the broader possibilities of AI in the formation of livable, future-ready cities. Table 5 highlights the integration of AI surveillance in smart city contexts, emphasizing contributions to mobility, safety, disaster management, and environmental resilience.

Table 5. Smart City Applications of AI Surveillance

Domain	AI Application	Societal Benefit
Traffic Management	Real-time video analytics, signal optimization	Reduced congestion, lower emissions
Crowd Management	Density monitoring, anomaly detection	Prevention of stampedes, public safety
Disaster Response	Drones with AI vision, geospatial analysis	Faster rescue, situational awareness
Environmental Monitoring	Air quality sensors, waste detection	Healthier urban environments
Infrastructure Safety	AI-embedded sensors in bridges/tunnels	Prevention of accidents, resilience

Benefits of Streamlining Law Enforcement Operations

The other significant benefit of using AI surveillance is that it will facilitate the internal workflow of law enforcement organizations. Historically, police departments have been overwhelmed by the time-intensive process of watching live video feeds, paperwork, and data streams. AI helps curb these inefficiencies by automating repetitive and routine actions so that the human officers can make complex decisions, go out in the field, and work with the community.

As an example, automatic license plate recognition can read thousands of cars in an hour, helping to identify a stolen car or a suspect much more efficiently than its paper counterparts. On the same note, the identity verification systems supported by AI streamline background checks, thus clearing people involved in an investigation or other events related to the maintenance of safety in the public. These devices also minimize mistakes likely to transpire when human exhaustion sets in throughout the long working hours of screening.

Integration with digital record management further enhances efficiency. Cross-jurisdictional AI systems can cross-reference forensic evidence, criminal histories, and intelligence reports, enabling investigators to quickly draw connections in transnational crimes. This interoperability not only speeds up resolutions of cases, but it also enhances cooperation among various agencies, starting with the local police departments to the international security departments. Resource allocation may also be facilitated through predictive workload management tools so that the number of officers deployed and at what time meets the expected surge of crime or emergency.

The net effect is a more cost-effective and faster policing model. It is not a topic of discussion, but AI enables agencies to optimize resources and reduce administrative burdens, thus maximizing operational effectiveness without necessarily increasing the size of their staff or funding. Meanwhile, AI-driven law enforcement also creates a new frontier of accountability as automated logging and auditing capabilities allow tracking of every decision made by algorithms, offering oversight capabilities that were frequently missing in the older workflows.

ETHICAL, LEGAL, AND REGULATORY DIMENSIONS

The widespread deployment of AI in surveillance raises profound ethical, legal, and regulatory challenges. Such systems are mostly acceptable because they help to keep society secure and maintain national security, but simultaneously, they are widespread, which threatens to undermine the most basic rights and freedoms. The main issues are the questions of consent, proportionality, fairness, and accountability, which become more central to the discussions about AI surveillance.

Intrusions into Personal Freedoms and Data Misuse

The nature of AI surveillance requires the massive gathering, processing, and retention of personal data. A major difference between traditional surveillance that may target a certain group of people suspected of a crime and AI systems is that the latter can be indiscriminate, collecting data on whole population groups. This will produce a scenario in which its citizens will always be under surveillance, even in day-to-day undertakings, like commuting, shopping, or even participating in social life. The detail of data gathered, biometric data, such as facial scanning and fingerprints, and behavioral data, such as gait scan, emotional scan, and voice data, implies that the surveillance tools could develop a reasonable, lifelong picture of the person.

Potential abuse of the data is especially acute when there are no distinct legal or institutional protections. Leaked information may be reused with unintended purposes, i.e., political power, business use, or governmental manipulation. As a case in point, surveillance data can be used to influence consumer behavior through targeted advertising campaigns on one hand and monitor political opponents or silence dissent on the other hand by governments using the same data sets. In addition to purposeful abuse, data storage and transfer vulnerabilities put people at risk of hacking, identity theft, and third-party access.

These risks are aggravated by the transparency of most AI systems. Black-box models tend to be complex algorithmic models that do not allow people to learn how their data is collected, processed, and deployed. Lack of transparency makes it almost impossible to hold organizations accountable for overreach or abuse. As a result, the uncontrolled application of AI surveillance is a root issue to individual freedom and autonomy, and it is questionable whether individuals can participate in practices that they do not see or understand. Table 6 summarizes the primary ethical risks posed by AI surveillance, with examples illustrating how these risks manifest in practice.

Table 6. Key Ethical Risks in AI Surveillance

Ethical Concern	Description	Example of Manifestation
Privacy Intrusion	Indiscriminate collection of biometric and behavioral data	Tracking commuters via facial scans
Data Misuse	Repurposing of sensitive data beyond original intent	Commercial profiling, political targeting
Security Vulnerability	Insecure storage and weak safeguards exposing sensitive data	Hacking of surveillance databases
Lack of Transparency	Opaque algorithms and unclear decision-making processes	Black-box systems flagging "suspicious behavior"
Chilling Effects	Surveillance pressure alters individual and collective behavior	Reduced protest participation, self-censorship

Risks of Algorithmic Bias, Discrimination, and Over-Policing

The quality of AI surveillance systems depends as much on the data it is trained on as it does on the data it depends on. It is a shame that historical datasets can attest to deep-rooted discrimination in policing and in governance. When this data is entered into predictive policing software or facial recognition software, it does not just remain neutral; instead, it recreates and amplifies the inequalities that already exist. As an example, the historically highly policed areas are labeled as high-risk zones, after which they receive even more attention in terms of surveillance and policing. This is a process referred to as a feedback bias that enslaves some communities in this big loop of scrutiny and criminalization.

One of the most well-documented cases is the rate at which facial recognition technologies misidentify people. Research has revealed that such systems often have problems with precision in the recognition of women and ethnic minorities. The risks of the implementation of biased systems in practice have already been observed in wrongful arrests in cities like Detroit. Such mistakes not only victimize the innocent but also destroy the confidence between the law-enforcing institutions and the community members. When augmented by AI, over-policing builds a setting in which the population feels constantly victimized and stigmatized, which further divides the citizens and the government.

Offering discriminatory ability of algorithmic systems is not confined to the police. The systems based on the data of the AI surveillance can also be biased in employment screening, immigration checks, and welfare fraud. In cases of unfair flagging of people because of unsuccessful datasets or discriminatory algorithms, the repercussions spill out to missed opportunities, stigmatization, and inclusion into the system. In this way, algorithm bias in surveillance is not simply a technical defect but an underlying ethical and social problem that needs immediate redress.

Chilling Effects on Free Speech and Democratic Participation

The ubiquity of surveillance has produced a chilling effect where people self-censure their words, associations, and actions because they fear being spied on. This is especially harmful in a democratic society where free expression and open participation are the value systems. When people feel they are constantly being watched, they can avoid holding open protests, and they can not join interest groups or even talk online about politics. With time, this undermines pluralism and constrains the multitude of voices in the state of affairs.

The influence is most apparent during times of political instability. Demonstrators in places with high levels of facial recognition cameras usually run the risk of being located, registered, and punished in the future. There have also been incidents where tracking information has been used to retroactively discover people who attended protests and led to personalized harassment, discrimination at the job site, or legal proceedings. The awareness of such practices deters the engagement in civic life, which compromises the right to assemble peacefully.

The minority, journalists, and activists become more vulnerable. Site monitoring systems may be tactically turned to be turned against them and reduce their resistance and critical voices. As an illustration, it is possible to trace the communication network of activists and find out how they plan to organize, and, accordingly, authorities can intervene. On the same note, press freedom can be undermined because the journalists reporting sensitive matters can find their sources compromised. Long-term AI surveillance can jeopardize not only individual liberties but the very well-being of the institutions of democracy itself, as this would set the balance of power at a significant level in favor of the state over civil society.

Cross-Border Surveillance and Global Privacy Concerns

AI surveillance can hardly be constrained by geography. In the contemporary globalized society, the border of surveillance technologies takes a global path, via the international data flows, international collaborations, and corporate networks. As an illustration, the data that is obtained by the sensors in a given country can be stored in data centers in another country where other privacy and security policies are applicable. This jurisdictional issue also leaves their accountability in loopholes, as people usually have minimal options when their data is being processed outside of their national laws.

The increasing issue is the export of surveillance equipment by states whose protection of human rights is weak. Totalitarian regimes tend to sell AI-enhanced surveillance technology, i.e., facial recognition software, predictive policing systems, high-tech monitoring devices, etc., to other regimes. These exports not only reproduce the intrusive patterns but they are also globalize it. These tools can become entrenched in the systems of governments of countries that do not have strong democratic controls, and such tools come to be adopted without any substantive discussion.

The absence of unified global frameworks of governance makes the situation worse. Although global associations such as the UN and OECD have promoted international digital rights safeguards, their implementation has been spotty and spotty. Different cultural and political contexts further complicate consensus on acceptable practices. Consequently, international privacy principles are being compromised by a mosaic of policies, where the least protective usually rule. The AI surveillance presents a potential for normalizing invasion into personal freedom globally without further enhancement of cross-border coordination.

Need for Transparency, Accountability, and Fairness in Algorithms

One of the most urgent ethical issues in the area of surveillance governance is the lack of transparency of the AI systems. Algorithms sometimes act as black boxes, and it is not possible to give any explanations that are available to policymakers, oversight agencies, or the general public. Such non-transparency complicates the identification of the sources of bias, detecting the errors, or holding the developers to account. When facing citizens with AI-based decisions, in policing, immigration, or other areas of the government, there is usually no effective means of recourse or redress.

In response to this, explainable AI (XAI) and independent auditing are the mechanisms of transparency that should become common. Explainable AI is aimed at solving the incapacity to interpret how algorithms make decisions, allowing oversight agencies to know the reasons outcomes are made. Equally, independent algorithmic audits will help demonstrate systemic bias or weaknesses before technologies are implemented on a mass basis. These precautions enhance accountability and assist in making sure that mistakes are noticed in time instead of being identified at a later stage when damages are already caused.

Equal justice in AI monitoring does not just need technical solutions. It entails institutional systems that ensure fair treatment among all mental demographic groups. As an example, there is the importance of guaranteeing diversity in training datasets, but this cannot suffice when institutions implementing the systems have biased enforcement practices. It is important to install mechanisms like the algorithmic impact assessments, citizen panels, or judicial review processes, to make fairness not only technical but also procedural. Civic confidence in AI surveillance will be contingent upon whether people believe that systems are not only comprehensible but also are refutable, with real channels of redress.

Existing Legal Frameworks and Their Limitations

The laws regulating surveillance differ tremendously depending on the region, and this has major consequences when it comes to monitoring with AI. In other jurisdictions (like the European Union), the personal data is well-protected through powerful tools, such as the General Data Protection Regulation (GDPR), which comes with rights to consent, transparency, and redress. Nevertheless, even GDPR is not able to explain the predictive and pervasive power of AI systems, which is beyond the traditional definitions of data protection. Automated profiling and predictive policing, e.g., are in gray law jurisdictions where the current regulations do not provide full coverage.

Surveillance laws in other regions of the world are either feeble, old-fashioned, or too permissive. Most governments have extensive discretionary powers to keep the people under little surveillance. In other situations, emergency legislation or national security exemptions are cited and used in justification of large-scale data collection without court review. This makes the citizens susceptible to the uncontested state power. Furthermore, the current laws are usually not enforced in line with the development of novel technologies, thus providing a legal loophole enabling the faster spread of surveillance technologies than the implemented governing tools can react.

Such a motley set of safeguards points to the dire state of legal frameworks that should be harmonized to specifically cover AI-based surveillance. Legislation should be developed not only to include general data protection but also should consider the concerns of algorithmic accountability, predictive analytics, and cross-border transfers of data. In the absence of such reforms, the current body of laws will still be poorly prepared to deal with the realities of AI monitoring. Table 7 compares surveillance regulations in major regions, highlighting strengths and gaps.

Table 7. Comparative Legal Frameworks for AI Surveillance

Region / Jurisdiction	Key Regulations	Strengths	Weaknesses / Gaps
European Union (EU)	GDPR, Draft AI Act	Strong consent provisions, high accountability	Gaps in predictive policing and biometric mass use
United States (US)	Sectoral/state-level laws, patchwork	Some state-level bans (e.g., San Francisco facial rec.)	No federal framework, fragmented protections
China	Cybersecurity Law, Data Security Law	Comprehensive state control, centralized enforcement	Emphasis on state power, limited individual protections
Canada	Privacy Act, proposed AI & Data Act	Expanding individual rights protections	Still in draft stage, weak enforcement mechanisms
Global South (e.g., India, Brazil)	Emerging AI ethics guidelines, draft bills	Recognition of human rights and privacy importance	Limited enforcement capacity, slow legislative process

Human Rights Perspectives and International Governance Debates

Ethically and legally, the issue of AI surveillance is more profound to contend with on the human rights aspect. Basic rights which are directly involved include the right to privacy, freedom of expression, and freedom of assembly. Widely spread international bodies such as the United Nations Human Rights Council and the Council of Europe have issued multiple warnings that the uncontrollable use of AI surveillance systems is a threat to the very principles of democratic nations. According to reports by the UN Special Rapporteur on the right to privacy, the phenomenon of mass surveillance is fundamentally incompatible with human rights norms unless it passes stringent tests of legality, necessity, and proportionality.

The world is finding itself in a greater challenge of trying to find a way of striking a balance between the needs of legitimate security and the need to preserve the basic rights of freedom. Whereas in some nations the incidence of terrorism and crime is claimed to be so severe that drastic monitoring strategies are necessary to address the problem, elsewhere it is claimed that such reasons are typically stretched thin to the point of unreasonably encroaching on the life of the civilian population. National security issues have been used by authoritarian states, especially to warrant the extensive surveillance of political opponents, journalists, and minority groups.

It has been hard to come up with universal principles. The existence of different political systems, cultural values, and security interests makes it difficult to agree on a binding international arrangement. However, recent debates in forums like the UN, OECD, and G20 reveal an increased realization of worldwide standards. A human rights-based approach should always be the priority, so AI surveillance technologies should have legitimate security purposes without diminishing the dignity, autonomy, and freedoms of people across the world.

Role of Standards, Oversight Bodies, and Regulatory Innovation

The future of the governance of AI surveillance will rely on the development of efficient standards, monitoring institutions, and new forms of regulation. Independent oversight institutions can become central in the audit control of the AI systems, overseeing the adherence to ethical principles, and hearing complaints of victims of the surveillance. These bodies should be placed in a position of not only possessing technical expertise, but also possessing legal powers to make sure there is accountability in practice and not only in theory.

Already, standard-setting bodies, including the International Organization of Standardization (ISO) and the Institute of Electrical and Electronics Engineers (IEEE), are working on a set of guidelines to address AI ethics, transparency, and accountability. Such frameworks could be useful to both governments and corporations to give them useful benchmarks. Standards, however, cannot be relied on in the absence of enforcement mechanisms. Transparency and accountability binding requirements should be adopted by national legislatures with stiff penalties for non-compliance.

There should also be regulatory innovation. Innovations, like algorithmic impact assessment tools, which will help measure possible risks prior to releasing an AI system, or data trusts, which will enable collective control over sensitive datasets, can be considered promising. Equally, participatory designs that include civil society, academic specialists, and impacted communities have the potential of improving legitimacy and trust. The solutions to the problem of effective governance will necessarily have a multilayered approach: (a) national law to ensure short-term protection, (b) global collaboration to solve transnational issues, and (c) active participation of civil society to make sure that the implementation of surveillance technologies is organized responsibly and consistently with democratic principles.

RESPONSIBLE AND BALANCED AI SURVEILLANCE

The main question is not whether the implementation of AI-based surveillance will become more (and more) widespread; rather, the main question is how the implementation of such surveillance can be conducted responsibly. Governments, private organizations, and civil societies have the task of finding a balance between the undeniable positive security of tightening security and the necessity to protect civil liberties, which must be regarded as equally important. To meet this balance, there is a need to use rights-respecting approaches and principles, and collaborative governance, which is capable of adapting to the changing technological environment.

Strategies for Rights-Respecting Deployment of AI Tools

Ethical and legal protection at all levels of the lifecycle of the AI should begin with its responsible implementation, i.e., starting with the collection of the information the algorithm is going to operate with. One fundamental idea in this respect is privacy by design as a means of ensuring that the control measures, like minimization, anonymization, and encryption of data, are presented in the surveillance systems at the very beginning. This will minimize the risk of unnecessary intrusion into personal information and protect people against possible abuse. The other important protection is algorithmic auditing, where independent and regular evaluations of the system of surveillance are done to ascertain bias, track the mistake rate, and establish whether the system affects marginalized or vulnerable populations disproportionately. In the absence of these audits, AI-based surveillance may lead to the furthering of large-scale inequalities within the system or produce biased results.

The principle of informed consent and transparency is also of equal importance. The mode of data collection, processing, and retention of data related to surveillance should be made clear to the citizens. They are also to be offered practical access to challenge any erroneous results, e.g., mistaken identity or unfair profiling. Open procedures not only make citizens but also increase the validity of the surveillance programs. Lastly, successful implementation should have good mechanisms of accountability, so that mistakes, abuses, or unwanted harms can be attributed to negligent actors and remedied by corrective actions. By defining clear lines of responsibility, diffusion of blame can be avoided, and a framework of oversight can be developed. With these practices embedded into the design and functionality of AI surveillance systems, governments and organizations can overcome the risks of misuse significantly and can increase the level of trust of people in the use of security mechanisms based on AI.

Principles for Balancing Security Needs and Privacy Protection

One has to follow a number of principles towards a more moderate approach to monitoring AI and make sure that technological progress will be associated with democratic values and human rights principles.

The first one is proportionality, which demands that surveillance should be employed to the extent required to attain legitimate security goals. Uncontrolled or random surveillance threatens to compromise individual rights, as well as break the trust in governmental agencies. Intimately connected is the necessity principle, which notes that the use of AI surveillance must be to a definite and convincing community interest. It should not be implemented as a standard instrument of governance or for the convenience of administration.

The other consideration is equity. The design, testing, and auditing of the systems should work to reduce the discriminatory effects of the surveillance systems so that no community is discriminated against or disproportionately affected. Fair distribution safeguards those with little power and avoids the stabilization of system-wide disorders. The other principle is transparency and explainability. The AI systems are required to generate an output that can be easily understood and scrutinized by the regulators, courts, and common individuals. This helps to instill accountability and protect against misuse or abuse.

Last, human supervision should be one of the pillars of AI surveillance. Human review should always be made available in automated decisions in sensitive areas like law enforcement or border control. This helps avoid the risks of unchecked automation and leaves the moral discretion in the process of decision-making. Collectively, these principles allow one to develop guidelines on how to lead the use of AI surveillance responsibly by balancing the security needs with the rights of its people.

Recommendations for Policymakers, Technologists, and Civil Society

Responsible and balanced AI surveillance can only be achieved through the coordinated efforts of multiple stakeholders, and each of them should also make their contribution to the development of safeguards that can protect security and fundamental rights.

The policymakers are at the heart of the process through the enactment of comprehensive laws covering AI surveillance. Privacy safeguards in such laws must be strong, limits on data retention must be well defined, and there must be independent oversight to deter misuse. Since data flows are global in nature, international collaboration is also critically needed to standardize the norms and avoid cross-border violations that may undermine faith in governance. The design and application of surveillance systems should incorporate ethics, which should be the responsibility of technologists. This is in the form of ensuring fairness, accountability, and transparency in algorithms and collaborating with interdisciplinary professionals like ethicists, lawyers, and social scientists. Technologists can mitigate the risk of discrimination, prejudice, or harm to unsuspecting communities by foreseeing the effects on the whole society.

It is civil society and advocacy groups that act as watchdogs on this landscape by ensuring that there is a democratic inquiry into the practices of surveillance. They create awareness and keep a watchful eye on the practices of the government and corporations, and represent the interests of the most vulnerable through intrusive surveillance. Their involvement means that the policy discussions capture a wide range of opinions and realities of communities. When these stakeholders collaborate, they develop a system in which security imperatives can be achieved without violating the privacy, dignity, and freedom. This equilibrium is decisive in building the trust of the population and making the practices of AI surveillance compatible with democratic principles and respect for human rights.

CONCLUSION

The swift adoption of artificial intelligence in surveillance systems is a radical change in how societies regulate, protect, and engage with their social and personal spaces. Facial recognition AI, behavioral analytics, and predictive policing have shown explicit advantages in the context of increasing safety, optimizing law enforcement processes, and aiding national security efforts. However, as the chapter has demonstrated, these benefits are associated with some serious moral, legislative, and social privileges. The problem of loss of privacy, algorithm bias, and chilling effect on democracy participation demands the necessity of frameworks that prioritize human rights in technological innovation.

Moving forward, the future of AI monitoring will be determined by the decisions that societies take today. When implemented without proper monitoring, the surveillance technologies can become institutionalized to give credence to authoritarian tendencies and subdue basic freedoms. On the other hand, when used responsibly, they can also be the instruments of security and strength without violating personal rights. This balance is to be achieved through transparency of the algorithms in decision-making, strong legal protection, and accountability attributed to governments, industry, and civil society.

After all, the problem is not only technical but also very political and moral. The development and deployment of AI surveillance should be conducted in a manner that indicates democracy, upholds civil liberties, and preserves trust among the populace. Through embracing concepts of proportionality, fairness, and oversight, societies can forge a way to establish security systems that are effective and rights-respecting. The future of AI surveillance, then, depends on the combination of efforts to make sure that the innovation is paired with responsibility, and that the quest to purchase security does not imply the sacrifice of freedom.

REFERENCES

Bacalu, F. (2021). Digital Policing Tools as Social Control Technologies: Data-driven Predictive Algorithms, Automated Facial Recognition Surveillance, and Law Enforcement Biometrics. *Analysis and Metaphysics*, *20*(0), 74. Advance online publication. DOI: 10.22381/AM2020215

Benbouzid, B. (2019). Values and consequences in predictive machine evaluation. A sociology of predictive policing1. *Science & Technology Studies*, *32*(4). Advance online publication. DOI: 10.23987/sts.66156

Berk, R. A. (2021). Artificial Intelligence, Predictive Policing, and Risk Assessment for Law Enforcement. In *Annual Review of Criminology* (Vol. 4, Issue 1). DOI: 10.1146/annurev-criminol-051520-012342

Fan, W. Q., Ismail, A. S., Mohammed, F., & Mukred, M. (2025). AI-Driven Smart City Security and Surveillance System: A Bibliometric Analysis. In *Current and Future Trends on AI Applications: Volume 1* (pp. 305–328). Springer. DOI: 10.1007/978-3-031-75091-5_17

Fontes, C., Hohma, E., Corrigan, C. C., & Lütge, C. (2022). AI-powered public surveillance systems: Why we (might) need them and how we want them. *Technology in Society*, *71*, 102137. Advance online publication. DOI: 10.1016/j.techsoc.2022.102137

Goel, A., Goel, A. K., & Kumar, A. (2023). The role of artificial neural network and machine learning in utilizing spatial information. In *Spatial Information Research* (Vol. 31, Issue 3). DOI: 10.1007/s41324-022-00494-x

Hall, S. W., Sakzad, A., & Choo, K. R. (2022). Explainable artificial intelligence for digital forensics. *WIREs Forensic Science*, *4*(2), e1434. Advance online publication. DOI: 10.1002/wfs2.1434

Hamilton, M. (2021). Predictive policing through risk assessment. In *Predictive policing and artificial intelligence* (pp. 58–78). Routledge. DOI: 10.4324/9780429265365-4

Hussain, A., Khan, S. U., Khan, N., Shabaz, M., & Baik, S. W. (2024). AI-driven behavior biometrics framework for robust human activity recognition in surveillance systems. *Engineering Applications of Artificial Intelligence*, *127*, 107218. Advance online publication. DOI: 10.1016/j.engappai.2023.107218

Khan, F. A., Li, G., Khan, A. N., Khan, Q. W., Hadjouni, M., & Elmannai, H. (2023). AI-Driven Counter-Terrorism: Enhancing Global Security Through Advanced Predictive Analytics. *IEEE Access : Practical Innovations, Open Solutions, 11*, 135864–135879. Advance online publication. DOI: 10.1109/ACCESS.2023.3336811

Khoei, T. T., & Singh, A. (2024). A survey of Emotional Artificial Intelligence and crimes: Detection, prediction, challenges and future direction. *Journal of Computational Social Science*, *7*(3), 2359–2402. DOI: 10.1007/s42001-024-00313-3

Koormala, H., Reddy, C. K. K., Balusa, V. S., Jillapalli, N., & Hanafiah, M. M. (2025). Enhancing urban safety: AI-driven security solutions for smart cities. In *Information Security Governance using Artificial Intelligence of Things in Smart Environments* (pp. 146–163). CRC Press. DOI: 10.1201/9781003606307-7

Kostka, G., Steinacker, L., & Meckel, M. (2021). Between security and convenience: Facial recognition technology in the eyes of citizens in China, Germany, the United Kingdom, and the United States. *Public Understanding of Science (Bristol, England)*, *30*(6), 671–690. Advance online publication. DOI: 10.1177/09636625211001555 PMID: 33769157

Mahor, V., Bijrothiya, S., Rawat, R., Kumar, A., Garg, B., & Pachlasiya, K. (2022). IoT and Artificial Intelligence Techniques for Public Safety and Security. In *Smart Urban Computing Applications*. DOI: 10.1201/9781003373247-5

Meddeb, H., Abdellaoui, Z., & Houaidi, F. (2023). Development of surveillance robot based on face recognition using Raspberry-PI and IOT. *Microprocessors and Microsystems*, *96*, 104728. Advance online publication. DOI: 10.1016/j.micpro.2022.104728

Mishra, A. K., Tyagi, A. K., Dananjayan, S., Rajavat, A., Rawat, H., & Rawat, A. (2024). Revolutionizing Government Operations. In *Conversational Artificial Intelligence*. DOI: 10.1002/9781394200801.ch34

Monika, E., & Kumar, T. R. (2024). Advancements in AI-based Crime Detection and Prediction. *2024 8th International Conference on Electronics, Communication and Aerospace Technology (ICECA)*, 1557–1562.

Montasari, R. (2023). The Application of Big Data Predictive Analytics and Surveillance Technologies in the Field of Policing. In *Advances in Information Security* (Vol. 101). DOI: 10.1007/978-3-031-21920-7_5

Moriuchi, E. (2021). An empirical study of consumers' intention to use biometric facial recognition as a payment method. *Psychology and Marketing*, *38*(10), 1741–1765. Advance online publication. DOI: 10.1002/mar.21495

Mugari, I., & Obioha, E. E. (2021). Predictive Policing and Crime Control in The United States of America and Europe: Trends in a Decade of Research and the Future of Predictive Policing. *Social Sciences (Basel, Switzerland)*, *10*(6), 234. Advance online publication. DOI: 10.3390/socsci10060234

Pinney, J., Bentotahewa, V., & Tomlinson, M. (2024). Exploring Applications and Implications of Big Data Predictive Analytics in Policing Cyberspace. In *Navigating the Intersection of Artificial Intelligence, Security, and Ethical Governance: Sentinels of Cyberspace* (pp. 1–18). Springer.

Strikwerda, L. (2021). Predictive policing: The risks associated with risk assessment. *The Police Journal*, *94*(3), 422–436. Advance online publication. DOI: 10.1177/0032258X20947749

Syllaidopoulos, I., Ntalianis, K., & Salmon, I. (2025). A Comprehensive Survey on AI in Counter-Terrorism and Cybersecurity: Challenges and Ethical Dimensions. *IEEE Access : Practical Innovations, Open Solutions*, *13*, 91740–91764. DOI: 10.1109/ACCESS.2025.3572348

Thakur, N., Nagrath, P., Jain, R., Saini, D., Sharma, N., & Hemanth, D. J. (2021). Artificial Intelligence Techniques in Smart Cities Surveillance Using UAVs: A Survey. In *Studies in Computational Intelligence* (Vol. 971). DOI: 10.1007/978-3-030-72065-0_18

Yun, M. H., Rhiu, I., Kim, W., Lee, Y., & Kim, Y. M. (2022). AI in human behavior analysis. In *Human-Centered Artificial Intelligence* (pp. 191–204). Elsevier. DOI: 10.1016/B978-0-323-85648-5.00010-4

Zhong, Y., Oh, S., & Moon, H. C. (2021). Service transformation under industry 4.0: Investigating acceptance of facial recognition payment through an extended technology acceptance model. *Technology in Society*, *64*, 101515. Advance online publication. DOI: 10.1016/j.techsoc.2020.101515

Chapter 4
Cyber Warfare and the Role of Artificial Intelligence:
Emerging Threats, Strategic Defense, and Ethical Challenges

M. R. Ramesh
https://orcid.org/0000-0002-1648-9387
IGCAR, India

ABSTRACT

This chapter explores the evolving landscape of cyber warfare in the age of Artificial Intelligence (AI), examining how AI technologies are both weaponizing and defending digital domains. As AI enables advanced cyber-attacks through automated intrusion, data manipulation, and adaptive malware, it simultaneously empowers robust defense mechanisms including threat detection, real-time response, and predictive analytics. The chapter delves into emerging threats posed by AI-driven cyber operations, the strategic applications of AI in national and global cybersecurity frameworks, and the escalating arms race in cyber capabilities. It also critically analyzes the ethical dilemmas of autonomous cyber weapons, accountability in AI decision-making, and the need for international norms and governance. Through case studies and expert insights, this chapter highlights the dual-use nature of AI in cyberspace, emphasizing the urgent need for balanced strategies that safeguard security while upholding human rights and ethical integrity.

DOI: 10.4018/979-8-3373-3611-4.ch004

1. INTRODUCTION: THE CONVERGENCE OF AI AND CYBER WARFARE

1.1 Overview of Cyber Warfare as a Modern Geopolitical Tool

Cyber warfare has emerged as one of the most disruptive and impactful forms of conflict in the 21st century, reshaping how nations engage in geopolitical struggles. Unlike traditional warfare, which typically involves physical combat and territorial boundaries, cyber warfare operates within the digital landscape, where the boundaries between military, economic, and civilian infrastructures often blur. This form of conflict can target critical national infrastructure, financial systems, and even individual citizens, all while remaining largely anonymous and difficult to trace.

In the digital age, the Internet has become the backbone of global commerce, governance, and communication, making it an ideal battleground for adversaries. Nation-states are increasingly turning to cyber tactics as a means to influence political outcomes, disrupt enemy operations, and defend national interests without the risks and visibility of conventional military action. The ability to launch attacks that can sabotage energy grids, manipulate financial systems, or alter the public opinion with misinformation campaigns has turned cyberspace into an essential dimension of modern warfare (Binnendijk, & Libicki, 2020).

The concept of cyber warfare goes beyond just hacking into systems; it encompasses a wide range of tactics including espionage, sabotage, disinformation campaigns, and even cyber-attacks designed to destabilize governments. These attacks, often invisible and occurring at lightning speed, present new challenges for governments, military entities, and organizations seeking to safeguard national security and private interests.

Prominent instances of cyber warfare in recent years include the 2007 cyber-attacks on Estonia, the Stuxnet worm that targeted Iran's nuclear facilities, and Russian interference in the 2016 U.S. presidential elections through hacking and information warfare. These examples highlight the potential power of cyber warfare in shaping geopolitical outcomes, and they emphasize the importance of developing robust defense mechanisms in cyberspace.

1.2 Introduction to AI Technologies Relevant to Cybersecurity

Artificial Intelligence (AI) technologies have become central to cybersecurity, enabling more sophisticated and responsive defense strategies in the face of evolving cyber threats. In the past, cybersecurity largely depended on predefined rules, signature-based detection, and human monitoring. However, as cyber-attacks have become more complex and difficult to predict, AI has emerged as a critical tool to enhance the efficiency, adaptability, and resilience of cybersecurity frameworks (Cummings, 2019).

Table 1. Key AI Technologies and Their Cybersecurity Applications

AI Technology	Cyber Defense Applications	Cyber Offense Potential
Machine Learning (ML)	Anomaly detection, behavior analysis	Targeted phishing, evasive malware
Natural Language Processing (NLP)	Email filtering, social media monitoring	Disinformation campaigns, social engineering
Autonomous Systems	Real-time automated threat response	Autonomous attack execution
Predictive Analytics	Forecasting potential threats, proactive defense	Anticipating countermeasures
Threat Intelligence & Automation	Streamlined incident response, automated patching	Automated vulnerability exploitation

AI technologies in cybersecurity can be divided into several categories, each contributing to different aspects of threat detection, analysis, and defense. These technologies include:

- **Machine Learning (ML)**: Machine learning algorithms can analyze vast amounts of data from networks, identifying patterns and anomalies that suggest malicious activity. ML can detect previously unknown threats by learning from historical data and adapting to emerging attack techniques. This proactive approach helps identify vulnerabilities before they are exploited.
- **Natural Language Processing (NLP)**: NLP algorithms enable AI systems to interpret and analyze human language, including text-based data from social media, emails, or dark web forums. This is especially useful in identifying disinformation campaigns, phishing attempts, and other social engineering tactics that often accompany cyber-attacks.
- **Autonomous Systems**: Autonomous AI systems can be deployed to make real-time decisions in the defense of networks and critical infrastructure. These systems are capable of automatically identifying, mitigating, and responding to threats without human intervention, making them particularly valuable in high-speed, high-stakes environments.
- **Predictive Analytics**: AI-powered predictive analytics can forecast potential cyber threats based on historical data and trends. By analyzing the attack vectors of past incidents, AI can help identify new vulnerabilities and predict when and how attacks may occur, allowing organizations to proactively strengthen their defenses.

- **Threat Intelligence and Automation**: AI can process and analyze data from multiple sources to create actionable intelligence about potential cyber threats. Additionally, AI can automate routine cybersecurity tasks, such as vulnerability scanning and patch management, improving efficiency and reducing the burden on human experts.

Table 2. AI Technologies in Cyber Defense

AI Technology	Application in Cyber Defense	Description / Benefit
Machine Learning (ML)	Threat detection, anomaly detection	Learns normal behavior and flags deviations or malicious activities
Natural Language Processing (NLP)	Phishing email detection, intelligence gathering	Analyzes text data to detect malicious content and extract threat intel
Deep Learning (DL)	Intrusion detection systems (IDS), malware classification	Accurately classifies complex attack patterns using large data sets
Reinforcement Learning	Dynamic threat response, autonomous decision-making	Learns optimal defense strategies through trial and error
Expert Systems	Automated response systems, security policy enforcement	Applies rules to mimic human cybersecurity analysts
Computer Vision	Face and behavior recognition in secure zones	Enhances physical and biometric security
AI-Driven Automation	Patch management, log analysis, incident response	Reduces time to detect, respond, and mitigate threats

Table 3. AI Technologies in Cyber Offense

AI Technology	Application in Cyber Offense	Description / Threat Potential
Generative AI (e.g., GPT)	Creating realistic phishing emails, deepfakes	Mimics human-like communication for social engineering attacks
Adversarial ML	Bypassing ML-based security systems	Exploits weaknesses in AI models used for detection
Automated Reconnaissance	Target profiling, vulnerability scanning	AI collects and analyzes data on targets faster than manual methods
Botnets with AI Control	Coordinated DDoS attacks, adaptive malware distribution	Uses AI to dynamically modify attack paths and vectors
AI-Driven Malware	Self-learning, polymorphic malware	Learns how to evade traditional detection tools
Voice Cloning & NLP	Impersonation in voice-based attacks	Can impersonate executives or officials to execute fraud or breach security
Swarm Intelligence	Coordinated multi-point attacks	Distributed AI agents that attack simultaneously and adapt strategies in real-time

These AI technologies enable cybersecurity teams to be more proactive and effective in preventing, detecting, and responding to cyber-attacks. However, as AI becomes a more integral part of cybersecurity, it also opens the door for adversaries to exploit the same technologies for malicious purposes, creating new challenges in the realm of cyber warfare (Allen & Chan, 2017).

1.3 Historical Precedents and Emerging Trends in AI-Enabled Cyber Conflict

The integration of AI into cyber warfare represents the next frontier in the evolution of digital conflict. While the use of artificial intelligence in cyber operations is still in its early stages, historical precedents have already demonstrated the potential for AI to disrupt traditional notions of warfare and security (Fitzgerald & Jenkins, 2020).

The first significant instances of AI-enabled cyber conflict can be traced back to the early 2000s when state-sponsored cyber-attacks began to target critical infrastructure. One of the most notable examples is the Stuxnet attack, which took place in 2010. The Stuxnet worm was a sophisticated piece of malware that specifically targeted Iran's nuclear enrichment facilities. It caused significant damage to the machinery of the facility by manipulating industrial control systems. Stuxnet was a prime example of a cyber weapon that integrated traditional hacking techniques with advanced AI algorithms to cause physical damage.

Since then, AI has increasingly been used to enhance the sophistication of cyber-attacks. In particular, machine learning techniques have allowed cyber-attacks to evolve beyond traditional "one-size-fits-all" methods. AI can now help adversaries conduct more personalized and targeted attacks, bypassing traditional security measures and exploiting vulnerabilities that would otherwise go unnoticed. Additionally, AI enables the automation of cyber-attacks, allowing for highly efficient and scalable operations. This can create a significantly greater volume of attacks, making it harder for defenders to keep up (Heath, 2019).

Table 4. Comparison of Traditional vs. AI-Enhanced Cyber Warfare

Aspect	Traditional Cyber Warfare	AI-Enhanced Cyber Warfare
Speed	Human-dependent, slower response	Real-time, autonomous decision-making
Adaptability	Predefined rules and patterns	Dynamic learning and adaptation
Scale of Attacks	Limited by human resources	Large-scale, automated
Sophistication	Rule-based attacks	Intelligent, targeted, evolving
Attribution Difficulty	High	Even more complex due to obfuscation

Another emerging trend in AI-enabled cyber conflict is the rise of deepfake technology, which uses AI to create realistic but fake audio and video content. Deepfakes have become a tool for information warfare, allowing adversaries to manipulate public perception, spread disinformation, and influence political processes. These technologies can be used to impersonate political leaders, make false statements, or create fake evidence of malicious activities. As deepfake technology improves, the implications for national security and public trust could be profound, making it harder to distinguish between fact and fabrication.

As we move into the future, AI is expected to play an even greater role in cyber warfare. Autonomous AI-driven cyber weapons are already being researched by various nations, which could potentially conduct complex attacks without human oversight. These weapons, capable of learning and adapting to countermeasures, would represent a new era of warfare, where human involvement in strategic decision-making could be minimal (Brundage, et al. 2018).

Emerging trends also point to AI-assisted cyber defense mechanisms, including AI-based threat hunting, real-time intrusion detection, and adaptive countermeasures that could evolve alongside cyber-attacks. The integration of AI into cybersecurity systems is essential for defending against increasingly sophisticated and autonomous cyber threats. However, this also raises concerns about the potential for AI to be weaponized by malicious actors, further complicating the security landscape (Buchanan, 2020).

The convergence of AI and cyber warfare presents an evolving set of challenges for both military strategists and cybersecurity professionals. It is clear that AI will not only enhance offensive cyber capabilities but also fundamentally change the way nations and organizations approach the defense of critical digital infrastructure (Nissenbaum & Van den Hoven, 2020).

2. AI-DRIVEN OFFENSE IN CYBER WARFARE

Cyber warfare is an emerging battlefield where both state and non-state actors leverage advanced technologies to gain strategic, military, economic, and political advantages. The rapid advancement of Artificial Intelligence (AI) has significantly altered the dynamics of cyber warfare. AI is no longer just a tool for defense but has evolved into a powerful weapon in the offensive arsenal of cyber attackers. In this chapter, we will explore how AI-driven technologies are being used for offensive purposes in cyber warfare, covering the role of AI in malware optimization, automated reconnaissance, deepfakes, social engineering, and more. Through real-world and hypothetical case studies, we will demonstrate the potential capabilities of AI in attacking cyber infrastructures and discuss the ethical, legal, and technical challenges in attribution and accountability for these malicious activities (Taddeo & Floridi, 2019).

2.1 Offensive Uses of AI in Cyber Warfare

2.1.1 Malware Optimization

Malware, a common weapon in cyberattacks, has evolved significantly with AI. Traditional malware required human intervention for updates, tweaks, or optimizations to evade detection by antivirus software or security protocols. With AI, however, malware can automatically adapt to different environments, learn from its interactions with defense mechanisms, and improve its evasion strategies. This adaptive capability makes AI-driven malware much more sophisticated and difficult to detect and neutralize.

Table 5. Comparison of Traditional vs. AI-Driven Malware

Feature	Traditional Malware	AI-Driven Malware
Adaptability	Static or manually updated	Self-learning and adaptive
Evasion	Signature-based evasion	Behavior-based and polymorphic
Spread Mechanism	Manual or scripted	Autonomous and intelligent

AI algorithms like machine learning (ML) and deep learning (DL) are used to create malware that can automatically change its code to avoid signature-based detection systems, a method known as polymorphic malware. For example, an AI-driven piece of malware can observe the types of antivirus signatures it encounters and modify its structure to bypass those specific threats. Moreover, AI can be used to create self-replicating malware that propagates itself autonomously across different systems, accelerating the spread of an attack exponentially.

2.1.2 Automated Reconnaissance

Reconnaissance is a critical first step in any cyberattack. In traditional cyberattacks, attackers spend time manually gathering information about their targets—whether it's through social engineering or probing for vulnerabilities in network systems. However, AI has revolutionized this process by enabling automated reconnaissance that can scan vast amounts of information in real time (Danks & London, 2017).

AI-powered systems can automatically crawl through open-source databases, social media, and other online resources to gather intelligence. Natural language processing (NLP) models can sift through public documents, forum discussions, or even social media profiles to gather data that reveals potential weaknesses, such as outdated software or misconfigured network settings. Additionally, AI tools like reinforcement learning can assist in identifying zero-day vulnerabilities by continuously learning from the system's interactions, which can then be exploited in a later stage of the attack (Tolk, et al 2020).

2.1.3 Deepfakes

Deepfake technology, powered by generative adversarial networks (GANs), has opened up a new frontier in cyber warfare. Deepfakes use AI to manipulate audio, video, or images to create highly convincing fake media. This technology can be used for misinformation campaigns, disinformation warfare, or as part of broader social engineering attacks (Zhou & Kim, 2021).

In cyber warfare, deepfakes can be used to create videos of political leaders or military personnel making false statements, potentially leading to public unrest, diplomatic tensions, or even influencing election results (European Union Agency for Cybersecurity (ENISA), 2020). This kind of AI-driven attack has serious implications for the integrity of public discourse, national security, and democratic processes. Furthermore, deepfakes can be used to impersonate high-ranking officials within an organization or government, manipulating lower-level employees or systems into granting unauthorized access.

2.1.4 Social Engineering

Social engineering exploits human psychology rather than technical vulnerabilities in systems. AI can significantly enhance the efficiency and success of social engineering attacks. By analyzing personal data and behavior patterns, AI-driven systems can craft highly personalized phishing attacks or spear-phishing emails that have a much higher chance of success than generic attempts.

Table 6. AI Applications in Social Engineering

Technique	AI Application Example
Spear Phishing	Tailored emails based on user behavior
Vishing	Voice cloning for scam calls
Chatbot Attacks	NLP-powered chat deception

Machine learning algorithms can analyze data from social media, email correspondences, and even voice patterns to predict an individual's responses or behavior. For example, AI can monitor communication patterns to create highly convincing and personalized scam emails or phone calls, making it increasingly difficult for individuals to distinguish between legitimate and malicious actors (International Committee of the Red Cross (ICRC), 2021). This form of AI-driven social engineering can be used to bypass two-factor authentication, steal credentials, or trick individuals into transferring large sums of money.

2.2. Case Studies

2.2.1 Stuxnet 2.0 (Hypothetical)

Stuxnet, the sophisticated worm that targeted Iran's nuclear enrichment facilities, is one of the most infamous examples of a cyberattack with clear geopolitical consequences. If Stuxnet were to be powered by AI in its hypothetical 2.0 version, it would represent a new era in cyber warfare.

In this scenario, AI would allow the worm to adapt and learn from its environment, dynamically adjusting its actions to avoid detection and disable a wider array of industrial control systems (ICS) with greater precision. Unlike its predecessor, which required human oversight for modifications, Stuxnet 2.0 would operate autonomously, navigating through different environments and learning how to bypass cybersecurity measures on the fly. For example, AI-driven capabilities could allow it to identify and disable backup systems or alter control systems in real-time without triggering immediate alarms.

Additionally, Stuxnet 2.0 could use AI-powered reconnaissance to identify new targets within the same network and prioritize the most critical systems to attack. The inclusion of AI would make such attacks harder to predict and counter, potentially disrupting critical infrastructure on a global scale.

2.2.2 AI-Assisted Ransomware

Ransomware attacks, where attackers encrypt a victim's data and demand a ransom for its release, have become a common form of cyber extortion. When AI is integrated into ransomware, the malware becomes far more sophisticated, dynamic, and evasive.

AI-assisted ransomware could use machine learning algorithms to analyze the behavior of the victim's network and identify the most sensitive data to encrypt, maximizing the impact of the attack. It could also adapt to the defenses in place, evolving in real-time to avoid detection by antivirus software and even anticipating responses from security teams.

For example, AI could enhance the efficiency of file encryption by predicting the file types that are most valuable to the victim (e.g., personal data, financial records, or intellectual property) and prioritizing their encryption. This leads to faster, more effective attacks that could cause significant damage to organizations and individuals. Additionally, reinforcement learning algorithms could help ransomware evolve through repeated attack cycles, learning which methods are most successful at bypassing defenses and generating higher ransoms.

2.2.3 Botnets Using Reinforcement Learning

Botnets—large networks of infected devices used to carry out cyberattacks—are a staple tool for cybercriminals. AI-powered botnets, however, present a more advanced and dangerous threat. Traditional botnets follow predefined rules, making them relatively easy to track and dismantle. With AI, particularly reinforcement learning, botnets can evolve and learn from each attack, improving their tactics and making them harder to detect.

Reinforcement learning allows botnets to learn from the feedback they receive during attacks, modifying their behaviors to avoid detection and improve efficiency. This could make botnets far more resilient and capable of launching more sophisticated distributed denial-of-service (DDoS) attacks, making it increasingly difficult for cybersecurity teams to neutralize these threats.

2.3 Challenges in Attribution and Accountability

One of the most significant challenges in AI-driven cyber warfare is attribution. Determining the origin of an attack and holding the responsible parties accountable is often an arduous task. The use of AI technologies, particularly in automated reconnaissance and social engineering, can obscure the identity of the attacker. This anonymity creates substantial hurdles for law enforcement and intelligence agencies.

AI-powered attacks could be launched by state actors, non-state actors, or even individuals who employ sophisticated tools to hide their tracks. The integration of AI in cyber attacks makes it harder to trace the attack back to a specific entity, as the AI algorithms can adapt and mask their activities in real time. Moreover, the rise of decentralized and distributed networks, such as botnets or AI-assisted systems, further complicates the identification of attackers.

Table 7. Attribution Challenges in AI Cyber Warfare

Challenge	Description
Obfuscation	AI hides origin through proxy routing or spoofing
Autonomous Operation	Lack of direct human control
Distributed Architecture	Attacks launched from global decentralized nodes

Accountability is also difficult to enforce because AI-based attacks are often executed autonomously, without human intervention, making it harder to pinpoint legal responsibility. This raises critical questions about the ethics of AI-driven warfare: Who is accountable when an AI system causes significant harm? Should the developers of the AI systems be held responsible for their creation, or should accountability lie with the entity deploying the technology?

3. AI-ENHANCED CYBER DEFENSE MECHANISMS

The increasing sophistication of cyber threats has raised new challenges in safeguarding digital infrastructure, particularly in the face of cyber warfare. Cyber-attacks are no longer just disruptive acts but have evolved into tools of geopolitical strategy, posing significant risks to national security, economic stability, and critical infrastructure. As such, traditional cyber defense mechanisms struggle to keep pace with these evolving threats.

Artificial Intelligence (AI) has emerged as a transformative solution, reshaping the landscape of cyber defense. By enhancing detection, prediction, and response capabilities, AI-driven systems are being integrated into cybersecurity protocols to provide more robust, adaptable, and scalable defense mechanisms. This chapter delves into the role of AI in cybersecurity, focusing on AI-enhanced cyber defense mechanisms, including intrusion detection, threat intelligence, real-time response systems, vulnerability prediction, and patch management. The limitations and potential adversarial threats against AI-based defense systems are also explored.

3.1 Role of AI in Intrusion Detection Systems (IDS)

One of the core functions of cybersecurity is identifying and preventing unauthorized access to systems or data. Traditional intrusion detection systems (IDS) are rule-based and depend on known attack signatures to detect intrusions. While these systems are useful for recognizing known threats, they often struggle to detect novel or sophisticated attacks, particularly those involving zero-day vulnerabilities.

AI-enhanced IDS, however, leverages machine learning (ML) algorithms to recognize and respond to previously unseen patterns in network traffic, user behavior, and system activities. These systems can detect anomalies and identify malicious activity by analyzing vast amounts of data in real-time. Machine learning techniques such as supervised learning, unsupervised learning, and reinforcement learning are particularly useful in recognizing patterns and outliers that deviate from normal operations, enabling the system to flag suspicious behaviors even in the absence of known attack signatures.

Table 8. Key Benefits of AI-Enhanced IDS:

Feature	Traditional IDS	AI-Enhanced IDS
Detection of Known Threats	High	High
Detection of Unknown Threats	Low	High
False Positive Rate	High	Low
Adaptability	Low	High
Data Correlation Capability	Low	High

For example, AI can be used in network traffic analysis to identify deviations in packet flow, data exfiltration, or unauthorized access attempts based on an organization's baseline activity. By leveraging deep learning algorithms, AI-driven IDS can continuously adapt and evolve, improving their ability to detect new attack vectors over time. Additionally, AI systems can enhance anomaly detection by correlating multiple data points and generating a more accurate profile of what constitutes "normal" behavior within the network.

Furthermore, AI-powered IDS can drastically reduce the number of false positives compared to traditional systems. By distinguishing between legitimate activity and actual threats, AI systems ensure that security teams are not overwhelmed by unnecessary alerts, thus enabling a more efficient use of resources.

3.2 AI in Threat Intelligence

The rapidly changing landscape of cyber threats necessitates a dynamic and proactive approach to cybersecurity. Threat intelligence refers to the collection, analysis, and dissemination of information regarding potential cyber threats, enabling organizations to defend against emerging attacks. AI plays a crucial role in augmenting threat intelligence by automating the processing of vast amounts of data from various sources—such as security logs, vulnerability databases, social media, dark web forums, and intelligence reports (Kott & Arnold, 2017).

AI-powered threat intelligence systems use natural language processing (NLP) and data mining techniques to analyze unstructured data and extract actionable insights. By using AI to process and categorize data at scale, these systems can identify patterns, track trends, and predict future attacks with a level of accuracy that is not possible through manual analysis. For example, AI can scan social media and hacker forums to detect early signs of cyberattack plans or identify vulnerabilities being exploited by advanced persistent threats (APTs).

Table 9.

Data Source	AI Technique	Outcome
Dark Web Forums	NLP, Sentiment Analysis	Early identification of planned attacks
Security Logs	Clustering, Classification	Detection of anomalies
Threat Databases	Correlation Analysis	Historical pattern recognition

Another key aspect of AI in threat intelligence is the ability to automate the dissemination of information. AI can prioritize alerts, ensuring that the most pressing threats are communicated to the relevant stakeholders in real-time. This allows organizations to respond faster to emerging risks, preventing attackers from exploiting vulnerabilities before they can be patched.

Machine learning algorithms can also help in threat attribution by analyzing attack vectors and correlating them with known threat actors, thus enabling organizations to better understand the motivations and methods of attackers. This enhanced insight into the tactics, techniques, and procedures (TTPs) used by adversaries allows for more precise defenses to be implemented.

3.3 Real-Time Response Systems Powered by AI

Real-time response systems, which provide automated defense mechanisms against active cyber-attacks, are an essential component of modern cybersecurity. AI is pivotal in enhancing these systems by enabling rapid detection, assessment, and mitigation of threats (Lin, 2016).

In a typical AI-enhanced real-time response system, the AI continuously monitors network traffic and system activities, detecting anomalies in real-time. When an attack is detected, the system evaluates its severity and initiates an appropriate defensive action without requiring human intervention. For example, AI-powered systems can automatically isolate compromised devices, block malicious IP addresses, or initiate a lockdown to prevent further intrusion.

The use of AI allows response systems to operate at speeds far beyond human capabilities, which is critical during an ongoing cyber-attack. In the case of Distributed Denial-of-Service (DDoS) attacks, for instance, AI can immediately detect the abnormal traffic surge and initiate countermeasures to mitigate the impact. Similarly, in the event of a ransomware attack, AI systems can quickly identify the malicious payload and initiate a lockdown, minimizing the potential for system-wide encryption.

AI-driven systems also allow for dynamic and adaptive responses based on the attack's nature. By analyzing past data and attack patterns, AI can adjust its defense mechanisms in real-time, ensuring the response is tailored to the specific type of threat being faced.

3.4 Predicting Vulnerabilities and Automating Patch Management

One of the most significant advantages of AI in cybersecurity is its ability to predict vulnerabilities before they are exploited. Machine learning models can analyze vast datasets, including software code, network configurations, and historical attack data, to identify potential vulnerabilities. By learning from previous breaches and analyzing patterns in system behavior, AI can help predict where vulnerabilities are likely to exist in a network or software application.

This predictive capability is especially valuable in the context of zero-day vulnerabilities, which are unknown to vendors and security teams. AI-driven vulnerability prediction systems can help security teams focus their efforts on high-risk areas, thus enabling them to address potential weaknesses before they are exploited by attackers.

AI can also automate the patch management process, which is traditionally a time-consuming task. Once vulnerabilities are identified, AI systems can prioritize patching efforts based on the severity and potential impact of each flaw. Automated patch management can reduce the time between identifying a vulnerability and deploying a fix, which is crucial in minimizing the window of opportunity for attackers.

3.5 Limitations and Adversarial Threats Against AI-Based Defense

While AI has immense potential in cyber defense, it is not without its limitations and risks. One of the primary challenges is the vulnerability of AI systems themselves to adversarial attacks. Adversarial machine learning, a form of attack in which malicious actors manipulate the input data to fool AI systems, poses a significant threat to AI-driven cybersecurity (National Institute of Standards and Technology (NIST), 2018).

For example, attackers may feed AI systems with specially crafted data designed to mislead the algorithms, causing them to misclassify threats or fail to detect malicious activity. Adversarial attacks can compromise the integrity of AI-based intrusion detection systems and threat intelligence platforms, making them less effective at preventing cyber-attacks.

Additionally, the "black-box" nature of many AI algorithms poses another challenge. In many cases, AI systems operate without providing clear explanations for their decision-making processes, which can make it difficult for cybersecurity professionals to understand why certain actions were taken or failed. This lack of transparency can be problematic when it comes to identifying and rectifying errors in AI-driven defense mechanisms.

Table 10. Risks and Mitigations

Risk	Description	Mitigation Strategy
Adversarial Inputs	Input crafted to deceive AI	Use of adversarial training
Model Drift	Outdated models due to evolving threats	Regular retraining and monitoring
Bias in Training Data	Incomplete or unbalanced datasets	Diversification and validation of datasets

Another significant limitation is the need for vast amounts of high-quality training data. AI models require extensive datasets to learn and improve, and the lack of diverse, representative, and labeled data can hinder the accuracy of AI predictions. Moreover, the continuous evolution of cyber threats means that AI systems must be constantly updated and retrained to keep pace with new attack vectors.

4. ETHICAL AND LEGAL DILEMMAS

Cyber warfare, an evolving and increasingly significant facet of modern conflicts, brings forth complex challenges related to the deployment of artificial intelligence (AI). While AI promises numerous advancements in the realm of defense, surveillance, and security, its integration into military strategies raises several ethical and legal dilemmas that need to be addressed. From questions of autonomy versus accountability to the risks posed by algorithmic bias and the need for international legal frameworks, AI in cyber warfare challenges traditional norms of warfare and security policies (Singer & Friedman, 2014). This chapter delves into these issues, exploring the multifaceted ethical and legal considerations of AI in the context of cyber warfare.

Table 11. Human vs. AI Accountability in Military Operations

Criteria	Human Operated	AI Operated
Decision Control	Human Commanders	Algorithms & Systems
Legal Accountability	Clear (based on chain of command)	Ambiguous
Moral Responsibility	Assigned to Individuals	Diffused/Shared
Error Attribution	Human Error	Programming/Design Error

4.1 Autonomy vs. Accountability: Who Is Responsible for AI Decisions?

One of the most pressing ethical questions surrounding AI in cyber warfare is the issue of responsibility and accountability. As AI systems are increasingly integrated into military and defense operations, the question arises: who is responsible when an AI makes a decision that leads to unintended or harmful consequences? (Taddeo & Floridi, 2019)

In traditional warfare, accountability lies with human commanders and leaders who make decisions based on strategic interests and military doctrine. However, as AI begins to take a more autonomous role—such as in cyberattacks, drone warfare, or surveillance operations—accountability becomes more difficult to assign. When an AI system autonomously launches an attack on a target, who is held responsible if the attack causes unintended collateral damage or violates international law?

One argument posits that responsibility should still rest with human operators, as they are the ones who program, monitor, and manage AI systems. This human-in-the-loop model ensures that accountability is not completely relinquished to machines. On the other hand, proponents of full autonomy in military systems may argue that AI's ability to make decisions in real-time, without the emotional biases or fatigue that affect human soldiers, could lead to more efficient and objective outcomes.

In either case, questions of accountability remain crucial. If an autonomous AI system makes a decision leading to civilian harm or the violation of international humanitarian law (IHL), can the creators, programmers, or military commanders be held liable? How do we ensure that AI systems are programmed with sufficient oversight to adhere to legal and ethical norms?

The issue of accountability is not only a matter of legal responsibility but also one of moral responsibility (Thealla, et al, 2024). In the future, if an AI system operates independently in the battlefield and causes harm, should the decision be viewed as the machine's "fault," or should blame be placed on the human agents involved in the creation, oversight, and deployment of the technology?

This conundrum is magnified in the realm of cyber warfare, where the target of an AI-driven attack may not be a physical entity but instead a network or an infrastructure that, if compromised, may lead to long-term political, economic, or social consequences. This brings us to another pressing issue: risk of algorithmic bias and misuse of predictive profiling.

4.2 Risk of Algorithmic Bias and Misuse of Predictive Profiling

Another key ethical dilemma in the deployment of AI for cyber warfare is the risk of algorithmic bias. AI systems, especially those relying on machine learning and predictive analytics, are only as good as the data fed into them. If the datasets used to train these systems contain biases—whether racial, political, or socioeconomic—there is a significant risk that the AI will inherit these biases, potentially leading to harmful, unfair, or discriminatory outcomes.

Table 12. Examples of Bias in AI Systems

Type of Bias	Description	Cyber Warfare Implication
Racial Bias	Disproportionate targeting of ethnic groups	Misidentification of threats
Geopolitical Bias	Training based on politically skewed data	Escalation of geopolitical tensions
Socioeconomic Bias	Prioritization of threats from poorer regions	Unjust profiling of vulnerable communities

In cyber warfare, where AI is often used to predict threats, target vulnerabilities, and determine the most effective strategies, this bias can be particularly problematic. For instance, if an AI system is used to predict which groups or countries may pose a cyber threat, and the data used to train the system is biased towards certain racial, ethnic, or national characteristics, the AI might unfairly target specific groups or regions. This could lead to increased geopolitical tensions, as well as violations of human rights, particularly if the AI system is used in surveillance operations or to justify preemptive attacks.

Furthermore, AI systems used for predictive profiling—especially in intelligence gathering—can inadvertently lead to the surveillance, criminalization, or oppression of certain populations. A poorly designed or biased algorithm may overstate the potential threat posed by certain individuals or groups based on patterns of behavior that are not necessarily indicative of harmful intent (United Nations Group of Governmental Experts (UN GGE), 2021) . This could, for example, disproportionately affect marginalized communities or lead to the wrongful targeting of specific individuals for surveillance or punitive actions.

The ethical implications of these biases in AI systems are profound. Not only do they raise concerns about fairness and justice, but they also touch on issues of sovereignty and privacy. When a nation-state deploys an AI-driven cyberattack against a perceived threat based on biased or flawed data, it risks not only violating international law but also infringing upon the rights of innocent civilians and other states.

In response to these concerns, researchers and policymakers are calling for greater transparency in the design and deployment of AI systems, as well as improved mechanisms for auditing AI algorithms to ensure fairness, accuracy, and accountability. However, achieving this goal remains a significant challenge, especially when the AI systems in question are classified or used in military operations.

4.3 International Law and Norms: Geneva Convention in the Cyber Era, NATO Policies, and UN Resolutions

The deployment of AI in cyber warfare also raises critical questions about international law, particularly the application of existing norms to the cyber domain. The Geneva Conventions, which govern the conduct of war and aim to protect civilian populations, were developed in the context of traditional military conflicts. However, these conventions were created before the advent of cyber warfare and AI technologies, leaving a gap in international law regarding the ethical and legal frameworks for AI in warfare.

Table 13. Applicability of International Law to AI-Cyber Warfare

Legal Principle	Geneva Conventions	AI-Cyber Warfare Applicability
Civilian Protection	Yes	Complicated (infrastructure attacks)
Distinction	Yes	Difficult in cyberspace
Proportionality	Yes	Needs reinterpretation
Attribution of Attacks	Assumed human agency	Challenging with anonymous cyber actors

The Geneva Conventions explicitly prohibit attacks on civilians and civilian infrastructure, and they mandate that military forces distinguish between combatants and non-combatants in all operations. However, the use of AI in cyber warfare complicates this distinction. AI-driven cyberattacks may target critical infrastructure, including healthcare systems, transportation networks, and energy grids, which may be essential to civilian life. This raises important questions about whether such attacks violate IHL, particularly if they result in widespread harm to civilian populations.

As part of the broader effort to address the challenges of cyber warfare, NATO and the United Nations have begun to explore the implications of AI and cyberattacks on international peace and security. NATO's policy on cyber defense emphasizes the need for a collective response to cyber threats, including the use of AI in both offensive and defensive operations. However, NATO's policies remain somewhat vague when it comes to the ethical implications of using AI in military operations, and more clarity is needed on how the organization plans to address the risks associated with AI-driven cyber warfare.

Similarly, the United Nations has been increasingly focused on the need for international cooperation to regulate cyber warfare. In recent years, the UN Group of Governmental Experts (GGE) on Developments in the Field of Information and Telecommunications in the Context of International Security has called for the creation of international norms and guidelines to govern the use of cyber technologies in warfare. However, there is still a lack of consensus on how existing international law, including the Geneva Conventions, can be applied to the cyber domain and AI-driven warfare.

A key challenge in this regard is the fact that cyber warfare, unlike traditional warfare, is often decentralized and operates in the shadows, with states or non-state actors engaging in attacks that are difficult to attribute. The anonymity of cyberattacks complicates the process of enforcing international law and norms, as it may not always be clear who is responsible for a given attack.

This challenge highlights the need for new international legal frameworks that specifically address AI in cyber warfare. The current state of international law is insufficient to address the unique challenges posed by AI-driven cyberattacks, and there is a pressing need for collaboration between governments, international organizations, and the private sector to develop a robust and coherent legal response.

5. GLOBAL POWER DYNAMICS AND CYBER DETERRENCE

The nature of warfare has evolved dramatically over the past few decades, and at the forefront of this transformation is cyber warfare. What began as a fringe area of military strategy has now become a central aspect of national defense for countries worldwide. One of the key forces driving this evolution is Artificial Intelligence (AI), which has the potential to reshape not only the tactics used in cyber warfare but also the broader global power dynamics that influence international relations and national security policies. The integration of AI into cyber deterrence, arms race scenarios, and asymmetric warfare introduces new threats, challenges, and opportunities for both state and non-state actors.

This chapter will explore the ways in which AI is influencing global power dynamics, particularly within the context of cyber deterrence, arms race scenarios, and asymmetric warfare. Additionally, it will discuss the roles of superpowers and non-state actors in shaping the future of cyber conflict, and how AI is impacting military doctrines, intelligence strategies, and defense capabilities on a global scale.

5.1 AI and the Evolution of Cyber Deterrence

Cyber deterrence refers to strategies and policies designed to prevent hostile actors from engaging in cyber attacks by threatening retaliatory actions. Traditionally, deterrence in military strategy has been based on the threat of conventional or nuclear retaliation; however, in the digital age, this concept is undergoing a radical shift. The introduction of AI into this sphere presents both new challenges and opportunities for nations seeking to defend themselves against increasingly sophisticated cyber threats.

5.1.1 The Role of AI in Strengthening Cyber Defense

AI can enhance the capabilities of cyber defense systems in several ways. Machine learning algorithms can be used to identify potential threats in real-time, analyzing vast amounts of data to detect patterns and anomalies that may indicate an impending attack. Additionally, AI can automate responses to cyber incidents, allowing for faster mitigation of risks and reducing the burden on human operators. By improving the speed and accuracy of these processes, AI can significantly enhance deterrence by ensuring that nations are better prepared to defend themselves against cyber attacks.

Table 14. Applications of AI in Cyber Defense

Application	Function	Impact on Deterrence
Threat Detection	Identifying malware and anomalous behavior	Early warning and prevention
Automated Response	Real-time neutralization of threats	Reduced response time and damage control
Simulation and Forecasting	Predicting attack vectors and vulnerabilities	Enhanced preparedness
Threat Attribution	Identifying likely perpetrators	Stronger basis for retaliation

Moreover, AI-driven systems are capable of simulating potential cyber attack scenarios, allowing nations to develop more effective defense strategies. These simulations can help identify vulnerabilities in existing cybersecurity frameworks, providing valuable insights for improving national security policies and defense infrastructure. The increased resilience offered by AI-based systems enhances the credibility of deterrence, making it more likely that adversaries will refrain from launching attacks.

5.1.2 AI and Attribution of Cyber Attacks

One of the most challenging aspects of cyber warfare is the difficulty in attributing attacks to specific actors. Traditional methods of attribution—such as tracing the origin of physical weapons—are much less effective in the cyber domain, where attackers can obfuscate their identities and locations through various means. AI can aid in overcoming this challenge by improving the accuracy of attribution. By analyzing patterns in cyber attack behaviors, AI systems can help identify likely perpetrators, thereby strengthening the deterrent effect.

This capability of AI could fundamentally change the deterrence calculus. In the past, ambiguity surrounding the identity of the attacker made it difficult to respond proportionally to cyber threats. With AI's enhanced ability to track and attribute cyber activities, states can more effectively deter adversaries by signaling a strong and targeted response to cyber aggression. This could include preemptive or retaliatory cyber operations, further complicating the strategic environment and encouraging adversaries to reconsider launching attacks.

5.2 AI and the Cyber Arms Race

As AI continues to shape the landscape of cyber warfare, it is driving a new kind of arms race—one not based on traditional weapons but on cyber capabilities. Much like nuclear arms races of the past, the pursuit of cutting-edge cyber capabilities has led to increasing investments in AI-driven cyber tools by both state and non-state actors.

5.2.1 Superpowers and AI-Driven Cyber Capabilities

At the forefront of this arms race are the world's superpowers, particularly the United States, China, and Russia. Each of these nations is heavily invested in developing AI-driven cyber capabilities to enhance their offensive and defensive operations in cyberspace. For example, the U.S. has developed sophisticated cyber tools as part of its Cyber Command, with a focus on both defense and offense. China, on the other hand, has integrated AI into its broader military modernization strategy, recognizing the critical role that cyber capabilities play in maintaining national security.

Table 15. AI-Driven Cyber Capabilities of Superpowers

Country	Focus Areas	Strategic Goals
United States	Cyber Command, automated threat mitigation	Defensive resilience, preemptive strike
China	Military modernization, cyber espionage	Strategic parity, influence projection
Russia	Disinformation, AI in malware development	Asymmetric advantage, global disruption

Russia, similarly, has developed advanced cyber warfare capabilities, leveraging AI and machine learning to conduct cyber espionage, disinformation campaigns, and cyberattacks on a global scale. These countries are not only developing their own cyber weapons but are also engaged in a form of strategic cyber escalation, seeking to gain the upper hand in what could be described as the "digital battlefield."

As nations race to develop AI-based cyber tools, there is a growing concern about the destabilizing effects of this competition. The proliferation of cyber weapons, combined with the rapid evolution of AI technologies, has created an environment where it is increasingly difficult to maintain control over the escalation of cyber conflicts. Much like the nuclear arms race during the Cold War, the AI-driven cyber arms race introduces significant risks of unintended escalation, cyber miscalculations, and global instability.

5.2.2 The Role of Non-State Actors

In addition to superpowers, non-state actors—including hacker groups, terrorist organizations, and other rogue entities—are increasingly leveraging AI for cyber warfare. These actors may not possess the same resources as nation-states, but they are using AI to launch highly sophisticated cyber attacks that can disrupt critical infrastructure, steal sensitive data, and cause widespread economic damage.

AI empowers these actors by providing them with advanced tools for identifying vulnerabilities, automating attacks, and evading detection. This democratization of cyber warfare—where non-state actors can access powerful AI-driven capabilities—poses significant challenges for traditional military deterrence strategies, which have primarily focused on state actors. The increasing involvement of non-state actors in cyber warfare further complicates global power dynamics and contributes to the growing uncertainty in the realm of cybersecurity.

5.3 AI's Influence on Military Doctrines and Intelligence Strategies

5.3.1 AI and Military Doctrines

AI is fundamentally reshaping military doctrines worldwide, particularly in the realm of cyber warfare. In traditional warfare, doctrines were focused on conventional combat methods—land, sea, and air operations. However, with the advent of cyber threats, military doctrines must now incorporate the cyber domain, with a focus on both defense and offense. AI is becoming an essential component of these doctrines, with an emphasis on rapid decision-making, automated responses, and intelligence gathering.

Table 16. Non-State Actors and AI in Cyber Warfare

Actor Type	AI Use Case	Impact on Global Stability
Hacktivist Groups	Sentiment analysis, automated propaganda	Political disruption
Terrorist Cells	AI-generated malware, attack planning	Threat to critical infrastructure
Cybercriminals	AI in phishing, ransomware distribution	Eco

Countries are increasingly developing cyber warfare doctrines that prioritize the use of AI to secure national interests. For example, AI-powered systems are now being incorporated into command-and-control networks, allowing military leaders to make real-time decisions based on vast amounts of data from multiple sources. This shift toward AI-enabled decision-making enhances the speed and accuracy of military operations, giving countries an edge in modern warfare.

5.3.2 AI and Intelligence Strategies

AI is also transforming intelligence strategies, providing military and intelligence agencies with new tools for gathering, analyzing, and acting on information. AI systems can process large datasets from a variety of sources—such as satellite imagery, intercepted communications, and cyber activities—enabling intelligence agencies to detect threats faster and more accurately.

Table 17. Evolution of Military Doctrines with AI

Domain	Traditional Focus	AI-Enhanced Capabilities
Command and Control	Manual decision-making	Real-time, data-driven decisions
Cyber Defense	Reactive policies	Predictive, preemptive actions
Combat Operations	Physical platforms	Autonomous and semi-autonomous systems

In the cyber domain, AI is being used to analyze patterns of behavior, identify potential attackers, and predict future threats. This predictive capability allows intelligence agencies to take proactive measures, rather than merely reacting to cyber incidents as they occur. AI's ability to automate the processing of large datasets and its predictive capabilities give nations a significant advantage in the cyber intelligence realm, reshaping the strategic calculus of national security.

Table 18. AI in Intelligence Gathering and Analysis

Intelligence Activity	AI Role	Strategic Advantage
Surveillance	Real-time pattern recognition	Early threat identification
Signal Intelligence (SIGINT)	Automated data mining from multiple sources	Comprehensive threat landscape
Behavioral Analysis	Predictive modeling	Anticipating adversary actions

6. AI TECHNOLOGIES AND THEIR APPLICATIONS IN CYBER DEFENSE AND OFFENSE

Artificial Intelligence (AI) has revolutionized multiple sectors, and cybersecurity is no exception. As cyber warfare intensifies globally, AI technologies have become critical tools in both cyber defense and offense. AI's ability to process vast datasets, identify patterns, and autonomously execute tasks has introduced unprecedented capabilities and complex challenges in cyberspace. This chapter explores how AI technologies are applied in cyber defense and offense, the emerging threats associated with these applications, and the ethical considerations that must guide their use.

6.1. AI in Cyber Defense: Enhancing Detection and Response

6.1.1 Automated Threat Detection

Traditional cybersecurity methods struggle to keep up with the rapid evolution of cyber threats. AI enhances cyber defense by enabling automated threat detection through anomaly detection and behavior analysis.

- **Anomaly Detection:** AI models learn normal system behaviors and flag deviations indicative of malicious activity, such as unusual login times or data transfers.
- **Malware Analysis:** Deep learning models analyze executable files to detect known and zero-day malware variants by examining code structure and behavior.
- **Phishing Detection:** NLP-powered AI systems analyze email content, URLs, and sender information to detect phishing attempts before they reach users.

These AI-driven defenses reduce detection times drastically, enabling proactive incident response.

6.1.2 Incident Response and Mitigation

AI systems are increasingly integrated into Security Orchestration, Automation, and Response (SOAR) platforms, enabling:

- **Automated Incident Triage:** AI prioritizes alerts by severity, reducing human workload.
- **Response Automation:** Scripts triggered by AI can isolate affected systems, block IP addresses, or apply patches autonomously.
- **Threat Intelligence Integration:** AI aggregates data from multiple sources to provide contextual understanding and predict attacker movements.

Table 19. Comparison of Traditional vs AI-Driven Cyber Defense Capabilities

Capability	Traditional Methods	AI-Driven Methods
Threat Detection Speed	Minutes to hours	Seconds to minutes
Adaptability	Limited	High (continuous learning)
False Positives	High	Reduced via pattern recognition
Incident Response	Manual	Automated and real-time

6.2 AI in Cyber Offense: Empowering Attack Capabilities

6.2.1 Autonomous Cyber Attacks

AI's offensive capabilities are becoming a significant threat in cyber warfare. Autonomous AI systems can:

- **Conduct Reconnaissance:** AI crawls target networks, identifying vulnerabilities faster than humans.
- **Develop Malware:** AI can generate polymorphic malware that adapts to avoid detection by traditional antivirus software.
- **Coordinate Botnets:** AI controls botnets intelligently to launch Distributed Denial of Service (DDoS) attacks, dynamically adjusting attack vectors.

6.2.2 Advanced Social Engineering Attacks

AI enables sophisticated social engineering through:

- **Deepfake Generation:** AI-generated synthetic audio/video content to impersonate trusted individuals and deceive targets.
- **Personalized Phishing:** AI tailors messages based on collected data to increase phishing success rates.
- **Automated Spear Phishing:** Using NLP and data mining, AI crafts convincing emails sent en masse with minimal human involvement.

6.2.3 AI-Powered Cyber Espionage

State and non-state actors employ AI to infiltrate networks and extract sensitive information using:

- **Stealth Malware:** AI-driven malware that modifies behavior to avoid detection.
- **Credential Theft Automation:** AI scripts that perform rapid password guessing and bypass authentication.
- **Data Exfiltration Optimization:** AI identifies optimal timing and methods for data theft to avoid triggering alerts.

6.3. Emerging Threats and Challenges in AI-Enabled Cyber Warfare

6.3.1 AI-Driven Attack Escalation

AI accelerates cyber conflict escalation by enabling rapid attack deployment and complex multi-vector campaigns. Autonomous systems may act unpredictably, increasing the risk of unintended consequences and collateral damage.

6.3.2 Adversarial AI and Model Manipulation

Attackers can exploit AI systems using adversarial inputs designed to mislead ML models, causing false negatives or positives. Such attacks include:

- **Poisoning Attacks:** Corrupt training data to degrade AI performance.
- **Evasion Attacks:** Slightly modifying inputs to bypass detection.
- **Model Extraction:** Stealing AI model parameters for reverse engineering.

6.3.3 AI Arms Race and Accessibility

The proliferation of AI tools lowers barriers for cybercriminals, fueling an AI arms race. Non-state actors gain access to powerful AI cyber weapons previously limited to advanced nations, complicating defense strategies.

6.4. Ethical Considerations and the Need for Governance

6.4.1 Accountability and Human Oversight

AI's autonomous actions in cyber warfare raise critical questions of accountability. Who is responsible when AI systems cause unintended harm or violate laws? Ensuring human-in-the-loop oversight is essential to maintain control and ethical standards.

6.4.2 Bias, Privacy, and Transparency

AI models may inherit biases from training data, leading to unfair targeting or privacy infringements. Transparent AI systems with explainable decision-making processes are needed to uphold ethical cybersecurity practices.

6.4.3 International Norms and Legal Frameworks

Developing global norms to regulate AI's use in cyber warfare is vital to prevent misuse. Laws must clarify the permissible scope of AI in cyber offense and defense, balancing security with respect for human rights.

6.5 Future Directions: Building Resilient AI-Enabled Cybersecurity Ecosystems

6.5.1 Advancing Explainable AI (XAI)

Research should focus on making AI decisions interpretable, allowing cybersecurity professionals to audit and trust AI recommendations, enhancing accountability.

6.5.2 Collaborative AI Defense Networks

Global collaboration through AI-enabled intelligence sharing platforms can improve collective defense capabilities against sophisticated AI-powered attacks.

6.5.3 Ethical AI Frameworks and Certification

Creating ethical certification standards for AI cybersecurity products will help ensure that these technologies are developed and deployed responsibly.

7. POLICY RECOMMENDATIONS AND FUTURE DIRECTIONS

In the ever-evolving landscape of cybersecurity, the increasing reliance on Artificial Intelligence (AI) has led to both unprecedented opportunities and complex challenges. As AI continues to be integrated into cyber warfare strategies, understanding its role in defense mechanisms, ethical dilemmas, and global governance becomes imperative. This chapter outlines the policy recommendations for managing AI's role in the cyber domain, with a focus on governance, multilateral collaboration, and the importance of ethical frameworks to guide the development and deployment of AI technologies.

7.1 Strategies for AI Governance in the Cyber Domain

AI's application in the cyber domain presents unique challenges, particularly in terms of autonomy, security, and accountability. As states and non-state actors increasingly turn to AI for cyber offense and defense, the need for robust governance structures is clear. AI systems can autonomously execute cyberattacks, launch malware campaigns, or disrupt critical infrastructures, which raises significant concerns about accountability and international security.

Regulation of Autonomous Cyber Systems: One of the most pressing issues is the regulation of autonomous AI systems in cyber warfare. AI systems that can execute attacks without human oversight pose significant risks, particularly when they are used in offensive operations. These systems can cause unintended harm, trigger escalation in international conflicts, or be used by malicious actors to exploit vulnerabilities in public and private sector infrastructures.

Table 20.

Aspect	Policy Measure	Expected Outcome
Autonomous cyber attacks	HITL/HOTL controls mandated	Reduced unintended escalation
Accountability	Legal responsibility frameworks	Clear liability for AI system actions
Offensive AI use	International limits & prohibitions	Mitigated risks of autonomous cyber warfare

To mitigate these risks, policymakers must prioritize creating and enforcing regulations that govern the development, deployment, and use of autonomous AI systems. A framework should be established that requires developers of AI-powered cyber defense systems to implement safeguards and maintain human-in-the-loop (HITL) or human-on-the-loop (HOTL) controls. Such mechanisms ensure that human oversight is maintained, particularly in decision-making processes involving critical defense systems.

Establishing Cybersecurity Standards: Standardization of AI-driven cybersecurity tools is essential for ensuring interoperability and effectiveness in both defense and response strategies. National governments, international organizations, and industry stakeholders should work together to develop and agree upon cybersecurity standards that outline best practices for AI applications in cyber defense. This would include agreed-upon methods for AI-based threat detection, response automation, and incident reporting. Regular audits and certification of AI systems could also be mandated to ensure compliance with these standards.

Table 21.

Area	Standardization Focus	Stakeholders
Threat detection	Accuracy, speed, bias mitigation	Governments, private sector
Response automation	Safety, reliability, human oversight	AI developers, cybersecurity teams
Incident reporting	Transparency, timeliness	Regulatory bodies, organizations

Building Trustworthy AI: As AI is increasingly used to defend against cyber threats, it is important to ensure that AI technologies are trustworthy, reliable, and resilient. National regulatory bodies and international organizations should establish protocols to verify that AI systems used in defense are secure, transparent, and free from biases that could compromise their decision-making processes.

Policymakers should promote research into the development of explainable AI (XAI), which ensures that AI's decisions and actions can be easily understood and audited. This is crucial for accountability, particularly in scenarios where AI systems are used in complex cyber warfare situations. Additionally, establishing ethical frameworks for the development of AI models will help safeguard against unintended consequences, such as algorithmic biases or adversarial exploitation of AI vulnerabilities.

7.2 Importance of Multilateral Collaboration and Transparency

AI in the cyber domain is inherently global, with threats crossing national borders and affecting the global commons. As such, multilateral collaboration is essential for the development of norms, regulations, and response mechanisms that can address the complex challenges posed by AI in cyber warfare.

Table 22.

Forum/Institution	Role	Focus Area
United Nations GGE	Norm setting	Responsible state behavior
International courts	Enforcement	Accountability in cyber warfare
Multilateral treaties	Legal framework	AI use in cyber conflict

Building International Consensus: At the heart of multilateral cooperation is the need for international agreements on the use of AI in the cyber domain. Existing frameworks, such as the United Nations (UN) Group of Governmental Experts (GGE) on Advancing Responsible State Behavior in Cyberspace, have begun addressing the role of AI in international cybersecurity. However, these agreements often lack the specificity needed to tackle the nuanced issues of AI-driven cyber warfare.

Governments, international organizations, and tech companies must come together to form treaties and norms that define acceptable use, set red lines, and agree on the consequences of malicious use of AI in cyber warfare. These frameworks could be modeled after the Geneva Conventions, ensuring that AI deployment in conflict is consistent with international humanitarian law. Such agreements should also address the accountability of both state and non-state actors using AI in offensive cyber operations.

Transparency and Information Sharing: Transparency is a critical element in building trust in the use of AI for cybersecurity. Multilateral cooperation should prioritize the exchange of information on AI-driven cyber threats, particularly in detecting new types of cyberattacks that exploit AI vulnerabilities. Governments and private sectors should collaborate on creating platforms for sharing intelligence on emerging AI-driven cyber threats in real time, ensuring that countries can swiftly detect, mitigate, and respond to AI-powered attacks.

Additionally, the private sector, especially technology giants responsible for developing AI, must be held accountable for disclosing vulnerabilities and collaborating with governments to mitigate potential risks. Public-private partnerships could play a crucial role in facilitating this information sharing and in ensuring that AI systems used in the defense sector adhere to national security standards and international legal frameworks.

Fostering Global AI Literacy and Capacity Building: One of the critical challenges in international collaboration is the uneven distribution of AI knowledge and resources across countries. Developing nations may face significant barriers to understanding and implementing AI-driven cybersecurity solutions. The international community must prioritize capacity-building initiatives aimed at enhancing AI literacy, cybersecurity expertise, and the technical capabilities of countries that lack the resources to develop their own AI infrastructure.

Table 23.

Capacity Building Area	Initiative	Target Beneficiaries
AI literacy	Training workshops, online courses	Developing nations, academia
Technical infrastructure	Grants for AI cybersecurity tech	Under-resourced countries
Collaborative research	Joint international projects	Multilateral partners

Multilateral organizations, such as the World Bank and the International Telecommunication Union (ITU), can play a pivotal role in providing funding, technical assistance, and educational resources to developing nations. By enhancing the global capacity for AI-driven cybersecurity, the international community can ensure that the benefits of AI are distributed equitably and that all countries are equipped to defend against emerging threats.

7.3 Proposals for Ethical AI Certification, Open-Source Models, and Public-Private Partnerships

To address the ethical challenges associated with AI in cyber warfare, several key initiatives must be implemented to ensure that AI systems are developed and deployed responsibly.

Ethical AI Certification: One of the most critical aspects of AI governance is ensuring that AI systems adhere to ethical principles that prioritize fairness, transparency, accountability, and respect for human rights. An ethical AI certification system should be established to assess AI technologies used in cyber defense and warfare. This certification would involve evaluating AI systems for their compliance with international norms, regulations, and human rights standards, particularly in relation to privacy, discrimination, and accountability.

Table 24.

Certification Criterion	Description	Impact
Fairness	Absence of bias and discrimination	Equitable AI decisions
Transparency	Explainability of AI operations	Accountability
Privacy	Protection of sensitive data	Respect for individual rights

Such certification could be issued by a recognized global body, such as the International Organization for Standardization (ISO), and would serve as a mechanism for assuring governments and the private sector that AI technologies are aligned with ethical guidelines. This would also incentivize AI developers to adhere to best practices in system design, ensuring that AI systems are robust, reliable, and fair.

Open-Source AI Models: In the spirit of transparency and global collaboration, the development and sharing of open-source AI models should be encouraged. Open-source AI initiatives can democratize access to AI-driven cybersecurity tools, enabling smaller states, academic institutions, and research organizations to build and enhance their own cybersecurity systems. Moreover, open-source models foster community-driven innovation, where security vulnerabilities are more likely to be identified and addressed through collective expertise.

Additionally, open-source models can promote ethical development by enabling third-party audits, ensuring that AI systems do not perpetuate biases or violate privacy rights. Public access to these models can also help accelerate the development of AI-powered defense systems that are both secure and transparent.

Public-Private Partnerships (PPPs): Given the complexity and scale of the cybersecurity challenges posed by AI, public-private partnerships (PPPs) will be essential in addressing AI-related threats. Governments and private-sector companies must work together to ensure that AI technologies are developed responsibly and deployed for the greater good.

Table 25.

Partnership Element	Role	Benefits
Data sharing	Real-time threat intelligence	Faster response, better defense
Joint research	AI tool development	Innovation, standardization
Regulatory collaboration	Policy development	Balanced governance

PPP frameworks can facilitate the sharing of data, research, and resources, enabling faster responses to emerging threats. Furthermore, PPPs can play a crucial role in the development of AI standards, ethical guidelines, and cybersecurity protocols that safeguard both national and global security. Public-private collaborations can also ensure that AI systems are developed with the necessary safeguards to prevent malicious actors from exploiting vulnerabilities in critical infrastructure.

8. CONCLUSION

As we conclude our exploration of *Cyber Warfare and the Role of Artificial Intelligence,* it becomes evident that AI is reshaping both the landscape of cyber threats and the strategies employed to combat them. The integration of AI into cyber warfare has introduced new dimensions of speed, sophistication, and scale in both offensive and defensive operations. While AI offers immense potential for enhancing cybersecurity measures, its misuse also presents significant risks, underscoring the dual-edged nature of this technology.

On one hand, AI's ability to analyze vast amounts of data, predict vulnerabilities, and automate defensive responses allows for a more proactive and dynamic defense strategy. Machine learning algorithms, for instance, can detect anomalies in network traffic, identify potential intrusions, and rapidly respond to emerging threats with unparalleled precision and speed. The role of AI in automating defense mechanisms and minimizing human error is critical, especially in high-stakes cyber warfare scenarios where timely decision-making can be the difference between a successful defense and catastrophic failure.

However, the use of AI in offensive cyber operations raises profound ethical, legal, and strategic concerns. AI-driven attacks, such as deepfake technology, automated phishing campaigns, and autonomous weaponized systems, have the potential to disrupt critical infrastructure, influence political systems, and destabilize societies. The increasing complexity of these AI-driven threats makes it more difficult for governments, international organizations, and cybersecurity experts to develop effective deterrence measures. As cyber warfare becomes more sophisticated, nations may find themselves engaged in a new form of arms race, this time centered around AI capabilities and their integration into cyber weapons.

Ethical challenges are at the forefront of this discussion, particularly in terms of accountability, transparency, and the potential for unintended consequences. AI systems, especially in the context of autonomous weaponry or offensive cyber tools, may operate without clear human oversight, leading to moral and legal dilemmas about responsibility for actions taken. The lack of global consensus on norms and regulations surrounding AI in warfare further complicates the path to ensuring responsible use.

In conclusion, while AI offers promising advancements in cybersecurity, it also presents unprecedented challenges in both defense and offense. As nations and organizations navigate this complex terrain, it is imperative that they develop not only advanced technical capabilities but also robust ethical frameworks and international agreements. The future of cyber warfare, shaped by AI, will demand a careful balance between innovation and responsibility, with an unwavering commitment to safeguarding global peace and security.

REFERENCES

Allen, G., & Chan, T. (2017). *Artificial Intelligence and National Security*. Harvard Belfer Center.

Binnendijk, H., & Libicki, M. C. (2020). *Cybersecurity and Cyberwar: What Everyone Needs to Know*. Oxford University Press.

Brundage, M., et al. (2018). *The Malicious Use of Artificial Intelligence: Forecasting, Prevention, and Mitigation*. Future of Humanity Institute.

Buchanan, B. (2020). *The Hacker and the State: Cyber Attacks and the New Normal of Geopolitics*. Harvard University Press.

Cummings, M. L. (2019). Artificial Intelligence and the Ethics of Cyber Warfare. *International Journal of Military Ethics*, *18*(2), 123–140.

Danks, D., & London, A. J. (2017). Algorithmic Bias in Autonomous Systems. *Proceedings of the 26th International Joint Conference on Artificial Intelligence*, 4691–4697.

European Union Agency for Cybersecurity (ENISA). (2020). *Threat Landscape for Artificial Intelligence*.

Fitzgerald, R., & Jenkins, L. (2020). AI in Cybersecurity: Opportunities and Threats in Warfare. *International Conference on AI and Security*, 103–117.

Heath, J. (2019). *The Ethics of Cyberwarfare*. Oxford University Press.

International Committee of the Red Cross (ICRC). (2021). *Autonomous Weapon Systems: Implications of Increasing Autonomy in the Critical Functions of Weapons*.

Kott, A., & Arnold, R. (2017). The Promises and Perils of Artificial Intelligence in National Security. *The Cyber Defense Review*, *2*(2), 79–93.

Lin, H. (2016). Attribution of Malicious Cyber Incidents. *Journal of National Security Law & Policy*, *6*(1), 1–22.

National Institute of Standards and Technology (NIST). (2018). *Framework for Improving Critical Infrastructure Cybersecurity* (Version 1.1). U.S. Department of Commerce.

Nissenbaum, H., & van den Hoven, J. (2020). Ethical Challenges in Cyber Warfare: The Role of AI and Autonomous Systems. *Ethics and Information Technology*, *22*(1), 17–34.

Singer, P. W., & Friedman, A. (2014). *Cybersecurity and Cyberwar: What Everyone Needs to Know*. Oxford University Press. DOI: 10.1093/wentk/9780199918096.001.0001

Taddeo, M., & Floridi, L. (2018). Regulate Artificial Intelligence to Avert Cyber Arms Races. *Nature*, *556*(7701), 296–298. DOI: 10.1038/d41586-018-04602-6 PMID: 29662138

Taddeo, M., & Floridi, L. (2019). "The Ethics of Cyberwarfare." *In Ethics in the Age of Technology*, Springer, 143-160.

Thealla, P., Nadda, V., Dadwal, S., Oztosun, L., & Cantafio, G. (Eds.). (2024). *Corporate Cybersecurity in the Aviation, Tourism, and Hospitality Sector*. IGI Global. DOI: 10.4018/979-8-3693-2715-9

Tolk, A., Diallo, S. Y., & Turnitsa, C. D. (2020). *Modeling and Simulation Support for System of Systems Engineering Applications*. Wiley.

United Nations Group of Governmental Experts (UN GGE). (2021). *Norms of Responsible State Behavior in Cyberspace*. United Nations Office for Disarmament Affairs.

Zhou, X., & Kim, J. (2021). "AI and Cyber Defense: From Deterrence to Active Defense." *Proceedings of the 13th International Conference on Artificial Intelligence and Cybersecurity*, 42–53.

KEY TERMS AND DEFINITIONS

AI Governance in Cybersecurity: AI Governance in Cybersecurity refers to the frameworks, policies, and ethical guidelines that oversee the development and deployment of AI technologies within the cybersecurity domain. It focuses on ensuring that AI systems are developed and used in a responsible, transparent, and accountable manner, while addressing issues such as algorithmic bias, security breaches, and the protection of human rights.

AI-Driven Autonomous Weapons: AI-driven autonomous weapons are weapon systems powered by artificial intelligence that can make targeting and operational decisions without human intervention. These systems are capable of operating autonomously in hostile environments, such as drones or robots, and pose significant ethical and strategic challenges in both warfare and defense.

Algorithmic Warfare: Algorithmic Warfare refers to the use of algorithms, particularly those driven by AI and machine learning, in military operations and cyber warfare strategies. This can involve automating decision-making in defense systems, such as the identification of cyberattack patterns or the development of autonomous weapons systems that are powered by AI algorithms for targeting and engagement.

Artificial Intelligence (AI): Artificial Intelligence (AI) refers to the development of computer systems capable of performing tasks that typically require human intelligence, such as reasoning, learning, problem-solving, and decision-making. In the context of cyber warfare, AI includes algorithms and machine learning models that can detect, prevent, or respond to cyber threats autonomously, analyze large datasets, predict potential vulnerabilities, and optimize security measures.

Artificial Intelligence in Cyber Defense: Artificial Intelligence in Cyber Defense refers to the application of AI technologies to enhance security measures against cyber threats. This includes the use of AI-powered tools for threat detection, vulnerability scanning, malware analysis, incident response, and the automation of security protocols to defend against cyberattacks in real time.

Autonomous Cyber Defense Systems: Autonomous Cyber Defense Systems are AI-powered systems designed to detect, respond to, and neutralize cyber threats without human intervention. These systems leverage real-time data, machine learning algorithms, and decision-making processes to analyze potential threats, assess risks, and implement protective measures such as firewalls, intrusion detection systems, and automated counterattacks.

Cyber Attribution: Cyber attribution refers to the process of determining the origin and identity of an attacker responsible for a cyber event or breach. Accurate attribution is crucial for both retaliation and legal action but remains a complex challenge in cyber warfare due to the anonymity of digital networks and the potential for false flag operations.

Cyber Espionage and AI: Cyber espionage, in the context of AI, refers to the use of AI technologies to infiltrate, monitor, and gather sensitive data from targeted entities for intelligence purposes. AI can be used to automate data collection, uncover vulnerabilities, and conduct stealthy surveillance on a massive scale, potentially enhancing the effectiveness of espionage operations.

Cyber Espionage: Cyber espionage involves the use of digital technologies to gather sensitive information from government entities, corporations, or individuals without their knowledge or consent. In cyber warfare, it often involves exploiting vulnerabilities in information systems to steal classified data, intellectual property, or strategic information for national security or economic advantage.

Cyber Warfare Doctrine: A Cyber Warfare Doctrine refers to a set of strategic principles and policies developed by a government or military entity to guide the use of cyber tools and tactics in warfare. This doctrine outlines the goals, rules of engagement, and ethical considerations in utilizing cyberattacks as part of a broader defense or offense strategy during conflicts.

Cyber Warfare: Cyber warfare refers to the use of digital technologies, including cyberattacks, cyber espionage, and other malicious activities, by nation-states or non-state actors to disrupt, damage, or manipulate the systems and infrastructure of adversaries. It includes activities such as hacking, spreading misinformation, or launching denial-of-service attacks that impact national security, economic stability, and social order. Cyber warfare can be directed at government institutions, military systems, critical infrastructure, or civilian sectors.

Cyberattacks: Cyberattacks are deliberate actions aimed at compromising the integrity, confidentiality, or availability of computer systems, networks, or data. Types of cyberattacks include malware deployment, phishing, ransomware, Distributed Denial of Service (DDoS) attacks, and hacking. Cyberattacks are central to the tactics used in cyber warfare and can target a wide range of entities from government institutions to private corporations.

Cybersecurity Frameworks: Cybersecurity frameworks are structured guidelines, policies, and best practices designed to protect organizations from cyber threats. Frameworks like the NIST Cybersecurity Framework (National Institute of Standards and Technology) provide a blueprint for identifying risks, implementing security controls, detecting incidents, and responding to cyberattacks.

Cybersecurity Threat Landscape: The cybersecurity threat landscape refers to the evolving spectrum of cyber threats, vulnerabilities, and attack vectors that organizations, governments, and individuals face. This includes new and emerging threats such as advanced persistent threats (APTs), zero-day exploits, and the potential impact of AI-driven cyberattacks. Understanding the landscape helps in developing better defenses and mitigation strategies.

Deep Learning: Deep Learning is a subset of machine learning that uses artificial neural networks with many layers (hence "deep") to analyze large datasets. In the context of cyber warfare, deep learning techniques can be used to enhance threat detection systems, improve malware classification, and support autonomous decision-making in defense operations.

Ethical Dilemmas in Cyber Warfare: Ethical dilemmas in cyber warfare refer to the complex moral questions that arise in the use of digital technologies for military and strategic purposes. These dilemmas include concerns about the legitimacy of preemptive cyberattacks, the collateral damage of civilian infrastructure, the transparency and accountability of AI-driven decisions, and the balance between national security and individual privacy.

Ethical Hacking: Ethical hacking refers to the practice of legally probing computer systems for vulnerabilities in order to identify potential weaknesses before malicious hackers can exploit them. Ethical hackers, often employed by organizations or governments, use techniques similar to those used by cybercriminals but aim to strengthen system defenses and ensure security.

Machine Learning (ML): Machine Learning (ML), a subset of AI, involves training computers to recognize patterns in large sets of data and make predictions or decisions based on those patterns. In the realm of cyber warfare, ML can be used to identify anomalies in network traffic, predict cyberattacks, and create adaptive defenses that evolve in response to changing threats.

Offensive Cyber Operations: Offensive cyber operations refer to proactive measures taken by nation-states or organizations to disrupt, destroy, or damage the digital infrastructure of adversaries. These operations can include cyberattacks, hacking, espionage, and data manipulation with the aim of achieving a strategic advantage.

Strategic Cyber Defense: Strategic Cyber Defense refers to the planning, implementation, and management of measures designed to protect a nation's digital infrastructure and information systems from cyber threats. This includes employing advanced technologies, policies, frameworks, and AI tools to ensure that critical sectors, such as defense, energy, communications, and finance, are safeguarded against cyberattacks, espionage, and other malicious activities.

APPENDIX

Additional Reading

"Cybersecurity and Cyberwar: What Everyone Needs to Know" by P.W. Singer and August Cole

This book provides a comprehensive overview of the evolving landscape of cyber warfare, including the rise of AI-driven cyber threats. Singer and Cole explore the implications of AI for both offensive and defensive cybersecurity strategies and discuss the potential risks posed by cyber weapons in the hands of state and non-state actors.

"Artificial Intelligence and National Security" edited by Greg Allen and Taniel Chan

This collection of essays explores the dual-use nature of AI technologies and their role in national security. It discusses the intersection of AI, military strategy, and defense capabilities, highlighting the challenges in harnessing AI for defense purposes while mitigating its risks, particularly in cyber warfare scenarios.

"The Ethics of Cybersecurity" by Markus Christen, Bert Gordijn, and Thea O'Keefe

This book addresses the ethical challenges posed by cybersecurity, including AI in cyber warfare. The authors explore ethical concerns such as privacy, autonomy, accountability, and the moral responsibility of deploying AI in both offensive and defensive cybersecurity.

"Cyber War: The Next Threat to National Security and What to Do About It" by Richard A. Clarke and Robert K. Knake

Clarke and Knake provide an in-depth analysis of cyber warfare, focusing on the strategic implications of AI and its application in cyber conflict. The book examines real-world cyber threats, highlighting case studies of state-sponsored cyberattacks and the emerging role of AI in these activities.

"Artificial Intelligence in Cyber Defense: A Review" – IEEE Access

This research paper reviews the role of AI in enhancing cybersecurity defense mechanisms. It discusses AI-based intrusion detection systems, automated threat analysis, and the use of machine learning algorithms for anticipating and mitigating cyberattacks. The paper also examines the ethical and operational challenges involved in AI-driven defense systems.

"Artificial Intelligence and the Future of Cyber Warfare" by Brian V. McKeon and Kenneth A. Schultz (Harvard Kennedy School)

This article explores the strategic implications of AI in cyber warfare, including its use in reconnaissance, attack, and defense. The authors argue that AI will reshape the landscape of cyber conflict, both in terms of capability and escalation risks. They also delve into the ethical concerns of AI-driven cyber warfare.

"Ethics of Artificial Intelligence and Cyberwarfare" – International Journal of Information Security

This paper explores the ethical dilemmas surrounding AI in cyber warfare, including accountability for actions taken by autonomous systems, the potential for AI to escalate conflicts, and the risks of AI being used to violate human rights. The paper advocates for the development of international regulations and ethical frameworks for AI in warfare.

Thealla, P., Nadda, V., Dadwal, S., Oztosun, L., & Cantafio, G. (Eds.). (2024). *Corporate cybersecurity in the aviation, tourism, and hospitality sector*. IGI Global.

This paper explores the ethical dilemmas surrounding AI in cyber warfare, including accountability for actions taken by autonomous systems, the potential for AI to escalate conflicts, and the risks of AI being used to violate human rights

Chapter 5

Ethical Leadership Effect on the Regulation of AI in Cyber Security by Mediating OCB by Collaborative Governance in Ethiopia

Jesu Antony Arockia Venice
https://orcid.org/0009-0005-6115-960X
DMI-St.Eugene University, Zambia

Wako Jio
https://orcid.org/0009-0003-6192-459X
Bule Hora University, Ethiopia

Shashi Kant
https://orcid.org/0000-0003-4722-5736
DMI-St. Eugene University, Zambia

Sandeep Sharda
https://orcid.org/0009-0003-6235-9414
Symbiosis Institute of Operation Management, Symbiosis International University, Pune, India

Shashank Mittal
https://orcid.org/0009-0007-8643-4350
O.P. Jindal Global University, India

DOI: 10.4018/979-8-3373-3611-4.ch005

ABSTRACT

This chapter addresses the effects of ethical leadership to the regulation of artificial intelligence (AI) on cyber-security and the mediating role of Organizational Citizenship Behavior (OCB) as a part of the collaborative governance context in Ethiopia. The results could indicate a significant impact of ethical leadership on the effective control of AI in the field of cyber-security; OCB may also play a mediating role. This implies that leaders with ethics embedded in them facilitate citizenship culture amongst employees, hence creating harmonious relationship in collaborative governance. The shortcomings of these findings are broken down into the discussion of Ethiopia and its changing cyber-security system, whereby ethical leadership is important in the formulation of regulatory policies that maximize AI technologies. The chapter ends with the recommendations that policymakers and leaders in organizations may implement to ensure the facilitation of ethical governance behaviors that may stimulate OCB, which would eventually result in better AI regulation in the cyber-security.

INTRODUCTION

The pace and incorporation of the artificial intelligence (AI) technology in other sectors has elicited immense interest throughout the world especially in their establishment in the cyber-security (Negeri et al., 2025). AI can transform the process of threat detection, respond to threats, and manage security (Badada et al., 2025). Nevertheless, the growing complexity and independence of AI systems also imply significant ethical, regulatory, and governance issues happening around the globe (Vargas-Hernandez & González-Ávila, 2025). For it is through ethical leadership, that the concept is being used to help put integrity, accountability and transparency into focus so that they get used towards heading organizations that work in a very responsible manner regarding management of emerging technology (Ghaleb & Pardaev, 2025). It began in the theories of leadership based on moral philosophy and on organization behavior, Ethical Leadership is used as the basis of building trust and cultures of collaborations which are needed to navigate the technological ambiguities (Ibragimov & Kadagidze, 2025). The impact of Ethical Leadership on organizational outcomes and personal behaviors of employees (Da Veiga, 2025). Organizational Citizenship Behavior (OCB) is studied as a positive effect by empirical literature and it is the voluntary discretionary behavior aimed at organizational goals that are beyond the formal job framework (Hong et al., 2025). Likewise, the studies on AI regulation as applied to cyber-security have highlighted the importance of having efficient governance systems that can balance between innovation and ethics and risk reduction (Razmak et al., 2025).

Even though it has made plenty of progress, there are still a number of practical issues (Payne et al., 2025). Fragmentation of policies, fast-changing technological advancements, and inadequate collaboration between stakeholders are some factors that tend to limit the achievement of effective AI regulation by organizations (Nuseir et al., 2024). Also, although Ethical Leadership, OCB, and AI governance have been studied independently, researchers have not yet been able to understand the dynamics between these three factors in collaborative governance space to regulate the use of AI effectively (Al Kurdi et al., 2024). This lack is a missing point in the establishment of more detailed approaches through which leadership, behavioral, and regulatory approaches are incorporated (Usama et al., 2024). Besides, the majority of the research available currently gives the propensity to concentrate upon direct relationships at the expense of mediating mechanisms, e.g. the mediating role of OCB in converting the influence of leadership to regulatory effectiveness (Kant et al., 2025).

The purpose of this chapter is to fill these gaps by examining the mediation position of OCB by utilizing Collaborative Governance in connection between Ethical Leadership and Regulation of AI in cyber-security. The chapter combines both theoretical knowledge and empirical examination to provide a complex picture of the role of ethical leadership in promoting collaborative behaviors that are imperative in effective governance of AI.

The availability of AI in cyber-security systems has brought opportunities and challenging issues to governments, organizations, and societies across the entire world (Da Veiga, 2025). Cyber threats are being designed with a growing level of sophistication and AI can provide effective tools to identify, forecast and nullify attacks as they happen (Hong et al., 2025). Such technological improvements have however, created serious issues in privacy, bias, accountability, and control especially in nations with weak institutional structures (Razmak et al., 2025). In this new dynamic environment, ethical leadership has become more crucial in leading the responsible regulation and governance of AI (Ghaleb & Pardaev, 2025). Ethical leadership does not just mean observing the moral laws in the ruling process; it also includes shaping the political policies and functioning of the institutions as well as establishment of trust in the society (Nuseir et al., 2024). However, even though its significance has been realized, it is quite difficult to execute ethical leadership in AI governance especially in low- and middle-income nations (Al Kurdi et al., 2024).

It has been noted that Ethiopia has taken a significant step towards digital transformation and the formulation of cyber policy during the last decade (Kant et al., 2025). The government is investing in such initiatives as the National Digital Strategy and the foundation of the Ethiopian AI Institute, which testify to a high level of commitment to the adoption of technological innovation (Jio et al., 2025). Nevertheless, the laws and regulation instruments required to guide the utilization of AI in cyber-security are not fully built and are poorly enforced (Badada et al., 2025). The gaps between policy intentions and practicalities evident in the AI policy realm are reflected through ethical violations, the absence of transparency, and stakeholder involvement in AI policymaking (Vargas-Hernandez & González-Ávila, 2025). To illustrate, the reports over the use of facial recognition tools by security agencies with no clear guidelines or without consent of citizens attracted much attention to the aspect of violating the privacy of the citizens and the likelihood of misusing information (Payne et al., 2025). These problems show why the development and deployment of AI systems require ethical oversight in the spheres connected with the national security particularly (Usama et al., 2024).

A good real life example is the use of surveillance technologies being installed in Addis Ababa in the name of promotion of safety of the masses (Ibragimov & Kadagidze, 2025). Although there was an underlying motivation to employ AI-driven cameras as a crime prevention tool, a lack of ethical frameworks, poor data protection laws (Adula et al., 2024), as well as the failure to consult with the civil society contributed to the criticism of such actions by civil society organizations and privacy advocates (Plantinga et al., 2024). The described scenario can be seen as an example of how the lack of ethical leadership and collaborative governance leads to regulatory islands, the loss of people trusts in institutions, and the abuse of AI-based technologies (Ciolacu et al., 2204). In addition, the limited resources of regulatory institutions and state department siloed working process prevent the creation of effective AI governance systems (Sołtysik et al., 2024). Inter-agency cooperation and civil society are not included, which aggravates the situation and does not allow establishing a system of inclusive, ethical, and responsible governance (Mengesha et al., 2024).

OCB is an important mediator in such context (Mengesha et al., 2024). As leaders are inclined towards ethical values and enable employees to take action outside formal professional positions, contributing to ethical reviewing, making critical remarks on AI undertakings (Badada et al., 2024), or launching mutually targeting policy discussions, organizations become capable of developing strong and visible governance systems (Kant et al., 2025). Nevertheless, the contribution of OCB in closing the gap between the subject of ethical leadership and the regulation of AI is less of empirical data. In addition, not much research has been carried out to establish this relationship in developing countries where institutions, culture, and resource limitations create an extra challenge (Dugo et al., 2025).

This background creates a strong case to investigate the capacity of ethical leadership to regulate AI by using the mediating factor of OCB in the framework of collaborative governance. Ethiopia presents a case study which is timely due to the relevancy of the comprehension of the country; this case study is insightful providing information whose knowledge can be applicable to other nationalities that have similar issues. This research will, therefore, contribute to the theoretical development of the field as well as provide practical answers to one of the most challenging technology and ethics issues this era has ever faced by understanding the barriers to the ethical leadership implementation in AI governance and identifying the organizational behaviors that facilitate it.

This growing dependence on the utilization of AI technology in cyber-security has posed a great urgency in the deployment of appropriate regulation mechanisms that can guarantee an ethical, safe, and responsible application (Razmak et al., 2025). Optimally, organizations must be directed based on a greater Ethical Leadership that encourages collegial conducts among workers, which promotes the holistic and versatile AI governance (Nuseir et al., 2024). Such a model of improved state does not only involve embedding ethical standards in the leadership, but it also develops OCB (Mengesha et al., 2024), the voluntary cooperation facilitated by the leadership and fosters a stronger form of regulatory compliance and innovation (Da Veiga, 2025). But, there are studies showing conflicting results on whether Ethical Leadership directly influences AI regulation at least significantly or not (Tufa et al., 2025). In addition, the number of mechanisms in which leadership plays a role in the governance of AI is unspecified, and the mediating roles that behavioural aspects including OCB can take are hardly examined (Badada et al., 2024). This leads to inconclusive results which do not allow complete view on how leadership and collaborative behaviors can be incorporated into practice of AI regulation (Ghaleb & Pardaev, 2025).

There are also the still existing theoretical gaps especially that of existing between leadership theories and the technology governance (Vargas-Hernandez & González-Ávila, 2025). Although Ethical Leadership and OCB have been substantiated in institutional conduct science, the way of their integration and the influence they generate in the environment of AI-driven regulation of cyber-security is not sufficiently examined (Payne et al., 2025). As well, knowledge gaps include the degree at which collaborative governance models are able to operationalize these construct to enhance better regulatory outcomes (Al Kurdi et al., 2024). It has been suggested that contextual gaps exist since most of the available research has not been done in the environment of cyber-security (Dugo et al., 2025). There is little information regarding AI specifically in these types of AI environments where there is administrative instability due to the rapid change in technologies combined with high risk which necessitates agile and ethical governance systems (Ibragimov & Kadagidze, 2025). The landscape is also complicated by practical issues such as fragmented development of the policy, lack of coordination among stakeholders, and challenges of promoting ethical cultures that can promulgate both innovation and risk management (Hong et al., 2025). Most organizations fail to convert moral agendas into functional actions that can improve AI regulation since they have no clear indication on how to nurture collaborative citizenship among employees and inculcate it into the governance process through leadership styles (Badada et al., 2025).

Ethical Leadership Theory: Offers a theoretical perspective, and it states ethical leaders as those people who exhibit normatively desirable behavior, through individual behaviors, and in relation with other people and that, such behavior ought to be encouraged by communicating and making decisions. It is based on the moral philosophy and OCB definitions and proposes that it is specifically referred to the role of leaders to enhance ethical climates that have implications on other behaviors and attitudes such as, by the followers and discretionary behaviors such as OCB (Vargas-Hernandez & González-Ávila, 2025).

OCB Theory: It defines the kind of extra-role behaviors that are displayed by the employees outside the obligations of their formal jobs and are voluntary. Derived through organizational psychology, OCB theory emphasizes the role of such behaviors towards organizational effectiveness through cooperation, trust, and flexibility. Within the framework of the proposed study, OCB will serve as a cognitive process according to which ethical leadership can influence AI regulation indirectly by promoting cooperative and proactive effort among the members of the organization (Ghaleb & Pardaev, 2025).

Collaborative Theory of Governance: It gives thoughts on the involvement of various actors who are the stakeholder involved in the decision-making as a group would solve complex challenges. Originating within the realms of public administration studies and policy analysis, this theory reveals the necessity of promoting collectiveness, openness, and inclusiveness in governance which is essential in regulating AI technologies that cuts across many areas and interests (Ibragimov & Kadagidze, 2025).

Technology Acceptance Theory and Governance Theory: The processes by which organizations borrow and control new technologies are known through (such as the Technology-Organization-Environment (TOE) framework or socio-technical systems theory). The theories are concerned with the relationship between technological functions, organizational activities and external environmental issues and they have pointed out the importance of adaptive governing structures, which integrate both organizational ethics and behavior (Jio et al., 2025).

One of them is Ethical Leadership Theory, which would be the primary theoretical framework of the chapter. It gives a conceptual background of studying how leadership creates an impact on the organizational behaviors and the regulation outcome particularly via the ability to influence ethical climate and catalyze citizenship behaviors that are critical in governance of AI.

DEFINITION AND ORIGIN OF KEY TERMS

Ethical Leadership: The term is used to describe the behavioral demonstration of normatively appropriate behavior embodying integrity, fairness, and concern of others by the leaders, and to its communication to and reinforcement of the followers as well as applying the role modelling. It is a concept of moral philosophy which was later advanced in the study of organizational behavior to focus on the influence of the ethical standards of the leaders in shaping the behavior of the employees and building the organization culture (Badada et al., 2025).

OCB: It is adopted as optional employee acts not expressly realized in formal reward systems that however lead to positive contributions to organizations. Developed in the 1980s as part of organizational psychology, OCB includes assisting coworkers, arriving on time, promoting organizational change, and entails individual desire to pursue collective interests beyond their defined roles (Vargas-Hernandez & González-Ávila, 2025).

Collaborative Governance: It is a governance mechanism through which two or more stakeholders-in most cases belonging to different sectors, participate jointly in decision-making forums to resolve the problems affecting the people or their complexities. Founded in the late 20th century as the product of public administration and policy research, this term focuses on inclusiveness, decentralization, and cross-accountability as the aspects of effective governance particularly useful in the situations that involve cross-sector cooperation (Ghaleb & Pardaev, 2025).

AI regulation in Cyber-security: This is the policies, standards and procedures that are in place to guarantee that AI technologies applied in cyber-security is implemented ethically, safely and in a responsible manner. It is a somewhat recent concept as the fast progress of AI and an increase in concerns regarding vulnerability to attacks, privacy issues and ethical concerns have been rising, requiring a need to combine governance methods and find a balance between encouragement and risk reduction (Ibragimov & Kadagidze, 2025).

Ethical Leadership and AI in Cyber-security

Moral leadership consisting of elements of fairness, integrity, transparency, and interest towards societal welfare has been empirically associated with enhanced compliance (Payne et al., 2025), moral decision-making and responsible innovation

(Vargas-Hernandez & González-Ávila, 2025). In an environment where AI is used to control sensitive areas of security like surveillance, data protection, and threat detection, ethical leadership plays a very crucial role in making sure that regulatory practice become legal and moral (Badada et al., 2025). A number of studies confirm the beneficial effect of ethical leadership on the issue of technological governance (Ghaleb & Pardaev, 2025). Indeed, found out that ethical leadership was greatly beneficial in lessening the unethical use of technology, as well as supporting the norms of privacy of data in IT employees (Da Veiga, 2025). In the same line of reasoning, stressed that ethical role modeling by leader's builds organizations in which organizational actors are more inclined to favor fair and transparent implementation of technology (Hong et al., 2025). This form of leadership compliments the adoption of the human-centered concepts of AI governance, including fairness, accountability, and expandability in context of AI (Razmak et al., 2025). Ethical leadership can reduce risks in this sector as data science is an industry where the use of AI would be subject to various risks, such as a risk of civil liberty violations, discriminatory surveillance, and unintentional casualties (Nuseir et al., 2024). To take one example, researchers emphasize the importance of ethically embedded leadership in the production of AI to serve the purpose of public safety with the caveat that otherwise the technology could be deployed in an authoritarian or discriminatory mode (Al Kurdi et al., 2024). Empirical studies also reveal that workers in cyber-technology companies had higher possibilities of participating in whistles-blowing and inner checks once they saw their leaders to be ethical and willing to ethical discussions (Mengesha et al., 2024).

Nonetheless, although these insights can be mentioned, the empirical research particularly inclining ethical leadership to the regulatory aspect of AI in cyber-security is rather scanty (Badada et al., 2024). Most of the current literature is either about ethical leadership within the general contexts of organizations or about the ethics of AI design overlooking the actual processes of regulation, like compliance structures, stakeholder involvement and policy-formulation (Mishra et al., 2024). Besides, much of the empirical literature was done in developed countries whose governance systems are fully established like U.S., U.K and Germany, creating a huge gap on how such dynamics occur in emerging market (Ibragimov & Kadagidze, 2025). Also, there is a paucity of research that is concerned with how, in fact, ethical leadership comes to life in the form of organizational behaviors that are aimed at facilitating the regulation agendas (Kebede et al., 2024). In particular, the role of the mediating mechanism, that is OCB, in such relationship remains under-researched (Negeri et al., 2025). It has been demonstrated that OCB can reinforce ethical climate, and the final results of governance, yet its particular role in the context of AI regulation has been only seemingly applied, and not practically tested. In the same manner, the science of collaborative governance models encompassing ethical leadership which involves the involvement of various actors (Kant et al., 2025).

Ethical Leadership and OCB Collaborative Governance

The linkage between ethical leadership and the OCB has been well reported in the organizational behavior literature that the available empirical studies reveal how ethical leaders contribute to the culture of voluntarily pro-social behavioral culture among employees (Ghaleb & Pardaev, 2025). Value-based leadership by adopting a fair and moral approach emphasizing business ethics and stakeholder care have proven to be instrumental in influencing positive employee attitudes and behaviors above and beyond what is required immediately or directly by a job mandate (Da Veiga, 2025). Beth found that trust building, open communication, and psychologically secure climate using moral leadership other than formal job requirements promote OCB (Razmak et al., 2025). Ethical leaders have more chances of getting employees that are more helpful to each other, promoting ethical course of actions and joining activities aimed to the welfare of an organization in general and the community too (Nuseir et al., 2024). This relationship has always been affirmed by empirical research studies (Al Kurdi et al., 2024). As an example, they presented evidence that moral leadership is an important prognosticator of OCB in diverse organizational environments, more specifically by its impact on moral efficacy and organizational commitment (Badada et al., 2025). Ethical leaders also give moral signals and demonstrate their role models, which makes the employees internalize ethical standards and go the extra mile out of their free will (Ibragimov & Kadagidze, 2025). This evidence highlights the behavioral processes through which ethical leadership has an impact on organizational performance particularly in complex situations where voluntary contributions are an important necessity (Mengesha et al., 2024).

OCB can be assumed to be especially relevant in the power structures where collaborative governing is utilized, i.e. where, in the decision-making process, the government players are joined by the private and civil organizations (Badada et al., 2024). Collaborative governance is a kind of governance that is associated with shared responsibility, construction of consensus, and mutual accountability (Negeri et al., 2025). In these types of structures, ethical leadership is needed so that a high degree of transparency can be achieved, the repositories can be trusted and all (the stakeholders) can be included to develop inclusive participation (Jio et al., 2025). The empirical studies observe that ethical leadership is a factor-determiner of successful cooperation within the sphere of public administration because it strengthens the idea of commitment, equity, and mutual respect among sectors (Vargas-Hernandez & González-Ávila, 2025). An ethical leadership makes stakeholders more inclined to practice civic-minded behaviors other- volunteering to assist the policy implementation, involvement in discussions of regulations, and providing information- that can be viewed as twin aspects of OCB (Payne et al., 2025).

Additionally, ethics in leadership will increase the desire of the employees to engage in joint initiatives, particularly in the situations when working in the public service, by fostering honesty and transparency (Dugo et al., 2025). In cross-sector partnerships, the ethical leaders should create a context that employees and stakeholders both feel the incentive to give more than what they are being asked to institutionally, which enhanced the quality of the governance outcomes (Tufa et al., 2025). In a similar way, found that ethical leadership within the governmental agencies resulted in the greater involvement of employees in non-obligatory, citizenship-like activities supporting the inter-agency coordination and policy innovation (Hong et al., 2025). Although the knowledge base of this area is increasing, empirical research that links ethical leadership and OCB to collaborative governance is largely absent, especially those in non-Western and low-resource settings (Kant et al., 2025).

OCB Collaborative Governance and Regulation of AI in Cyber-security

Regulation of AI in cyber-security is gradually becoming a multi-actor project that needs powerful institutional structures besides combined procedures and spirited organizational actions (Nuseir et al., 2024). OCB voluntary and un-mandated efforts by staff that lead towards the enhancement in the functionality of the organization is indeed one of the main components whose implementation can bring about the required disparity between policy and the practice part of such a system of governance (Mengesha et al., 2024). Within the context of collaborative governance whereby various stakeholders engage with one another as part of the collective sharing of decision-making, OCB becomes a source of trust accumulation (Negeri et al., 2025). Although the combination of these constructs remains in development in the empirical studies, the amount of literature emphasizing their applicability to AI regulation in the area of cyber-security is steadily increasing (Razmak et al., 2025).

Research on inter-organizational governance and public administration have shown the role of OCB in determining the success of joint ventures (Jio et al., 2025). In one study, the researchers stated that high-level OCB leads to an increase in the likelihood of an employee in the public sector to indulge in primitive actions conducive to inter-agency coordination and policy innovation (Badada et al., 2025). On the same note, made it clear that the civic virtue and conscientiousness are among the most notable characteristics of OCB and this stood on the side of enhancing the effectiveness of governance networks by ensuring transparency, accountability, and the enduring engagement of stakeholders (Da Veiga, 2025). At a collaborative governance level, OCB enables workers and stakeholders to go beyond what is mandated and to volunteer in conducting ethical reviews, in providing policy decisions, and in resolving competing interests, which are essential in controlling complex and developing technologies such as AI (Ghaleb & Pardaev, 2025). Research with respect to AI regulation, specifically in cyber-security, empirical research is only now looking at the human and behavioral aspects that affect the regulatory process (Hong et al., 2025). Such as, stated that companies that had well developed ethical responsibility and citizenship behavior cultures were more prone to adopt AI systems that ranged in line with the fairness standards, non-discrimination, and privacy practices. In this regard, OCB would allow people to be proactive as regards to detecting algorthematic risks, and reporting unintended consequences, and adhering to ethical principles (Ibragimov & Kadagidze, 2025).

Collaborative governance also emphasizes the importance of OCBs in the process of AI regulation through their ability to make policy processes inclusive and participatory (Badada et al., 2024). contend that collaborative governance relies on the willingness of actors to cooperate in a voluntary effort to achieve common objectives and mutual accountability (Vargas-Hernandez & González-Ávila, 2025). Employees with a high OCB play a critical role in operationalizing ethical and technical standards through informal coordination, cross-sectoral participation (Badada et al., 2025). Nonetheless, little empirical attention has been given to the OCB in the context of collaborative governance systems with a specific reference to the regulation AI in the cyber-security arena and to developing countries scenarios (Payne et al., 2025). Large proportion of the literature available is based on western model of governance and does not fully consider the institutional, cultural, and infrastructural constraints established in countries with lesser income (Al Kurdi et al., 2024). Such gaps are of special concern since such countries are rapidly adapting AI technologies but do not develop regulatory and ethical capabilities (Negeri et al., 2025).

Ethical Leadership, AI in Cyber-security and OCB Mediation

The ability to integrate ethical leadership, AI regulation in the sphere of cyber-security, and OCB inside the context of collaborative governance is a relatively new field of potential empirical studies with the crucial value attached to it (Negeri et al., 2025). The more closely intertwined with national security infrastructure AI systems get, the more it is realized that the issue of technology regulation remains a critical, human, and very much not technical and legal exercise (Kant et al., 2025). The ethical leadership is fundamental as it establishes the moral norms and develops organizational cultures that would promote accountability, transparency, and social responsibility as key values that would make AI ethical and effectively governable (Badada et al., 2024). Ethical leadership combined with OCB and empowered by collaborative systems of governance, makes regulatory systems more impartial, dynamic and capable of withstanding turbulence (Mengesha et al., 2024).

The empirical evidence has developed significant association between ethical leadership and ethical technology governance (Al Kurdi et al., 2024). As an illustration, discovered that ethical leaders are entrusted and promote ethical values to be internalized by the followers, which is translated to responsible approaches in an organization (Nuseir et al., 2024). This kind of leadership is important in the high stakes areas such as in cyber-security where there is the need to ensure that AI is not used to cause abuse through surveillance, discrimination, or infringement of privacy (Payne et al., 2025). Leadership that is ethical makes employees aware of ethical norms as well as putting the employees in a position to take the ethical norms into actions (Kar et al., 2025). This empowerment is manifested in OCB whereby individuals are willing to take part in governance-related activities, do risk reporting, and take part in ethical deliberation--even going outside their specified job description (Kuwar et al., 2025).

The OCB as a mediator has been tested successfully in the organizational content, however, its transferability to the world of AI regulation is minimal, as demonstrated in which ethical leadership contributes to the boosting of the OCB through enhancing feelings of psychological safety, moral engagement, and organization ownership (Badada et al., 2025). According to Collaborative governance, such structural and operational framework provides the means in which collaborative governance can be implemented by ethics leadership and OCB in the regulation of AI (Razmak et al., 2025; Hong et al., 2025). In these characteristics, ethical leaders are major enablers and they encourage inclusive stakeholders and concentrate the various stakeholder interests in mutual ethical objectives (Da Veiga, 2025). OCB will also be more apparent and influential in the collaborative governance context because workers and partners are eager to bring their ideas and efforts to the ongoing surveillance of an essential nature in the adaptive governance of fast-changing AI technologies (Ibragimov & Kadagidze, 2025). Although these ideas are closely intertwined, empirical studies that explicitly establish the connection between the concepts of ethical leadership, OCB, and the regulation of AI through collaborative governance are limited, and in the developing countries (Ghaleb & Pardaev, 2025). Majority of the existing literature focuses on studying these constructs on their own, or in the context of Western corporate of public administration (Vargas-Hernandez & González-Ávila, 2025).

The chapter gives an in-depth insight on a crucial role that Ethical Leadership plays in shaping the Regulation of AI in Cyber-security through the mediating effect of OCB under Collaborative Governance systems. Through the analysis, it is evident that alone Ethical Leadership does not significantly and directly affect AI regulation, but contributes immensely to OCB, which, in turn, has a very strong and positive impact on the regulatory outcomes. Such a complete influence of the mediation stresses the significance of the behavioural and inter-relationship patterns in collaborative governance, where voluntary, at will actions of the organization members under the guidance of good moral leadership play a significant role in creating and implementing the regulations of AI. The evidence supports the idea that ethical leaders play a key role in establishing a culture of trust, collaboration, and willingness to take initiative, which is a necessity on the way towards each discovery in the ever-complicated and quickly changing field of AI and cyber-security. Additionally, the sound measurement model validity and reliability, together with strong model fit measures also support the theoretical framework used, which demonstrates the interrelatedness of leadership, collaborative citizenship, and regulation in the given case.

MANAGERIAL IMPLICATIONS

There are five valuable managerial implications to the organisations that want to have better control of the use of AI inside cyber-security by using effective leader and governing activities. Firstly, managers ought to consider Ethical Leadership very vital in organizational setting of trust, integrity, and collaboration, a fact that employees will be highly motivated to commit in the OCB. Through the advancement of ethical values and by providing good examples, managers may enhance voluntary and proactive behaviors that facilitate the consistency of regulatory compliance and enhance was governance processes. Second, the complete mediation effect of OCB points to the fact that managers are compelled to develop and maintain an atmosphere of cooperation, in which the emphasis is placed on the teamwork, mutual assistance, shared responsibility. The last one is not only to increase the effectiveness of regulations but also to increase the overall effectiveness of the organization and flexibility with regard to dealing with challenges of AI. Third, leaders should be trained in investment programs where special focus is put on leadership skills, and the ability to make good moral decisions and team interactions to find solutions to these complex ethical and technical concerns of AI in any cyber-security system. Lastly, the manager ought to incorporate collaborative governance mechanisms that foster free interactions and the collective problem-solving amongst the stakeholders, as a way to ensure that the regulation of AI is holistic, free, and competent. With these strategies, the organizations will be able to respond to the changing risks the AI technologies create and create a responsible and resilient approach to managing cyber-security.

PRACTICAL IMPLICATIONS

Practitioners should aim at developing ethical leadership at all the levels because this sort of leadership would lead to development of positive behaviors that are needed to move through the ethical complexities and security risks of AI technologies. Since the mediating role that OCB plays is demonstrated, compliance with regulation and effectivity of governance can be considerably better promoted by instilling a culture in which employees are willing to do more than required by their formal responsibility. Organizations are advised to use some policies and practices to help teams and departments managing AI in terms of supporting collaboration and transparency and joint accountability. Moreover, the training must be organized to increase ethical awareness and encourage collaborative interaction, so that personnel can easily determine and mitigate any security concerns related to AI on their own. These are some of the practical steps that may assist in filling policy-implementation gaps so that the regulation of AI would not just be well-designed but also successfully operationalized. Finally, the results of the research will help practitioners come up more ethical and resilient means of dealing with risks in the AI phenomenon in the field of cyber-security making safer and more reliable technological landscape.

THEORETICAL IMPLICATIONS

Current leadership and governance theory indicates that the effects of ethical leadership on innovative technological regulation are mostly indirect and it operates through behavioral mechanisms that promote voluntary and cooperative behavior among members of the organization. This insight fills knowledge gaps on how types of leadership can carry over into practice of regulation in the emerging professional practice areas like AI and cyber-security whereby formal structures might not be enough. The concepts of organizational behavior, ethics and information systems researches complement and are intertwined in the study, providing the multidisciplinary dimension to the issue, showing the necessity to appreciate the dynamics of collaboration in solving the issues related to technology. The validation of the measurement model and verification of the interrelationship among leadership, citizenship behavior and regulation provides the research with a basis to make a contribution to the future theoretical development and testing within the similar issues. On the whole, the study has theoretical implications that can contribute to scholarly discussions about leadership efficiency, collaborative governance, and technology regulation, offering a delicate discourse which could guide further research on issues of ethics and behavior in the management of AI.

Few recommendations are expected to improve the governance and leadership practices to regulate AI in cyber-security. Companies ought to focus on the development of Ethical Leadership by presenting ethics based training and developmental programs that focus on integrity, transparency and accountability. The promotion of the working environment that will support the OCB is important because the voluntary cooperative activity of employees is of great value in facilitating the reduction in the gap between the leadership intent and the regulatory results. Managers ought to design structures and procedures to allow collaboration and shared responsibility in such a way governance does not become only top-down activities. Also, the policy lords and heads of organizations are advised to come up with concise rules and guidelines that can combine ethics and the technological norms of AI use and deployment, where regulation also catches up with lightning speed in technology. New studies should consider the prospect of a longitudinal study to determine the changes in these relationships over time and determine the influences of cultural and situational contexts on leadership, OCB and AI regulation relationships. Adhering to these recommendations, organizations will enhance their ability to address the AI risks in a modulated manner and advance ethically and cooperative governance.

It is suggested that longitudinal studies will help to analyze these dynamics in future, as the sector of AI technology development and regulation environment evolves rather quickly. It is also possible to assume that in the future researchers might take into account moderating factors which, possibly, might affect the extent and character of these connections, including the organizational culture, the type of the industry, and the geographical location. The idea of considering other leadership styles or forms of governance may also help to get valuable insights on other possible mechanisms that influence the regulation of AI. In addition, the qualitative research, e.g. the interviews or the case studies, could provide deeper, more detailed insights into the way of ethical leadership practice and expression of OCB in different organizational contexts. In the last, considering how global the problem of AI and cyber-security currently seems, cross-cultural analysis might provide insight into how varying cultures and their values and norms influence leadership effectiveness and collaborative governance when it comes to the regulation of AI technologies. These new directions will assist in a larger and more context-sensitive approach of the relationship between leadership and behavior with technology governance.

REFERENCES

Al Kurdi, B., Alquqa, E. K., Nuseir, M. T., Alzoubi, H. M., Alshurideh, M. T., & AlHamad, A. (2024). Impact of cyber security and risk management on green operations: Empirical evidence from security companies in the UAE. In *Cyber security impact on digitalization and business intelligence: Big cyber security for information management: Opportunities and challenges* (pp. 151–167). Springer International Publishing. DOI: 10.1007/978-3-031-31801-6_9

Badada, B., Delina, G., Krishnaraj, R., & Thiruthuvanathan, M. M. (2024, April). Application of XAI in Integrating Democratic and Servant Leadership to Enhance the Performance of Manufacturing Industries in Ethiopia. In *International Conference on Innovations in Computational Intelligence and Computer Vision* (pp. 123-138). Singapore: Springer Nature Singapore. DOI: 10.1007/978-981-97-6995-7_10

Badada, B., Delina, G., Krishnaraj, R., & Thiruthuvanathan, M. M. (2025). Charting the Course of Leadership Through the Digital Era: A Synergy of Leadership Styles, Technology Integration, and Deep Learning. In *Leadership Paradigms and the Impact of Technology* (pp. 119-156). IGI Global Scientific Publishing.

Ciolacu, M. I., Marghescu, C., Mihailescu, B., & Svasta, P. (2024, May). Does Industry 5.0 need an engineering Education 5.0? Exploring potentials and challenges in the age of generative AI. In *2024 IEEE global engineering education conference (EDUCON)* (pp. 1-10). IEEE.

Da Veiga, A. (2025). Encouraging Creativity and Innovation in the Cybersecurity Culture of the Organisation for Sustainable Value and Growth. In *Diversity, AI, and Sustainability for Financial Growth* (pp. 1-28). IGI Global Scientific Publishing. DOI: 10.4018/979-8-3693-6011-8.ch001

Dugo, D., Kant, S., & Alemu, Z. K. (2025). Servant Leadership Influence on Organizational Citizenship Behavior with the Mediation Role of Emotional Intelligence: A Case of Public Universities in Ethiopia. In *Generation Alpha and Next Generation Leadership for Greener Futures* (pp. 269-292). IGI Global Scientific Publishing. DOI: 10.4018/979-8-3693-9281-2.ch014

Ghaleb, M. M. S., & Pardaev, J. (2025). Controlling Cyber Crime through Information Security Compliance Behavior: Role of Cybersecurity Awareness, Organizational Culture and Trust in Management. *International Journal of Cyber Criminology, 19*(1), 1–26.

Haque, S. (2025). Empowering Ethiopia's digital citizenship in early-career healthcare leadership. *PLOS Digital Health, 4*(5), e0000845. DOI: 10.1371/journal.pdig.0000845 PMID: 40333784

Hong, Y., Chen, T., & Zhang, Y. (2025). Individual intellectual capital, creative process engagement and information security policy compliance. *Journal of Intellectual Capital, 26*(6), 1–24. DOI: 10.1108/JIC-04-2025-0141

Ibragimov, I., & Kadagidze, L. (2025). Leadership and Its Correlation with Employee Affective Commitment: A Focus on LMX and OCB in Digital Transformation. *International Journal of Business and Social Science, 16*, 78–89. DOI: 10.30845/ijbss.v16p6

Jio, W., Kant, S., & Lemi, K. (2025). Ethical Leadership: Effect on Future of Organizational Citizenship Behavior by Mediation of Organizational Culture in Ethiopia. In *Generation Alpha and Next Generation Leadership for Greener Futures* (pp. 41-62). IGI Global Scientific Publishing.

Jio, W., Kant, S., & Lemi, K. (2025). The influence of ethical leadership on organizational citizenship behavior by the mediating role of organizational commitment in ethiopia. In *Humanizing the Hyperconnected Workplace* (pp. 221–248). IGI Global Scientific Publishing. DOI: 10.4018/979-8-3693-8171-7.ch008

Kant, S., Adula, M., & Badi, S. (2025). Leading With Wisdom: The Role of Wise Leaders in Ethiopia. In *Harnessing Happiness and Wisdom for Organizational Well-Being* (pp. 361-390). IGI Global Scientific Publishing.

Kant, S., Adula, M., Niguse, T., & Terefe, A. (2025). Future of AI on Job Markets by Mediation of Ethical Considerations in the Horn of Africa. In *Exploring AI Implications on Law, Governance, and Industry* (pp. 293-318). IGI Global Scientific Publishing. DOI: 10.4018/979-8-3373-3384-7.ch012

Kar, S., Yadav, M., & Panda, T. K. (2025). Inclusive organizational behaviour–the dynamic rules of building new workplaces. *VINE Journal of Information and Knowledge Management Systems, 55*(2), 492–510. DOI: 10.1108/VJIKMS-05-2022-0155

Kebede, D. A., Werke, S. Z., & Kebede, T. A. (2024). Strategic leadership practices in emerging economies: A systematic review and empirical investigation. *Cogent Business & Management, 11*(1), 2418425. DOI: 10.1080/23311975.2024.2418425

Kuwar, V., Sonavaney, V., Shankar, U., Yadav, A., Radhakrishnan, V., Upreti, K., & Jain, R. (2025). Workforce transformation and value creation in the era of Industry 4.0, 5.0 and 6.0: Challenges and enablers. *Int. J. Basic Appl. Sci, 14*(1), 314–324. DOI: 10.14419/r61ag136

Mengesha, G. H., Belay, E. G., & Adams, R. (2024). Social justice considerations in developing and deploying AI in Africa. *Data & Policy*, *6*, e65. DOI: 10.1017/dap.2024.73

Mishra, N., Habtemariam, G. M., Esseynew, S., Nayak, R. K., Tripathy, R., & Padhi, B. K. (2024). The Transnational ICT Leadership Assessment Based on the Available Infrastructure in the Governmental Organizations: A Case Study of the Ethiopian Northern Shewa Zone. In *Developments and Future Trends in Transnational Higher Education Leadership* (pp. 301-322). IGI Global. DOI: 10.4018/979-8-3693-2857-6.ch017

Negeri, D. D., Kant, S., & Huluka, A. T. (2025). Knowledge Management Effect on Customer Experience by Mediation of Strategic Leadership in Private Banks in Ethiopia. In *Demystifying Emotion AI, Robotics AI, and Sentiment Analysis in Customer Relationship Management* (pp. 105-128). IGI Global Scientific Publishing. DOI: 10.4018/979-8-3373-1867-7.ch006

Nuseir, M. T., Alshurideh, M. T., Alzoubi, H. M., Al Kurdi, B., Hamadneh, S., & AlHamad, A. (2024). Role of explainable artificial intelligence (EAI) in human resource management system (HRMS). In *Cyber security impact on digitalization and business intelligence: Big cyber security for information management: Opportunities and challenges* (pp. 249–263). Springer International Publishing. DOI: 10.1007/978-3-031-31801-6_15

Payne, B. K., Oesteraas, I., & May, D. C. (2025). Cybersecurity Students' Interest in Government Careers: Impact of Demographic Characteristics and Job Dynamics. *Journal of Applied Security Research*, *20*(1), 1–23. DOI: 10.1080/19361610.2023.2277513

Plantinga, P., Shilongo, K., Mudongo, O., Umubyeyi, A., Gastrow, M., & Razzano, G. (2024). Responsible artificial intelligence in Africa: Towards policy learning. *Data & Policy*, *6*, e72. DOI: 10.1017/dap.2024.60

Razmak, J., Refae, G. A. E., & Farhan, W. (2025). The role of AI applications in production and operations management: Complementing or replacing human labour. *International Journal of Economics and Business Research*, *29*(13), 1–28. DOI: 10.1504/IJEBR.2025.146325

Sołtysik, M., Gawłowska, M., Śnieżyński, B., & Gunia, A. (Eds.). (2024). *Artificial Intelligence, Management and Trust*. Routledge.

Tufa, G., Kinde, Z., & Kant, S. (2025). Strategic Leadership: Effect on Employee Performance With Mediation of Dynamic Capabilities in Case of Ethiopian Public Organizations. In *Generation Alpha and Next Generation Leadership for Greener Futures* (pp. 115-138). IGI Global Scientific Publishing.

Usama, M., Ullah, U., & Sajid, A. (2024). Cyber attacks against intelligent transportation systems. In *Cyber Security for Next-Generation Computing Technologies* (pp. 190–230). CRC Press.

Vargas-Hernandez, J. G., & González-Ávila, F. J. (2025). Organizational citizenship behavior: enhancing workplace dynamics. *Evolving Strategies for Organizational Management and Performance Evaluation*, 445-462.

KEY TERMS AND DEFINITIONS

Collaborative Governance: A governance method, which comprises several stakeholders, such as the public, the private, and the civil society individuals, that jointly participate in a collaborative process of decision-making with the likelihood of resolving complex problems.

Control in Cyber-security: The establishment and enactment of requirements, guidelines, and norms that would guarantee the ethical, safe, and efficient use of AI technologies in a cyber-security domain.

Ethical Leadership: Modeling of the normatively appropriate behavior in both personal behavior and interpersonal relations, and stimulating such behavior among the followers by communicating, reinforcing and making decisions.

Organizational Citizenship Behavior: Sense of collaboration and commitment Intentional, optional actions of employees that differ with those formal requirements of job and positively affect the organizational effectiveness.

Chapter 6
Future Directions: AI, Ethics, and Global Security

S. Ida Evangeline
https://orcid.org/0000-0003-2997-7897
Government College of Engineering, Tirunelveli, India

ABSTRACT

This chapter discusses the emerging nexus of artificial intelligence (AI), military ethics, and security in the future in a prospective model. As AI technologies are taking more independent roles in surveillance, targeting, cyber indicators, and decision-making, it is assailing core concepts of international humanitarian law and the just war theory. In the chapter, new capabilities including autonomous weapons, predictive targeting, and AI-enabled cyberwarfare are critically analyzed, presenting challenges to ideas of accountability, proportionality, and human control in a meaningful and ethical way. It also questions structural imbalances in world AI governance, which exclude Global South views and the concentration of technology in the hands of a few countries and corporations. These ethical and geopolitical dilemmas are answered by the chapter suggesting a normative framework of anticipatory governance that is built on the pivot of responsibility, transparency, inclusivity, precaution, and human dignity.

1. INTRODUCTION: THE FUTURE IS NOW

It is a major step towards an evolution in the character nature, extent, and morality of the modern war with the integration of artificial intelligence (AI) into the military systems. Because AI technologies are no longer used solely in traditional spheres of logistics and intelligence but are actively contributing to tactical and strategic decision-making, (and in some cases making tactical and strategic decisions

DOI: 10.4018/979-8-3373-3611-4.ch006

of their own) the distinction between human and machine agency is growing more and more blurry. It is not only the re-consideration of the stalwart military strategies and moral principles which is enforced by this development but a pressing need to explore future patterns of world security dictated by tech-enabled automation. Even the concept of war is redefined and, the AI is at the core of a paradigm shift that not only leaves the old systems of responsibility, sovereignty, deterrence, and humanitarian law but also disputes them (Rashid et al. 2023).

Although at the current juncture, most discussions of AI in the military context continue to revolve around its current state of development and how it can be likewise implemented on the case-to-case basis (autonomous drones, AI-enhanced surveillance, cyber activities), increased attention is being paid to the fact that ethical inquiry into the military application of AI in the future is simply an essential feature. The speed and uncertain nature of AI development is unlike those of other technological revolutions in the history of warfare, creating a distinct set of uncertainties that place stress on the moral and legal frameworks that are relied upon to formulate international norms of conflict. The black box nature of algorithmic decision-making, the possibility of the escalation of an activity, and the transfer of lethal power to inanimate objects all cast light on the questions that even the current legal frameworks and ethical guidelines are incompetent to answer (Bistron & Piotrowski, 2021).

This chapter proceeds on the basis that the ethical issues towards AI in warfare are not merely novel with respect to its type, but also to its time and scope. The main characteristic of AI is not its power to execute or perform at an efficient rate, but rather to respond within a dynamic and uncertain setting with a rising degree of autonomy typically implemented only in human combatants and commanders. This transition means a heavy burden of moral responsibility especially when it comes to either life and death of an individual or an action that can jeopardize the security of a region and the world at large.

Besides, the future of AI in warfare cannot be separated out of much larger systematic pressures: geopolitical conflict, economic struggles, technological dominance, and the concentration of power and resources in the world. Such forces affect not only the creation and usage of military AI systems but also ethical frameworks which they are applied and against which they are driven. In that way, the ethical future of AI use in the military needs not only a systems-level view but also to include the microdynamics especially of algorithmic interaction and the macrodynamics of global politics.

This chapter is aimed to deliver the conceptual and normative guide through these new challenges. It is not a retrospective or a case-based study but a forward-looking perspective that addresses the way in which AI can change not only the characteristics of operations in warfare, but also its moral and legal underpinnings.

The question is: What approaches our fundamental ethical ground lines the likes of proportionality, necessity, discrimination and responsibility, when machines take dominant positions within the kill chain? What can be done to make sure that AI-powered military systems are answerable to humankind values and international norms, especially when there is asymmetrical or transnational situation war? What global governance mechanisms are required to avert unregulated AI weaponized AI race and encourage ethical Don-Robotech?

The chapter will address these questions by referring to interdisciplinary knowledge of philosophy, international law, strategic studies, and the science and technology studies (STS) and to incorporate scenario-based analysis used to investigate future possibilities. It not only seeks to establish the hazards and predicament presented by AI against war itself but also to suggest positive ways out the same by ethical and government approaches, which are both predictive and accommodative.

This introduction, thus, creates a context in which the author will explore the ethical, legal, and stratagem issues of AI in international security in-depth. It says that we are overdue in coming up with speculative but based analysis that is not necessarily to know what is coming but to influence that which is coming in a way in which we say we are committed to notions of justice, peace, and human dignity.

2. TECHNOLOGICAL HORIZONS: MAPPING AI'S MILITARY TRAJECTORY

To comprehend ethical issues that the AI will present in future warfare, one must have a clear picture of the technologies that are in the pipeline and how they are redefining the shapes of military power. The AI angle to the military is no longer in isolated systems or instruments but it is becoming systemological—built into the very fabric of the defense planning apparatus, the command machinery involved in operations, and strategic deterrence. It is in this section that the current and projected trends of AI technologies applicable in the warfare will be tracked down not so as to list their inventions but to evaluate their ethical and geopolitical implications (Szabadföldi, 2021).

So-called modern Surveillance, Data fusion and decision support capabilities are already evident in modern AI systems in the military. Applications are often used to supplement human analysis, to, e.g., detect possible threats based on satellite imagery or suggest troop movements to realtime information flows. Yet, the further development of the use of AI in warfare is shifted toward the greater degrees of autonomy, integration, and the capacity to learn. An example of such evolution is landing autonomous weapons systems (AWS) that when deployed have the capability to select their own target and to engage them without any immediate intervention by a human being. Although current deployments remain scarce and mostly involved in some degree of human control, current research and development indicate a move towards more agile, adaptive and less predictive systems (Rickli & Mantellassi, 2023).

One of the fastest evolving spheres is the development of predictive targeting algorithms-AI that allow analyzing large amounts of information, such as social media, biometric data, and movement routes to learn the behavior of threats and potentially eliminate them long before the fact. Although such an ability can improve situational understanding and quick action, there is also the risk of due process undermining, the rise of false positives, and confusing suspicion with usable intelligence. Ethical implications create exponentially as predictive is combined with unmanned drones or killing robots, and the results are fatal on the basis of probability calculations, instead of confirmed intent (Oniani et al. 2023).

Also important is the use of AI in cyber warfare where autonomous or semi autonomous entities can scan, invade and lock networks within milliseconds; far out of the range of any meaningful human response. Because these cyber agents have the ability to replicate, adapt and respond to a threat in real-time, it creates the potential of unintended escalation or unintended collateral damage. The AI-powered cyber capabilities being actively developed by countries in both offensive and defensive applications create a further breakdown between war and peace as AI-facilitated activities have the potential to provide the impetus of kinetic conflicts where the conflicting parties can not be readily determined (Kania, 2022).

Along another front, AI-powered surveillance and reconnaissance, especially when implemented with satellite constellations, facial recognition systems and Internet-of-Things (IoT) devices. The tools allow continuous surveillance of the battlefield kinds and the civilian environment and propose several important questions regarding privacy, sovereignty, and ethics. Consent, transparency and protection of civilians are pressing when surveillance information is used to automate targeting, or when algorithms are programmed to conduct operations governed by specific decision rules (Agrawal & Saxena, 2024).

Moreover, the emergence of swarm intelligence the systems of autonomous actors whose communication is synchronous in real-time without centralized control creates some strategic opportunities with special ethical dangers. Swarms have the capability to overload defenses, perform distributed reconnaissance and launch distributed attacks, typically without a clear attribution of agency. The nature of these systems erodes the conventional aspects of command responsibility and accountability in the laws of armed conflict due to their opacity (Fisher, 2022).

It is necessary to underline the fact that technological feasibility does not warrant responsible use. The temptation of speed, efficiency, and supremacy proposed by AI level can shift the balance between military necessity and a humanitarian constraint. Besides, the proprietary and, in many cases classified, character of the military AI development hinders democratic control, public discussion and transnational regulation. Such difficulties are exacerbated by the dual-use nature of AI technologies, where civilian technology can be easily adapted to contribute to military applications, blur existing regulations and complicate any arms control regime (Xue et al. 2021).

During the mapping of these technological possibilities, this part of the discussion points out the importance of anticipatory ethical systems. There is a need to not only control what is there; the role of imagination and planning is to see and anticipate what can happen. It is only through comprehending the course of AI abilities that we can have the necessary foresight of what sort of moral quandaries, legal vulnerabilities and strategic threats are likely to appear and require immediate and long-term attention by scholars, policymakers, and world organizations alike (Wood, 2024).

3. DISRUPTING NORMS: ETHICAL TENSIONS IN AUTONOMOUS WARFARE

The growing use of artificial intelligence in warfighting is not just about new technologies but signals a fundamental challenge to long-held norms of conduct both ethically and under international law that have long regulated how armed conflict is fought. Driving such a disturbance is a collection of conflicts between millennia-old tenets of humanitarianism and the emergent-abilities of AI systems to operate quickly, without direction, and with untraceability. These strains cannot be relegated to the edges of our sense of agency, responsibility, and moral warrant of violence (Riesen, 2022).

The most present ethical issue is the outsourcing of taking the lives into the hands of machines. With its advanced weapons systems to autonomous weapons systems (AWS), or one may call it complete weapons automation systems; weapons systems can commence searching, identifying as well as targeting an object to engage it without human interaction in real-time. This throws those elements of meaningful human control in the air that already state that the decisions about the use of lethal forces should not be left under the discretion of a human operator. Whereas the proponents state the possibility of AWS minimizing human error, enhancing accurate results and others, the critics point out that such practice as outsourcing life-and-death decision-making to non-sentient agents diminishes the sense of moral duties and compromises the dignity of the people in question. The lack of a human in the loop decision-maker in war time is a moral break and the errors that can be made often are tragic and impossible to rewind (Hynek & Solovyeva, 2021).

Very closely connected to that is the question of accountability. Historical legal and moral systems have been premised on the concept of personification of responsible actors, persons or organizations who can be responsible in case of breachment of laws of war. However, it becomes hard to blame or search justice when the autonomous systems behave in ways that are not predictable or governed by the black box machine learning. The responsibility gap appears as the programmer, the commander or the machine cannot be easily blamed when the harmful result appears. This contravenes the fundamental principles of international humanitarian law in that the requirement to do no harm unnecessarily, and redress to victims should be provided is undermined (Konert & Balcerzak, 2021).

Additionally, the fact that AI is impossible to track operationally makes it hard to abide by the two principles of the just war theory and the Geneva Conventions: proportionality and distinction. Proportionality means that the military advantage of an action expected should dominate the harm likely to be affected on the civilians whereas distinction requires that fighters and non-fighters be distinct. AI systems and in general those driven by deep learning have become so-called black boxes- they generate outputs that even their designers cannot explain. Such obscurity presents serious obstacles to the verification and justification of combat decisions. In case an AI system misclassifies a civilian as a combatant or misjudges the probable collateral damage of an action, the normative framework upon which use of force is justified is null (Blanchard & Taddeo, 2024).

Asymmetric wars and urban warfare only increase the number of ethical issues since the division between the civilian and combatant is thinner than in other situations. In this case, the dependence on patterns, signals intelligence as well as probabilistic reasoning that is underpinned by AI brings about the potential of producing inaccurate or biased decisions. The biases are not mere hypothetical in nature, as they actually portray the fact that they worry about racial profiling, cultural misperception, as well as algorithmic discrimination which has already transpired in the civilian application of AI. In cases where the biases are brought into the battlefield settings, the outcomes may be disastrous (Koch, 2021).

The other normative tension is the temporal disjoint in relationships and relational disjoints created by AI. Actions based on human decision regarding warfare are usually tempered by a variety of emotions, moral reticence and a sense of oneness in being vulnerable to violence itself- which is an inhibitor of violence. Conversely, AI-based technology does not act out of fear, compassion or empathy. This could increase efficiency but decrease the underlying room to reflect morally and de-escalate an event. Ethical distance created between action and consequence with the human suffering produced by clinical precision of an algorithm has become a dangerous notion as the suffering might be hidden by the precision of the algorithm (Christie et al. 2024).

Moreover, AI is also associated with unintended escalation due to the unpredictable nature of its behavior, particularly, in hostile and complex environments. Machine learning systems use of adversarial inputs can result in unexpected output or the misinterpretation of actions and trigger other automatic action responses which generate additional issues. This risk is worse when there is no moral compass or contextual analysis surrounding this issue especially where just milliseconds make the difference and where human review is not always feasible (Johnson, 2022).

Overall, the emergence of autonomous military systems makes us feel confined that we might have to face the realization of assuming that our current ethical theories are not only stretched to their limits, but are possibly out of date. In case we are to be humanitarian in the era of AI we will be forced to reconsider some fundamental beliefs regarding agency, control, and ethical judgment. It does not mean that, in the age of autonomy, an ethical war is not possible-but that its requirements require the rearticulation in the light of the new technological conditions.

The second part will explore how such tensions go far beyond battlefield interactions to reconfigure global security structures, to the effect of de facto arms control, deterrence and strategic stability.

4. GLOBAL SECURITY IN FLUX: STRATEGIC AND GEOPOLITICAL IMPLICATIONS

Artificial intelligence is evolving to be an essential tool in military and intelligence and its effects are felt way beyond the battlefield tactics. AI is currently transforming the fabric of international security-modifying the rationale of deterrence, escalating a rivalry in armaments, and creating new weaknesses in international affairs. The increasing intertwining of AI and military forces has geopolitical repercussions of the most serious character, as it threatens the effectiveness of the current security mechanisms and brings into play the strategic processes which are as volatile to contend with as they are obscure to understand (Csernatoni et al. 2025).

The rise of an AI arms race between technologically advanced states is one of the most fateful ones. Countries like the United States, China, and Russia themselves have discovered an AI to be a vital priority and are investing in its military use. This rivalry does not stop at the procurement of a certain system or platform but involves the control over the entire AI ecosystem, including data infrastructure or computational power, recruitment of top talent, and dual-use technologies. The rush to be on the forefront of this race is not merely fuelled by the ambitions to achieve a battlefield superiority, but also by strategic obsolescence concerns: the portent of establishing the lead in AI into having a decreased presence on the international stage or becoming more susceptible (Sakr & Hakme, 2025).

The development of the AI race is not linear and predictable as observed in other conventional versions of an arm race, however. Due to their potential to be utilized both in the civilian and military sectors, it is challenging to regulate AI-based capabilities or even monitor them. Also, faster cycles of development of software-driven systems have become a challenge to slower cycles of arms control diplomacy. This introduces a perilous level of asymmetry: states can use systems whose long-term consequences are unclear, bumping up the chance of errors that will cause the accidental escalation of hostilities (Khan et al. 2024).

Among such places where such risks come into sharper focus is deterrence theory, more commonly referred to as the logic through which states deter others from aggression by demonstrating a credible threat of retaliation in case they stoop to aggression. Classical deterrence presumes rational actors, unmistakable signaling, and attribution of the attack. AI makes each of them more complex. Consider, by way of example, an autonomous cyberwarfare system that can operate more quickly than an adversary can, narrowing decision time and tempting preemption thereof. Attribution is also dicey: where the AI agents are deployed over decentralized networks or lead to proxy-engagements, then it may be hard to determine responsibility to an attack and this would compromise deterrence credibility (Schmid et al. 2025).

In addition, it is possible that automated decision-making will lead to a new form of conflicts, flash conflicts-the rapid automated conflicts caused by misinterpretation, bias in machine learning algorithms, or malicious inputs. Such situations are similar to flash crashes in financial markets where high-frequency trading algorithms combine in unpredictable ways resulting in instability in the system. Such feedback loops in a military scenario might result in actual real-life violence before human beings can react or defuse it. The externalisation of the command duty to AI agents, at least in nuclear command-and-control chains or defense of critical infrastructures, bring into doubt a fundamental level of being, that of a loss of meaningful control over the levels of conflict (Garcia, 2024).

The other disruptive capability of AI is the information warfare and psychological operation. They are increasingly causing a problem of genetically altered algorithms being used to manipulate opinion, to cause mistrust and disrupt democracy. Such techniques are not only comprised of propaganda, but also of deepfake videos, unfairly propagandized AI based campaigns and even microtargeting social engineering. The distinction between influence during peacetime and subversion during war break down and there is a constant state of hybrid conflict as states and non-state actors engage on a constant basis below the level of a full-blown war (Henrico, 2025).

Uneven access to AI technologies is also transforming international security. The technologically advanced powers are determining the speed and the standards of AI development and many states especially in the Global South, are left behind in the governance discourses or rely on external platforms. This generates an order of technological sovereignty that can impose further geopolitical imbalances. Furthermore, it is not only states but also commercial enterprises that are becoming influential players in the sphere establishing their own control over major AI infrastructures and formulating new global norms on the basis of proprietary systems and lobbying (Korkmaz, 2024).

Such changes are coupled with the weakening of multilateralism in security governance. With losing the trust in major powers, the attempts to create binding international frameworks involved in AI in warfare became stagnant. As an example, the United Nations Group of Governmental Experts (GGE) on Lethal Autonomous Weapons Systems (LAWS) has not reached any agreement with the states having various positions concerning definitions, legal thresholds, and scopes of bans or regulations. In the absence of concerted norms, the strategic environment can crystallize into a conflicted patchwork through unilateral doctrines and informal partnerships where the risk of conflict increases and with less collective restraint (Ruppert, 2024).

To conclude, AI does not only represent a new weapon in military arsenals: it is a force multiplier that transforms the environment of global security. It reduces the time of decisions, makes the responsibility unclear, and causes novel versions of strategic ambiguity. To deal with these challenges, more than just technical measures will be needed: international collaboration will also have to be reconsidered, as will the means of building trust and inclusive models of governance. Ethical governance of military AI will thus require the rootedness in a larger picture of global security with transparency, accountability, equitability of risk and gains ever in mind.

This part will then move to structural injustices that exist in the global AI regime, and will specifically highlight on how the voice of non-westerners is left out or marginalised in ethical discourses and governance systems.

5. STRUCTURAL INJUSTICES AND GLOBAL ASYMMETRIES

Although the discussed ethical debate concerning AI on the battlefield is related to technical controls, adherence to international humanitarian law, and battlefield behavior, it has the effect of hiding the structural inequalities that lie at the heart of the international order of AI. Geopolitical power imbalances, disparities of wealth, and longstanding exclusionary trends all have an acute influence on the making, operation, and regulation of military AI systems. The asymmetries pose serious issues concerning whose values are baked into AI systems,, who takes the risks of their application and who is heard in defining the morality and legal requirements under which they are put into action (Erskine, 2024).

One characteristic of modern developments in the field of AI is that it has resulted in a situation in which it creates a balance of technological power among few states and corporate enterprises, most of which are settled in the Global North. United States and China are leaders in the AI arms race not only by increasing budgets spent on defense but also by way of dominating data ecosystems, computing infrastructure, and AI research talent. Their huge influence throughout the technical architectures and normative assumptions that underlie the military AI are often not subjected to enough national and international oversight, by major defense contractors and technical firms. These Power structures result in an ethical monoculture one where structures are designed based on limited definitions of security, efficiency and strategic superiority, instead of pluralistic or humanitarian principles (Baresi, 2025).

Among the majority of the countries in the Global South, the level of AI governance is observed as a passive activity or the reactive activity. Such countries usually have no institutional ability, technical infrastructure, or geopolitical power to make a significant input into the high-level discussions on autonomous weapons, algorithmic responsibility, or AI restrictions on exports. Consequently, the ethical and policy norms are largely dictated by western liberal democracies, with occasional external input by competing authoritarian states, but little in substantive terms by peoples of Africa, Latin America, Southeast Asia, or Indigenous peoples. Such exclusion does more than marginalize other ethical traditions and epistemologies, it also runs the risk of creating a neo-colonialism of technology, imposing norms that are not consented to, and perhaps not culturally resonant (Sahebi & Formosa, 2024).

Besides, material risks of AI warfare are non-evenly spread. Less well-endowed states with less sophisticated defense networks will be susceptible to autonomous drone attacks, hacking to disrupt networks and data intelligence surveillance all facilitated by pioneered AI technology in other states. The deployment of autonomous systems could increase violence in areas of already political difficulties or active military conflicts, weaken state control and replace local methods of conflict resolution. Nevertheless, when it comes to discussing the ethical acceptability of such interventions, such communities are hardly consulted. The concept of free, prior, and informed consent, which underpins international human rights law, is also notably left unperceived with regards to the use of military AI deployments abroad or fragile nations (Enemark, 2025).

In the Global North, ethical discussion of AI is elitist and exclusionary, giving the voice of technologists, ethicists, and policymakers in elite institutions primacy. Strategic discussions often exclude the civil society actors and more so the actors in conflict areas or marginalized communities. Such a breach lends itself to an abstract morality, i.e., a morality that theorizes about damages and fairness without locating them within the experience or within social realities.

The other issue is the predominance of utilitarian logic that is applied in governance of AI particularly in military area. They are frequently performed at the expense of justice, dignity and historical accountability, which gives way to efficiency, strategic gain and risk minimisation. This favoritism could be used to justify AI-facilitated activities that are legally acceptable on the one hand, but ethically problematic in another- targeted assassinations, preventative actions, or algorithmic monitoring of qualified contentious entities. The normative landscape is still minimal without an opposition of views on restorative justice, decolonial thinking or non-Western philosophies (Burkhardt, 2025).

To overcome these structural injustices, it is important to reorient the way we think about, and practice, global AI governance. It requires a participatory morality- a moralizing that respects epistemic diversity, fair participation, and allocation/redistribution of risk/benefits. This may include empowering capacity-building efforts in less-represented nations, the establishment of multilateral platforms that give voice to marginalized groups and the integration of values of global justice into AI modelling and guidelines.

Importantly, it is imperative to underline that the future direction needs to abandon the idea that the moral power of technological mastery means moral mastering. The moral leadership should not be the right of the mighty but rather the duty of all corners of the world with respect to acknowledging the integrity, autonomy, and safety of everyone. What is needed is the removal of structural asymmetries so that a future where AI contributes to the cause of peace instead of preserving the hierarchies and damages of the past can be envisaged (O'Regan & Ferri, 2025).

With this critique in mind, the following section will suggest the normative principles and policy frameworks with which the anticipatory and inclusive governance of military AI can be approached.

6. NORMATIVE PATHWAYS: ETHICS FOR ANTICIPATORY AI GOVERNANCE

It is hard to avoid the disruptive force of AI and the asymmetries that global governance introduces structurally, and it is tempting to end this chapter by simply suggesting greater forward-looking normative efforts are necessary to respond. Reflections are necessary but not the ethical reflection only; there is the need that the anticipatory forms of governance should become an efficient model i.e. a governance model that aims engages technological advancement with widespread morality concepts, legal responsibility and democracy. Accordingly, this part will attempt to describe such a model through a synthesis of what philosophy, international law, policy analysis and critical theory each suggest, pieced together into a set of sensible guiding tracks (Lazaro & Rizzi, 2023).

A new ethical framework must be the core of any anticipatory governance effort based on principles beyond strategic and utilitarian lines of reasoning. These include (Mišić, 2021):

- Responsibility: Moral and legal responsibility should be clearly assigned in a system where AI is used. Developers, commanders, and policymakers should be responsible in designing, deploying, and the impact of the AI systems, especially in conflict zones. The concept of responsibility also means due care in determining the possible harms prior to adoption.
- Transparency: The logic behind the operation of the AI systems, primarily in the cases of use in surveillance, targeting and command control, is to be auditable and explainable. Transparency is important not only to the trust and reviews of the general population, but also regarding the principle of AI decision-making that complies with humanitarian principles and democratic needs.
- Inclusivity: governance should feature the perspectives of peoples and countries not usually incorporated in debates about AI on a global basis. These comprise the participation in policymaking, moral consultations, which are based on a multiplicity of cultural traditions, and the possibility of significant contribution of the Global South, civil society, and conflict-affected communities.
- Precaution: Precautionary approach should prevail where the risks associated with deployment of some forms of AI are not well understood. This could take the form of moratorium, international accords, or use of red lines surrounding very autonomous or destabilizing technology until it has adequate oversight mechanisms.
- Human dignity: In its essence, the subject of anticipatory ethics should be the protection of human dignity, the inherent value of a human being to which the calculations of the algorithm cannot take precedence. This involves not submitting to dehumanizing logics, including that which turns people into data points, targets, or collateral aspects.

The multi-layered policy architecture is necessary to implement such principles, so it can work at the level of a country, region, and world. On the country level governments should enforce strong limitations on the deployment of military AI such as human-in-the-loop protection, obligatory impact assessment and civilian oversight organizations. Improved use of defense R&D and procurement pipelines could include an ethical review system in the form of bioethics committees or environmental impact plans (Lysaght, 2022).

At a regional level, adjudication laws could be formed at an international level such as defense coalitions such as NATO or African Union through an agreed-upon collective ethical standards of application of AI to promote interoperability and avoid compromising human rights. These command structures might consist of a voluntary sharing of testing procedures, training of AI developers and AI commanders in ethics, and an early-warning system, to ensure the prevention of misuse or unintentional escalation (Urueña, 2021).

Worldwide, there is an urgent requirement to relaunch multilateral discussions about the autonomous weapons and AI norms. Other initiatives, like the UN GGE on Lethal Autonomous Weapons Systems, have collapsed but other regime-like mechanisms based on the Paris Agreement, the International Atomic Energy Agency, and others could provide flexible but binding settings to collaborate. Such platforms have to focus on capacity-building, transparency, and dispute resolution and need to respect sovereignty and cultural background of various stakeholders (Sigfrids et al. 2022).

Parallely, civil society and higher education institutes can play an important role. State behavior needs to be tracked by independent research organizations, ethics councils, and advocacy networks that drive towards open standards and create discussions in the form of public discourse which has the power to hold the power accountable. Critically, ethical innovation needs to be perceived not as a privilege but as a strategic requirement: as a bulwark against the corrosion of trust, stability and moral legitimacy in the era of AI-enhanced war (Ahern, 2025).

Lastly, anticipatory governance should be come-and-go and adjustive. It must understand that the ethical conclusions are changing depending on the technology and that the hardcoded policy of a top-down approach is not sufficient. Rather, ethical values should be integrated into design commitments (ethics by design), be comprehensively, constantly examined and evaluated in terms of their action outcomes (ethics in practice), and also be regularly reviewed and updated in the course of deliberative proceedings and which is constantly receptive to newly arising challenges (Umbrello et al. 2023).

Summing up, normative regulation of AI in global security affairs cannot be based only on abstract principles or proclamations. It should entail co-ordinated, realistic, and all inclusive action in various fields and jurisdictions. It is only in this way that efforts will be made to guarantee that the course of developing and deploying military AI is in line with the basic commitments to justice, peace, and human dignity that shape the principles of international law and ethical judgment.

The final (third) section will conclude the chapter by summarizing the underlying themes of the chapter and calling upon long-term international cooperation to create a safe and moral AI future.

7. CONCLUSION: TOWARD A JUST AND SECURE AI FUTURE

With the further penetration of artificial intelligence into the technological mechanisms of war, it is no longer adequate to question whether the technologies can boost the effectiveness of military forces. The more critical and complicated issue is whether they can be developed and implemented in a manner which fosters human dignity, limits consequences that create harm and fosters international safety. The chapter has explained that the moral dilemmas implied by military AI cannot be solved using the current paradigms. They require a re-conceptualization of our understanding of agency, responsibility, justice, and peace, in the era of algorithmic warfare.

Whether it is the faster rate of AI-based arms race, the uncertainties surrounding the lack of visibility of autonomous systems and destruction of the old forms of deterrence avoidance, one point has been made clear, AI is not just altering warfare, it is altering the structure of international order itself. These changes have the threat of destabilization, unintentional escalation and a rise in global inequalities. They also undermine fundamental tenets of humanitarian law and moral philosophy especially insofar as accountability, proportionality and the protection of the non-combatant is concerned.

Of equal urgency are the structural imbalances that determine who builds, controls and is impacted by military AI. Marginalisation of Global South voices, the hegemony of elite technocratic discourses and the privatization of defense innovation are all indicative of a system of governance not merely ethically deficient, but restricted in its epistemic terms as well. The fair AI future should become the redistribution of not only the power but the voice as well-making ethical deliberation global, inclusive, and allowing to take on board the diverse worldviews.

In response to such challenges, this chapter has offered a model of anticipatory and inclusive governance with its five organising principles of responsibility, transparency, inclusivity, precaution and human dignity. It has also demanded the operationalization of these values by using multi level governance structures, effective legal protection and persistent popular control. They are not utopian dreams but viable requirements, if humanity does not want to face a future where our own creations will become smarter than us not only in terms of ethical priorities but also regarding strategicmeans of controlling anything.

Indeed, the destiny of AI in warfare is not already settled. It will be influenced by the decisions done today, through politics, technology, legal and moral decisions. Through investing in foresight, creating international collaboration, and holding morality and ethics into every part of the growth and implementation of AI, we can create a path such that we can bolster the security of individuals without being an impediment to justice. This is a technological policy issue not only but it is an ethical obligation that we all have to fulfill.

REFERENCES

Agrawal, N., & Saxena, A. (2024). Artificial intelligence (AI) equipped edge internet of things (IoT) devices in security. In *Advanced IoT Technologies and Applications in the Industry 4.0 Digital Economy* (pp. 296–308). CRC Press. DOI: 10.1201/9781003434269-16

Ahern, D. (2025). The new anticipatory governance culture for innovation: Regulatory foresight, regulatory experimentation and regulatory learning. *European Business Organization Law Review*, *26*(2), 241–283. DOI: 10.1007/s40804-025-00348-7

Baresi, U. (2025). Neo-colonial intelligence: How AI risks reinforcing spatial injustices in a digitally divided world. *Cities (London, England)*, *166*, 106232. DOI: 10.1016/j.cities.2025.106232

Bistron, M., & Piotrowski, Z. (2021). Artificial intelligence applications in military systems and their influence on sense of security of citizens. *Electronics (Basel)*, *10*(7), 871. DOI: 10.3390/electronics10070871

Blanchard, A., & Taddeo, M. (2024). Autonomous weapon systems and jus ad bellum. *AI & Society*, *39*(2), 705–711. DOI: 10.1007/s00146-022-01425-y

Burkhardt, A. (2025). Infrastructural Perspectives on Artificial Intelligence—on the Implications of AI Infrastructures for Global. In *Justice. In Transnational Infrastructures and the Transformation of Global Orders* (pp. 81–96). Springer Nature Switzerland. DOI: 10.1007/978-3-031-74846-2_6

Christie, E. H., Ertan, A., Adomaitis, L., & Klaus, M. (2024). Regulating lethal autonomous weapon systems: Exploring the challenges of explainability and traceability. *AI and Ethics*, *4*(2), 229–245. DOI: 10.1007/s43681-023-00261-0

Csernatoni, R., Broeders, D., Andersen, L. H., Hoijtink, M., Bode, I., Lindsay, J. R., & Schwarz, E. (2025). Myth, Power, and Agency: Rethinking Artificial Intelligence, Geopolitics and War. *Minds and Machines*, *35*(3), 37. DOI: 10.1007/s11023-025-09741-0

Enemark, C. (2025). Loyal Wingmen, Artificial Intelligence, and Cognitive Enhancement: A Warning Against Cyborg-Drone Warfare. *Journal of Military Ethics*, *24*(1), 1–17. DOI: 10.1080/15027570.2025.2507458

Erskine, T. (2024). Before algorithmic Armageddon: Anticipating immediate risks to restraint when AI infiltrates decisions to wage war. *Australian Journal of International Affairs*, *78*(2), 175–190. DOI: 10.1080/10357718.2024.2345636

Fisher, K. (2022). The role of gender in providing expert advice on cyber conflict and artificial intelligence for military personnel. *Frontiers in Big Data*, *5*, 992620. DOI: 10.3389/fdata.2022.992620

Garcia, D. (2024). Algorithms and decision-making in military artificial intelligence. *Global Society*, *38*(1), 24–33. DOI: 10.1080/13600826.2023.2273484

Henrico, I. (2025). Modern approaches in military geoscience: Leveraging advanced geospatial technologies for strategic advantage. *Geology Today*, *41*(4), 166–175. DOI: 10.1111/gto.12522

Hynek, N., & Solovyeva, A. (2021). Operations of power in autonomous weapon systems: Ethical conditions and socio-political prospects. *AI & Society*, *36*(1), 79–99. DOI: 10.1007/s00146-020-01048-1

Johnson, J. (2022). The AI commander problem: Ethical, political, and psychological dilemmas of human-machine interactions in AI-enabled warfare. *Journal of Military Ethics*, *21*(3-4), 246–271. DOI: 10.1080/15027570.2023.2175887

Kania, E. B. (2022). Artificial intelligence in China's revolution in military affairs. In *Defence Innovation and the 4th Industrial Revolution* (pp. 65–92). Routledge. DOI: 10.4324/9781003268215-4

Khan, K., Khurshid, A., & Cifuentes-Faura, J. (2024). Is artificial intelligence a new battleground for cybersecurity? *Internet of Things : Engineering Cyber Physical Human Systems*, *28*, 101428. DOI: 10.1016/j.iot.2024.101428

Koch, W. (2021). On digital ethics for artificial intelligence and information fusion in the defense domain. *IEEE Aerospace and Electronic Systems Magazine*, *36*(7), 94–111. DOI: 10.1109/MAES.2021.3066841

Konert, A., & Balcerzak, T. (2021). Military autonomous drones (UAVs)-from fantasy to reality. Legal and Ethical implications. *Transportation Research Procedia*, *59*, 292–299. DOI: 10.1016/j.trpro.2021.11.121

Korkmaz, S. C. (2024). Emerging Technologies and Power Asymmetry in International System: An Analysis over Artificial Intelligence. *Artificial Intelligence*, 84–99.

Lazaro, C., & Rizzi, M. (2023). Predictive analytics and governance: A new socio-technical imaginary for uncertain futures. *International Journal of Law in Context*, *19*(1), 70–90. DOI: 10.1017/S1744552322000477

Lysaght, T. (2022). Anticipatory governance and foresight in regulating for uncertainty. *The American Journal of Bioethics*, *22*(1), 51–53. DOI: 10.1080/15265161.2021.2001111

Mišić, J. (2021). Ethics and governance in the digital age. *European View*, *20*(2), 175–181. DOI: 10.1177/17816858211061793

O'Regan, J. P., & Ferri, G. (2025). Artificial intelligence and depth ontology: Implications for intercultural ethics. *Applied Linguistics Review*, *16*(2), 797–807. DOI: 10.1515/applirev-2024-0189

Oniani, D., Hilsman, J., Peng, Y., Poropatich, R. K., Pamplin, J. C., Legault, G. L., & Wang, Y. (2023). Adopting and expanding ethical principles for generative artificial intelligence from military to healthcare. *NPJ Digital Medicine*, *6*(1), 225. DOI: 10.1038/s41746-023-00965-x

Rashid, A. B., Kausik, A. K., Al Hassan Sunny, A., & Bappy, M. H. (2023). Artificial intelligence in the military: An overview of the capabilities, applications, and challenges. *International Journal of Intelligent Systems*, *2023*(1), 8676366. DOI: 10.1155/2023/8676366

Rickli, J. M., & Mantellassi, F. (2023). Artificial intelligence in warfare: military uses of AI and their international security implications. In *The AI wave in defence innovation* (pp. 12–36). Routledge. DOI: 10.4324/9781003218326-2

Riesen, E. (2022). The moral case for the development and use of autonomous weapon systems. *Journal of Military Ethics*, *21*(2), 132–150. DOI: 10.1080/15027570.2022.2124022

Ruppert, L. (2024). Geopolitics of technological futures: Warfare technologies and future battlefields in German security debates. *Geopolitics*, *29*(2), 581–606. DOI: 10.1080/14650045.2023.2174431

Sahebi, S., & Formosa, P. (2024). Artificial Intelligence (AI) and Global Justice. *Minds and Machines*, *35*(1), 4. DOI: 10.1007/s11023-024-09708-7

Sakr, G., & Hakme, O. (2025). The Impact of Artificial Intelligence on Military and Security in the MENA. In *AI in the Middle East for Growth and Business: A Transformative Force* (pp. 363–383). Springer Nature Switzerland. DOI: 10.1007/978-3-031-75589-7_21

Schmid, S., Lambach, D., Diehl, C., & Reuter, C. (2025). Arms race or innovation race? Geopolitical AI development. *Geopolitics*, *30*(4), 1–30. DOI: 10.1080/14650045.2025.2456019

Sigfrids, A., Nieminen, M., Leikas, J., & Pikkuaho, P. (2022). How should public administrations foster the ethical development and use of artificial intelligence? A review of proposals for developing governance of AI. *Frontiers in Human Dynamics*, *4*, 858108. DOI: 10.3389/fhumd.2022.858108

Szabadföldi, I. (2021). Artificial intelligence in military application–opportunities and challenges. *Land Forces Academy Review*, *26*(2), 157–165. DOI: 10.2478/raft-2021-0022

Umbrello, S., Bernstein, M. J., Vermaas, P. E., Resseguier, A., Gonzalez, G., Porcari, A., Grinbaum, A., & Adomaitis, L. (2023). From speculation to reality: Enhancing anticipatory ethics for emerging technologies (ATE) in practice. *Technology in Society*, *74*, 102325. DOI: 10.1016/j.techsoc.2023.102325

Urueña, S. (2021). Responsibility through anticipation? The 'future talk'and the quest for plausibility in the governance of emerging technologies. *NanoEthics*, *15*(3), 271–302. DOI: 10.1007/s11569-021-00408-5

Wood, N. G. (2024). Explainable AI in the military domain. *Ethics and Information Technology*, *26*(2), 29. DOI: 10.1007/s10676-024-09762-w

Xue, Y., Fang, C., & Dong, Y. (2021). The impact of new relationship learning on artificial intelligence technology innovation. *International Journal of Innovation Studies*, *5*(1), 2–8. DOI: 10.1016/j.ijis.2020.11.001

KEY TERMS AND DEFINITIONS

Algorithmic Accountability: The necessity of AI systems to be open, duplicable and be on oversight particularly at times when outlay of decisions made by them has a big ethical, legitimate or geopolitical consequence. It is relevant in a military context concerning the traceability of lethal decision and attribution of responsibility.

Anticipatory Governance: An active form of regulation that attempts to anticipate and prevent ethical, legal and social consequences of new technologies before people are adversely affected. It highlights anticipatory and responsive thinking and policymaking that is not restrictive.

Artificial Intelligence (AI): Computer science worked on inventing machines that could perform the activities that ordinarily required the intervention of intelligence e.g. learning, reasoning, decision making and pattern recognition. As an application of AI in the army, the systems include surveillance, targeting, logistics, and autonomous systems.

Autonomous Weapons Systems (AWS): Armaments where the weapon, once activated, can target and attack targets without other human manual input. Their application brings up serious moral and true questions of responsibility, proportionality and the sobering maintenance of human control over life-or-death choices.

Design Ethics: The effort of the ethical consideration by directly integrating it into the formation of AI systems. Applied to military AI, it means ensuring that artificial intelligence (AI) systems are built to support norms of human rights, transparency and conflict prevention.

Dual-Use Technology: The technologies with dual civilian and military uses. The use of AI is an excellent ample in that the upgrading of language models, robotic, or image recognition technology could find use as a means of defense and complicate the process of regulation and accountability.

Global South: This is a colloquialism referring generally to those countries in Africa, Latin America, Asia and Oceania that are usually ignored in the making of decisions affecting the world. In the ethics AI it has emphasized the need to integrate non-Western voices and the need to fight against technological neo-colonialism.

International Humanitarian Law (IHL): A framework of international law that can regulate the way armed conflict is carried out and tries to safeguard individuals who do not take part in fighting. The use of opaque and autonomous AI systems contravenes the principles of distinction, proportionality, and necessity of IHL.

Predictive Targeting: AI to predict possible risks or foes behavior through analysing large data such as movement routes, social sites, and biometrics data. Although it can contribute to preemptive defense, it can create a confusion between probable and intentional thus leading to unfounded strikes.

Real Human Control: A regulative rule that holds that humans should be in active and deliberate control of some crucial roles and activities of AI-enabled systems, most importantly the deployment of life-taking violence. It acts as a form of defense against unaccountable or inadvertent unintentions of autonomous warfare.

Strategic Stability: One of the situations within international relations, in which none of the states is interested in initiation of the conflict because of the deterrence capabilities of the others. AI may disrupt this balance by increasing the speed of decision making, making attribution difficult, and getting ahead of escalation or making an accidental escalation.

Technological Asymmetry: The non-equal dispersion of the technological capacities of states and regions, which more frequently than not results in the accumulation of power in the context of global governance, security, and control of the level of ethical standards. It is a mirror of inequality in access to data, in computation infrastructure, and research power.

Chapter 7

Right to Privacy and State Surveillance:

An Analysis of the Legal and Ethical Challenges Concerning State Surveillance

Manu Mariyan Abraham
https://orcid.org/0000-0002-2196-3645
Christ University, Bangalore, India

Shampa Dev
Christ University, Bangalore, India

ABSTRACT

The conflict between state surveillance and the fundamental right of privacy is apparent even at the conceptual level. The rise of advanced surveillance mechanisms has been another abetting factor to this conflict while on the other hand many theorists have been at work to find a harmonisation between them. Surveillance techniques and mechanisms have indeed been helpful in thwarting the threats to national security and keeping the integrity of a nation. The chapter analyses whether the collective good that upholds state surveillance tends to override the individual interest that advocates the right to privacy. It considers the criteria or procedures followed to arrive at such a decision and whether the authorities could have been advised to find a better solution through harmonization rather than neglecting one in favour of the other. It explores the morality behind surveillance, including the panopticon model by Bentham, which was an example of promoting moral behaviour through surveillance.

DOI: 10.4018/979-8-3373-3611-4.ch007

INTRODUCTION

Protecting the privacy of citizens has been an enormous task for every government. Most of the nations have integrated right to privacy into their Grundnorm including India. The concept of privacy is deeply embedded in various legal systems and international conventions. It encompasses the right of individuals to control their personal information and to be free from unwarranted intrusions into their private lives. Privacy safeguards individuals' autonomy, fosters trust in social interactions, and protects their ability to express themselves freely without fear of reprisal. While there is no explicit guarantee of privacy in the Indian Constitution, courts there have interpreted other rights—most notably the right to life and liberty, found in Article 21—to give rise to a (limited) right to privacy through a series of rulings over the years. In the Puttaswamy case (Justice K.S. Puttaswamy (Retd.) & Anr. vs. Union of India & Ors., 2017), filed in 2015, this interpretation was contested and forwarded to a bigger Bench of the Supreme Court. As part of the freedoms protected by Part III of the Constitution, the right to privacy is now a fundamental right and an integral component of Article 21, which safeguards people' lives and liberties.

On the other hand, state surveillance plays a crucial role in preventing and detecting criminal activities, safeguarding national security interests, and ensuring public safety. Governments employ various surveillance techniques, ranging from physical monitoring to electronic surveillance, to gather intelligence and track potential threats. However, the extent of state surveillance powers often raises concerns about the potential for excessive intrusion into individuals' lives and the erosion of privacy rights. The surveillance framework in India is regulated by section 20(2) of Telecommunications Act, 2023 and section 69 of the Information Technology Act, 2000 (IT Act 2000) and the accompanying rules framed under these statutes.

The debate between privacy and state surveillance is further complicated by the evolving technological landscape. The rise of the internet and digital technologies has created vast troves of personal data, making it easier for governments to collect, store, and analyse information about their citizens. While these advancements have undoubtedly enhanced surveillance capabilities, they have also raised concerns about the potential for mass surveillance and the misuse of personal data.

If right to privacy of an individual is considered absolute, it would place an automatic restraint on the surveillance activities of the state. Thus, it has to be determined how much intrusion is lawful. The surveillance mechanisms set up by the state are actively participating in several types of monitoring activities where in different sorts of data are identified, monitored and processed. These help in identifying threats to the nation and also helps in neutralising elements which endanger national security. The argument for surveillance mechanisms stems from its sheer necessity. We could call it a necessary evil, designed to help maintain peace and public order. It is the responsibility of the law maker to keep it necessary and stop it from turning evil. Another argument would be posting collective good vs the individual interests. It has long been considered that concept of privacy revolves around individual interest. The right is there to protect an individual from unwanted intrusion from others. But on the other hand, surveillance mechanisms work for the common good of the people. It helps protect the nation as a whole at the expense of intruding into the lives of each citizen. There is also the debate of targeted and untargeted surveillance, wherein an untargeted mass surveillance could easily be justified compared to a targeted surveillance since it doesn't see anyone as criminals. Some argue that in a wide range of cases untargeted surveillance treats people less like suspects than more targeted alternatives (Hadjimatheou, 2013). There have been situations wherein the individual interests take a back seat wherein surveillance mechanisms have operated without any restraints while overriding right to privacy. This paper aims to analyse whether it was possible for the authorities to have been advised to find a better solution through harmonization rather than neglecting one in favour of the other. The paper argues that a working line can be determined to avoid a conflict between surveillance and ethics. It explores the morality behind surveillance, including the panopticon model by Bentham, which was an example of promoting moral behaviour through surveillance. Additionally, the paper examines whether moral and religious sanctions are a better alternative to the use of surveillance techniques to combat crime as propounded by Bentham.

UNDERSTANDING SURVEILLANCE ETHICS

Many opponents of surveillance have framed their arguments in terms of rights, particularly as an infringement on one's right to privacy. When the Snowden revelations were gradually made public, they incited outrage since they demonstrated the extent of privacy loss suffered by Americans and, in reality, a large number of other citizens. Much advocacy in support of human rights, particularly privacy, was sparked by the discoveries. Despite the uproar, a growing number of people seem to be accepting of the idea of a surveillance state, claiming that privacy is unachievable in this day and age of increased digitization. This phenomenon has been dubbed "surveillance realism" by Linna Dencik and Jonathan Cable (Dencik & Cable, 2017). The rise in highly sensitive personal data being stored in databases by more public and private organisations and the variety of uses to which they can be put has given rise to "surveillance realism." In fact, it is becoming more and more difficult to conduct business with many institutions without disclosing this kind of information. By providing vast amounts of personal data to private technology companies like Facebook and Google, who then mine this data for information that is helpful to them financially, many people forfeit their right to privacy. Consequently, the challenge has shifted well beyond control mechanisms based on states. Sharing too much personal data online has become commonplace, which feeds the monitoring state's appetite. The selfie has emerged as the defining characteristic of a generation of internet users fixated on creating egotistical, even narcissistic, digital personas. These actions have grown to be ingrained in what David Lyon has dubbed "surveillance culture," in which individuals are willing to participate in the gathering and use of personal data about themselves (Lyon, 2017). It will be challenging, if not impossible, for activists to create successful opposition tactics until they comprehend the extent to which monitoring is ingrained in the routine meaning-making processes of an increasing number of individuals. The reason for this is that these strategies usually concentrate on the legal or political aspects of surveillance, ignoring the benefits that individuals derive from increasing their visibility (like fulfilling their desire for acceptance and connection in a world where social disintegration has become more commonplace) and what they can do to modify these behaviours to reduce the risk of data misuse (Lyon, 2017).

Privacy sceptics have questioned why someone should worry about maintaining privacy if they have nothing to hide and have not done anything illegal, given how commonplace and inevitable surveillance seems. Citizens will never know when they require the right to privacy, which is the flaw in this reasoning. Also irrevocable are invasions of privacy. Something can never be undiscovered once it is discovered. Political activists, for example, who are more prone than others to question the distribution of power in society, are change agents who especially need the right to privacy. They thus run a higher risk of drawing the anger of the authorities, who might be highly motivated to monitor their activities using the state's surveillance capabilities.

A universal understanding of privacy has been articulated by academics like Colin Bennett in response to the growing issue of unauthorized surveillance and the need for a shared tool to combat it. Nevertheless, he has contended that for a number of years now, privacy has been acknowledged as a socially valuable concept and has even entered the public domain (Bennett, 2011). Former privacy sceptic David Lyon has also come to see that the fight against monitoring needs a unifying concept, and privacy offers precisely that (Lyon, 2015). The existence of the right to privacy may not prevent countries from witnessing relatively uncontrolled growth in monitoring if privacy is not revitalized. Proponents of surveillance would only need to identify a social issue for the right to become moot (Steeves, 2009). However, given how much the right to privacy is already burdened by worries about both unreported surveillance and public safety as well as terrorism, would highlighting the sociality of this right be sufficient to save it from becoming irrelevant in the actual world? What kind of legislation is required to thwart efforts to transform nations into "surveillance societies," in which individuals are unable to act or even think for fear of being observed by influential figures who might not be acting in their best sake? Due to their potential to ignore the social justice implications of surveillance, such as social sorting based on discrimination, social conceptions of privacy may still be lacking (Lyon, 2015). Privacy may even make surveillance possible because it can lead to organisations checking privacy boxes while essentially carrying on with their operations unchecked. The issue with the "turn to the social" in privacy studies is that it can become depoliticized, even as highlighting the social content of the right makes privacy supporters more capable of defending it against restrictions based on national security. That is to say, it is devoid of a political analysis of the issue, particularly with regard to power dynamics in society, and how the right will persist in being targeted for attacks on both a personal and a collective level until the political motivations behind these attacks are recognized and resolved. Given its focus on progressive social transformation, a critical political perspective—which includes a Marxist perspective—is especially crucial in this context. It should also point out the shortcomings of a rights-based analysis. To put it another way, resisting unjustified monitoring involves more than just standing up for one's right to privacy; it also entails altering the way the powers that monitor society are distributed.

ETHICS AND OVERSIGHT IN STATE SURVEILLANCE

Surveillance by the state is widespread across the globe. States usually market it as a tool for maintaining national security and combating threats, ranging from terrorism to cybercrime. Proponents are of the view that sophisticated surveillance mechanisms are necessary in order to identify and pre-empt possible threats to society and hence maintain public safety. However, this limited approach ignores the significant and pervasive influence that such actions have on individual privacy rights. Article 12 of the Universal Declaration of Human Rights and Article 17 of the International Covenant on Civil and Political Rights defend privacy as a fundamental human right. It is an important bulwark to safeguard people from unjustified intrusion by the state or other organisations.

To fully grasp the delicate balance between collective security and individual privacy, we must closely examine the criteria and procedures guiding surveillance practices. First, the legal framework governing these actions needs careful inspection to ensure it aligns with constitutional principles and international human rights standards (Macnish, 2014). A strong legal framework should not only allow monitoring but also create a good balance by defining clear limits, strict guidelines for collecting and storing data, and strong safeguards against potential abuse. This should involve explicit definitions of what constitutes a "threat" that warrants surveillance, standards for triggering such activity, and restrictions on the scope and duration of data gathering.

In addition, having good oversight structures is not only desirable but also important for holding people accountable and increasing transparency in surveillance activities. Effectively scrutinizing the operations of governments - concerning surveillance - requires independent oversight mechanisms that are different from the executive branch and have adequate authority. In the event of infringements, this means having the authority to conduct independent investigations, obtain classified information, and implement legally binding corrective actions. Transparency in surveillance activity, in meeting legitimate security requirements, is also instrumental in the establishment and maintenance of public trust. This involves disclosing the general extent and character of surveillance activities to enable informed public discourse and to hold powers to account for abuse. Without transparency, the "black box" effect ensues, engendering distrust and perhaps chilling legitimate criticism.

Ethical factors are very important in this argument. Decision-makers must take simple ethics such as proportionality, necessity, and consent into account when undertaking surveillance activities. According to proportionality, surveillance ought to be similarly intrusive as the actual threat it is meant to combat. According to need, monitoring cannot begin until less invasive options have failed. Although it is almost impossible to obtain explicit agreement for mass surveillance, the idea behind such measures is that they must be accepted by the people and have the legitimacy of democracy. Striking a delicate balance between security requirements and privacy rights requires careful consideration of these ethical dilemmas and a strong commitment to protecting human dignity and fundamental freedoms in the online world.

Legislators must first make sure that clear privacy rules and regulations are established before developing strategies to address the complex issues of state monitoring (Ross, 2002). Such laws must expressly guarantee accountability, openness, and democratic control. The growing role of new technology must be addressed. For example, new difficulties arise when Artificial Intelligence (AI) is used in surveillance, such as in real-time video analytics, facial recognition, and predictive policing. While AI has the potential to enhance threat detection, it also creates issues regarding algorithmic bias, harvesting large data without clear consent, and the possibility of further government oversight. The policies must thus concentrate on how AI is used and developed ethically in surveillance, with safeguards against discriminatory outcomes and unambiguous transparency on the use of AI-generated intelligence. In addition, with the increasing use of drones, biometric monitoring, and connected IoT devices for information collection, privacy legislation needs to be flexible and proactive, able to keep pace with advanced technology developments. This is because a forward-thinking approach must be taken in order to ensure that surveillance activity, however the technology is used, always remains within the strict parameters of the law and with considerable regard for human rights.

THE ETHICAL IMPLICATIONS OF MODERN SURVEILLANCE

In modern times, surveillance—the methodical observation of populations or groups—has expanded. Despite the fact that surveillance is typically justified in the name of safety, security, and social order, it raises serious ethical questions about privacy, authority, and the interplay between individual liberty and the common good. One of the most pervasive and influential formulations of surveillance and its ethical implications is Jeremy Bentham's panopticon model.

Surveillance involves a range of practices and technologies used to observe, monitor, and manage people or groups. There are many varieties of surveillance, from CCTV and governmental surveillance programs to social media and workplace monitoring. At its core, surveillance is an exercise of power, whereby the people conducting the monitoring exercise control over the people being observed. The ethical problems with spying are rooted in this power dynamic.

The ethics of surveillance depend on a number of primary ethical principles. Firstly, privacy - the privacy right is an elementary ethical principle that is usually transgressed in surveillance practices. Privacy refers to individuals' capability to manage access to their personal information and activities without unwanted observation or intrusion. Surveillance violates privacy when it is coupled with the gathering, analysis, or release of individual information without permission or justifiable reason. Secondly, autonomy - describes how people can decide and act upon their own preferences, beliefs, and values without the pressure of external coercion or manipulation. Through the use of social pressure, conditioning through fear of being watched, or limiting people's choices and freedom, surveillance can undermine autonomy. Last but not least, monitoring has the potential to exacerbate social injustices and inequality. Ethnic minorities, immigrants, and political dissidents are among the marginalized and vulnerable groups that surveillance typically disproportionately targets, leading to harassment, discrimination, and persecution. Systemic inequities and social hierarchies are only strengthened by the excessive concentration of surveillance authority in the hands of the government.

THE PANOPTICON: SURVEILLANCE, POWER, AND THE EROSION OF LIBERTY

Jeremy Bentham's panopticon design, which was initially a prison blueprint, is a groundbreaking examination of the symbiosis between surveillance, power, and moral conduct (Bentham, 1843). The panopticon is a central watchtower set around single cells, with inmates having no way of knowing if or when they are under observation. This design structure generates a state of eternal doubt and latent observation, forcing prisoners to control their actions in expectation of being seen. The shape of the panopticon is based upon the concept of "invisible visibility," under which the observer is never seen but still retains the ability to monitor. This visibility asymmetry confers tremendous power on the observer, since the fact of possible observation instils self-regulation and compliance in the observed individuals. Bentham conceived the panopticon as a device for instilling moral conduct and social discipline by the internalization of observation.

For Bentham, the panopticon is a mechanism for producing behaviour that exercises disciplinary functions by taking advantage of the psychological impact of surveillance to mould and direct behaviour. By promoting an atmosphere of omnipresent surveillance and ever-present threat of punishment, the panopticon breeds within people a habitual obedience to societal norms and regulations. Surveillance is here portrayed as an instrument of social regulation and moral control that promotes compliance, conformity, and discipline among the surveilled masses (Burns et al., 1968). Bentham also believed that through being continuously monitored, the panopticon would increase production and efficiency in a variety of institutional settings, including factories, hospitals, schools, and prisons. He asserted that in addition to punishing abnormal behaviour, the panopticon's disciplinary mode could also be used to reward conformity and promote compliance. Thus, Bentham saw the panopticon as a means to encouraging moral conduct and social usefulness by the rational control of oversight.

Apart from Bentham's utopian view of the panopticon as a moral welfare state, the model has been the subject of deep ethical critique and anxiety. Such critiques revolve around some central matters. The individual's right to privacy and self-determination is violated by the panopticon's invasive surveillance, which subjects them to constant observation and control without their knowledge. People lose their ability to behave freely and make their own decisions when their privacy is violated because they are continuously watched over and controlled by outside forces. The panopticon has drawn criticism for establishing unequal power dynamics between the observer and the observed by consolidating authority in the hands of a single authority. Centralized control is more likely to offer potential for misuse since those in charge can utilize monitoring to suit coercive or repressive objectives, stifling dissent and opposition. Critics contend that the panopticon encourages uniformity at the price of individuality and dissent, despite Bentham's conception of it as a tool for advancing moral behaviour and social order.

Because people emphasize compliance and obedience to avoid criticism, the continual fear of monitoring and punishment may stifle critical thinking, creativity, and innovation. Additionally, the panopticon's indiscriminate observation may make already-existing injustices and inequalities in society worse. Harassment, persecution, and discrimination are the results of excessive targeting and intensified monitoring of marginal and vulnerable groups, such as racial minorities, socioeconomically disadvantaged groups, and political dissidents. A profoundly moral dilemma involving power, control, privacy, and individual liberty is the ethics of surveillance, as represented by Bentham's panopticon design. The morality of surveillance goes much beyond utilitarian considerations of public safety and utility, even though it may be justified on the basis of social order and security. The panopticon, with its focus on ongoing surveillance and internalized discipline, serves to demonstrate the intricate dynamics between surveillance regimes and moral control. As we move through the ethical challenges created by surveillance in the information age, it is necessary to maintain standards of privacy, autonomy, justice, and equality that ensure surveillance regimes respect and safeguard the core rights and dignity of people in society.

From Panopticon to Control Society

Some people have contended that the panopticon is an inappropriate metaphor for modern society. Certain theorists have noted that surveillance occurs on a far more distributed basis today than it did in the past and that a state-centric approach to surveillance studies is no longer appropriate in societies where there is a huge diversity of surveillance actors. These observations are based on the insights of postmodern studies, which problematize theories that advance one-sided narratives of how societies function. Rather, Kevin Haggerty has contended that the panopticon has been abused in surveillance studies and has gone so far as to suggest that the panopticon should be literally destroyed in order to loosen its hold on the field. He has made the point that, since the publication of Foucault's seminal work, surveillance has evolved to perform a multitude of tasks beyond merely monitoring the movements of troublesome individuals. It is untrue to argue that surveillance is just employed for social control because it is also utilized in healthcare and education. This implies that a definition of surveillance that is less judgmental and more impartial is now necessary.

Additionally, surveillance has become far more pervasive and is no longer only used to uphold social hierarchies against the poor or marginalized. The control argument is being unsettled by the fact that surveillance is now being focused on non-human beings. This type of surveillance has even benefited society. Not only the state, but also other social actors use surveillance. The democratization of surveillance technologies has also made it possible for common people to employ inverse surveillance, or "sousveillance," which involves using these tools to expose the abuses of power committed by the powerful (Mann et al., 2002). For example, protestors can capture police brutality with video cameras. When citizens are given these powers, the idea that all surveillance is unavoidably harmful is called into question. The literature on surveillance is full of further instances of neutral definitions (Allmer, 2012).

According to Haggerty, researchers examining surveillance have a tendency to overlook positive cases because they are too preoccupied with criticizing the practice to notice these things (Haggerty, 2006). Some have proposed alternate metaphors to the panopticon, arguing that Foucault did not anticipate the advent of consumerism and computerization, which have significantly increased the amount of space available for observation. Due to these advancements, there are now numerous locations rather than just one where surveillance occurs (Fuchs, 2011). Because it acknowledges these more recent developments, Thomas Mathiesen's term "the synopticon", where the many observe the few through the mass media has gained popularity in surveillance studies. Stated differently, the ability of large audiences to delve into the personal lives of celebrities and other public figures subjects them to unprecedented levels of scrutiny that the audiences themselves are shielded from (Mathiesen, 2019). But Mathiesen was not exactly upbeat about the impact of mass media on society, and he did not always suggest the synopticon as a substitute for the panopticon in fact, the two are related in that they are both still hierarchical institutions.

It has even been said that surveillance in modern society is a "surveillant assemblage," meaning that information is gathered from many sources and places rather than just one area of society (Lyon, 2015). Kevin Haggerty and Richard Ericson have suggested that distinct surveillance systems have merged, resulting in a rhizomic levelling of surveillance, drawing on the work of Gilles Deleuze and Felix Guattari. The panoptic metaphor argues that surveillance is now mostly carried out by states and is no longer top-down. Instead, computers can supplement human surveillance efforts and various media can be connected to pursue surveillance for various goals. Surveillance is carried out by dispersed centres of calculation, such as banks and police stations, and as a result, it crosses institutional borders (Haggerty & Ericson, 2000). Such surveillance has been dubbed "liquid surveillance" by Zygmunt Bauman and David Lyon, as it depends on the body being encoded with data and followed through several data flows (Lyon, 2010).

In the same way that computerization made continuous surveillance possible at a lower cost—enabling continuous control rather than periodic examination—Deleuze himself acknowledged that surveillance methods had altered from the early modern era about which Foucault wrote. Deleuze contended that modern cultures are more appropriately characterized as society of control than as disciplinary societies as a result (Deleuze, 2009). Stated differently, control over individuals can be exerted not only through rigid institutional structures but also through quick and portable ICTs that allow for "on-the-go" control, a type of control that is ideal for flexible societies. However, electronic tagging does not prevent surveillance from occurring in order to verify that people are in authorized areas (Deleuze, 2009).

Some theorists contend that Foucault's theories are still extremely applicable to the surveillance society of today and that he would not have been shocked by current initiatives to make monitoring ubiquitous through the use of the internet and other technologies. In contrast to Deleuze's theory that societies of control have supplanted disciplinary societies, the smartphone might be viewed as a portable panopticon because it makes it possible to follow and monitor users covertly (Galič et al., 2016). In actuality, Foucault has returned to prominence as a result of the Snowden leaks, with a growing number of academics arguing for his ongoing significance. They claim that his work has been unfairly disregarded, despite the fact that the panopticon may not accurately depict how the internet operates. Gilbert Caluya, for example, has contended that the Deleuzian turn in surveillance studies, with its seminal metaphor of the rhizomic surveillant assemblage, does not necessarily signify a substantial divergence from Foucault, who acknowledged that state-centric conceptions of power were a feature of modern society and recognized the multiplicity of forms of surveillance (Caluya, 2010).

In addition, although though the internet is a distributed medium, its current state permits the covert filtration of information as a means of gaining control, making it intrinsically surveillant. Governments can transition from direct law enforcement to more covert, decentralized, technology-driven forms of enforcement thanks to its surveillance capabilities. This is a perfect fit for Foucault's understanding of power. But modern monitoring is horizontal, vertical, and diagonal, and human participation is involved. Because of this additional aspect, David Lyon has maintained that scholars must seriously consider the cultures of surveillance in order to comprehend the conditions in which individuals voluntarily engage in surveillance activities through their use of social media and the internet (Lyon, 2015).

SURVEILLANCE VS. SANCTIONS: THE DEBATE OVER ETHICS AND CRIME CONTROL

A complex interaction of ethical, social, and practical concerns surrounds the debate over the morality of surveillance and its value in preventing crime in contrast to moral and religious condemnation. One of the most well-known instances in this discussion is Jeremy Bentham's panopticon design, which was created as an architecture for enforcing moral behaviour through observation. Proponents contend that surveillance serves as a deterrent, affecting behaviour by fostering a culture of constant awareness of the potential for being watched and held accountable. According to this perspective, the panopticon embodies a utilitarianism that emphasizes the larger good that comes from preventing crime (Walzer, 2006). It suggests that people are strongly motivated to abide by laws and social standards out of fear of being watched, which will ultimately result in a society that is safer and more structured (Baumgardt, 1952). On the other hand, critics raise serious ethical concerns with the implied meanings of thorough observation. They contend that only using observational methods hinders people's ability to form their own moral convictions and sense of responsibility. Surveillance does little to address the root causes of crime or promote true ethical development, but it might discourage some actions by creating a fear of punishment. Concerns regarding privacy, autonomy, and the possibility of power abuse are also raised by the invasive nature of surveillance. The panopticon's centralized management and lack of transparency, which give the people in charge of looking and monitoring significant authority, raise worries about discrimination, manipulation, and authoritarianism (Coates, 1997).

Advocates of moral and religious penalties, on the other hand, think that a more nuanced approach to combating crime is possible, one that centres on the growth of moral qualities and ethical ideals. Although this strategy does not rely on external monitoring systems, it does emphasize the development of a culture of individual accountability, empathy, and decency toward others. Religious and moral education set the standards for moral behaviour, guiding people to internalize values like justice, compassion, and honesty. Invoking people's innate moral sense and religious convictions, proponents contend that moral and religious penalties can guarantee genuine moral development and social integration. Furthermore, in contrast to surveillance that carries on by force and external control, moral and religious sanctions instil greater self-awareness of the consequences of one's actions as well as empathy for others.

But critics of dependence on religious and moral sanctions contend that these methods can be inadequate in solving multifaceted social problems and preventing criminal behaviour in an effective manner. They refer to the shortcomings of moral instruction and religious sermons in accessing everyone, especially in pluralistic and secular societies. In addition, the relative subjectivism of morality and religious beliefs creates doubts about whose values will be enforced and how. Without external checking mechanisms of control and responsibility, moral relativism and arbitrariness in the imposition of sanctions risk increasing. Moral/religious sanctions when contrasted against surveillance methods (traditional or modern) has its own demerits. Firstly, Surveillance methods can provide instant deterrence and identification of criminal activity, particularly in environments where moral and religious influences are absent or low. Yet, they might only treat symptoms of crime and not the roots of it. Moral and religious sanctions, by contrast, can seek to create long-term behavioural modification by targeting individuals' beliefs and values, and thus potentially lowering the likelihood of criminal activity in the first instance. Further, moral and religious sanctions emphasize the inherent value and dignity of people, respecting their conscience and autonomy. They promote moral development and self-control, which pave the way for a more just and peaceful society built on mutual respect and collaboration. Despite their claims to provide security and order, surveillance techniques frequently include grave violations of people's privacy and liberties. By encouraging a culture of suspicion and surveillance, they have the potential to undermine social cohesiveness and trust. Secondly, the efficacy of religious and moral sanctions as opposed to surveillance methods can be influenced by cultural, social, and historical contexts. Where religious or moral principles dominate the shaping of behaviour in societies, sanctions based on such values can prove to be more effective in ensuring social order and deterring crime. On the other hand, in progressively secular and multicultural societies, surveillance methods may be seen as more neutral and effective methods of social control. Thirdly, moral and religious sanctions support the causes of human rights and civil liberties through promoting the centrality of individual autonomy, conscience, and dignity. Surveillance methods, especially when carried out without proper safeguards and regulation, can violate these rights in terms of privacy, due process, and freedom of expression. Lastly, sanctions based on morality and religion can create a stronger and self-policing society by promoting virtuous virtues and instilling a sense of shared responsibility. Techniques of surveillance, though granting instant deterrence, can lead to a compliance culture and reliance on outside control methods, perhaps eroding citizens' ability for moral decision-making and self-government.

ETHICAL DIMENSIONS OF SURVEILLANCE

Surveillance practices, while often justified for security and public order, raise significant ethical questions that demand careful consideration. Several key principles are at stake, forming the foundation of this ethical debate:

- Privacy: Privacy is a fundamental human right, recognized in international legal instruments and human rights frameworks. Surveillance activities that infringe on this right without clear justification or consent are ethically problematic. The erosion of privacy can have a chilling effect on personal development, autonomy, and free expression, discouraging individuals from exploring new ideas or associating with different groups for fear of being watched.

- Autonomy: Surveillance poses a direct threat to individual autonomy, or the capacity to make free and informed decisions about one's life. People may have less freedom to act without worrying about criticism or retaliation if they are continuously watched or profiled. Whether overt or covert, this type of influence calls into question how much a person's decisions are really their own.
- Informed Consent: Informed consent is a fundamental component of responsible behaviour in many ethical theories. However, in the situation of mass surveillance, where data is gathered in vast quantities without the participants' knowledge, gaining meaningful permission is particularly challenging. In order to be deemed ethical, surveillance needs to be open, accountable, and, whenever possible, prioritize an individual's right to opt-out or withdraw their consent.
- Discrimination and Bias: Surveillance technologies, from algorithms to data analysis techniques, can perpetuate and even amplify existing societal biases and inequalities. These technologies run the potential of escalating systematic discrimination when they disproportionately target marginalized groups, such as immigrants, political dissidents, or members of ethnic minorities. Such biases must be deliberately avoided by ethical monitoring procedures, which also need to have strong accountability and redress systems in place to address any discriminatory results.
- Accountability and Transparency: Abuse of power can readily result from surveillance if sufficient accountability is not in place. To ensure legitimacy and preserve public trust, procedures for impartial supervision, open audits, and unambiguous rules of participation are crucial. To enable educated public debate and to hold authorities responsible for their actions, the goal, extent, and techniques of monitoring must be openly disclosed.
- Data Security and Integrity: The vast amounts of data collected through surveillance create significant risks for security and integrity. Strong encryption, anonymization, and rigorous adherence to pertinent data protection laws are all necessary for ethical procedures. Protecting this data is not just a technical necessity; it is also an ethical duty to stop abuse and keep people safe.
- Dual-Use Technologies: Many surveillance technologies have both legitimate and potentially harmful applications. This "dual-use" nature raises ethical concerns about their development, sale, and export, especially when they could be used by authoritarian regimes to facilitate human rights abuses or

suppress dissent. A responsible approach requires considering the potential for misuse at every stage of a technology's life cycle.

Conflicts and Challenges

Despite of attempts to maintain ethical standards in surveillance activities, tensions and difficulties arise:

- Security and Privacy Balance: One of the core challenges of surveillance ethics is balancing security and public safety with protection of privacy and civil rights. Security measures introduced in the interest of security can overstep individuals' rights and freedoms, thus creating tension between security needs and ethical values.
- Technological Determinism: Technological innovation in surveillance technologies, such as artificial intelligence, facial recognition, and biometric identification, accelerates beyond ethical contemplation and regulation. Technological determinism, where technological opportunity precedes and determines societal norms and practices, creates ethical concerns over the automatic technological growth without bounds.
- Globalization and Jurisdictional Issues: Surveillance now extends globally in nature, crossing national borders and jurisdictions. Ethical considerations in surveillance go beyond the laws and regulations of individual nations and call for international cooperation, norms, and standards to address transnational issues.
- Abuse of Authority and Power Imbalances: Surveillance technologies may increase power imbalances among individuals, business corporations, and governments, resulting in abuses of authority, censorship, and oppression. Ethical surveillance operations need to protect against the wielding of power in one central location and provide accountability, transparency, and checks and balances to avoid abuse.

Strategies for Mitigation

To tackle the ethical dilemmas that come with surveillance, it is necessary to have a multifaceted response. One stepping stone is the use of ethical impact assessments prior to new surveillance technology being implemented. These assessments ought to incorporate varied views from impacted societies and civil society and are likely to mitigate and identify possible harms and risks. All of this should be complemented by robust regulatory frameworks that offer clear legal rules conforming with human rights and democratic principles, so all surveillance activity safeguards the freedoms of individuals. In addition to these laws, technological safeguards must be built into the very construction of surveillance systems through the use of techniques such as privacy-by-design and encryption to keep personal information safe from the beginning. Importantly, public engagement and education are crucial; educating citizens on their digital rights allows them to lobby for ethical use and hold institutions to account. This process necessitates multistakeholder dialogue and cooperation between governments, industry, and the public to make common cause and set common ethical standards. Lastly, developing ethical leadership and governance in the organisations responsible for conducting surveillance is essential to ensure that a culture of transparency and accountability is promoted, which can be supported by effective codes of conduct as well as whistleblower protections.

AVOIDING CONFLICTS THROUGH HARMONISATION – THE WAY FORWARD

The changing environment of state surveillance poses an ongoing ethical tightrope walk that requires a subtle and increasingly refined methodology for protecting inherent rights in light of legitimate security issues. The ultimate challenge is finding a functional line preventing clashes between the advancement of technologically driven abilities and time-tested ethical standards.

Strong collaboration amongst various stakeholders (governments, civil society, technology developers, and legal experts), ongoing communication, and regular adaptation to meet new realities are all necessary to achieve this sustainable equilibrium. Maintaining fundamental ethical principles such as necessity—using surveillance only when less invasive methods are insufficient—transparency—letting the public know about and monitor surveillance within security perimeters—and proportionality—making sure that surveillance isn't more invasive than is required for the particular threat—are necessary to achieve this.

In addition, enacting strong legal systems consistent with constitutional safeguards and international human rights norms is most important. These structures need to be articulately, precisely formulated, and continuously revised to keep up with new emerging technologies, instead of playing catch-up. They need to delineate clear red lines of what surveillance is not allowed, set strict authorization procedures, and require independent watchdog bodies with actual influence to review and challenge government conduct. The legal regime needs to provide effective means of redress for victims of their rights being breached as well.

The argument stretches beyond the confines of mere legal obedience into the area of more profound social mores. The conflict between surveillance methods and religious and moral prohibitions ultimately focuses on rival visions of justice, liberty, and the proper function of the state as a manager of behaviour. While surveillance potentially provides a strong means of preserving order and deterring crime, its unrestrained use poses deep moral questions about individual privacy, autonomy, and the accrual of power in the state's hands. It has the potential to create a "chilling effect," wherein people self-censor or avoid legitimate activities for fear of observation or misinterpretation, thereby eroding democratic debate.

By contrast, moral and religious sanctions play on people's innate sense of ethics and personal responsibility, stimulating self-regulation and a shared endeavour for societal welfare. These mechanisms alone, though, may not be adequate to tackle the sophistication and magnitude of threats within a contemporary, interconnected society.

Hence, a real hope for the future is a balanced strategy that carefully blends insights from both external deterrence (through careful and moral surveillance) and internal moral cultivation (through education and the development of social responsibility).

Ultimately, surveillance and ethics will be shaped by our shared responsibility to seek out wise and compassionate solutions. It's about realizing that, in a society that is increasingly being watched, true security includes not just the lack of risk but also confidence, freedom, and respect for human dignity. Making ensuring that surveillance serves humanity's interests rather than undermining the very principles it is meant to protect is more important than putting a stop to it.

REFERENCES

Allmer, T. (2012). *Towards a Critical Theory of Surveillance in Informational Capitalism*. Peter Lang Verlag., DOI: 10.3726/978-3-653-01459-4

Aristotle, , & Crisp, R. (2014). *Nicomachean ethics*. Cambridge University Press. DOI: 10.1017/CBO9781139600514

Baumgardt, D. (1952). *Bentham and the ethics of today*. Princeton University Press.

Bennett, C. J. (2011). In defence of privacy: The concept and the regime. *Surveillance & Society*, *8*(4), 485–496. DOI: 10.24908/ss.v8i4.4184

Bentham, J. (1843). *The Works of Jeremy Bentham* (Vol. 1). William Tait.

Burns, J. H., Rosen, F., & Schofield, P. (1968). *The Collected works of Jeremy Bentham* (Vol. 4). Oxford University Press.

Caluya, G. (2010). The post-panoptic society? Reassessing Foucault in surveillance studies. *Social Identities*, *16*(5), 621–633. DOI: 10.1080/13504630.2010.509565

Coates, A. J. (1997). *The ethics of war*. Manchester University Press.

Deleuze, G. (2009). 9 'Postscript on the societies of Control.' In *Media studies*. (pp. 89–93). DOI: 10.1515/9781474473231-011

Dencik, L., & Cable, J. (2017). The Advent of Surveillance Realism: Public Opinion and Activist Responses to the Snowden Leaks. *International Journal of Communication*, *11*. http://orca.cf.ac.uk/97855/

Fuchs, C. (2011). How to define surveillance? *Matrizes*, *5*(1), 109. DOI: 10.11606/issn.1982-8160.v5i1p109-136

Galič, M., Timan, T., & Koops, B. (2016). Bentham, Deleuze and Beyond: An Overview of Surveillance Theories from the Panopticon to Participation. *Philosophy & Technology*, *30*(1), 9–37. DOI: 10.1007/s13347-016-0219-1

Hadjimatheou, K. (2013). The relative moral risks of untargeted and targeted surveillance. *Ethical Theory and Moral Practice*, *17*(2), 187–207. DOI: 10.1007/s10677-013-9428-1

Haggerty, K. D. (2006). Tear down the walls: on demolishing the panopticon 1 2. In *Theorizing surveillance* (pp. 23–45). Willan.

Haggerty, K. D., & Ericson, R. V. (2000). The surveillant assemblage. *The British Journal of Sociology, 51*(4), 605–622. DOI: 10.1080/00071310020015280 PMID: 11140886

Justice K.S. Puttaswamy (Retd.) & Anr. vs. Union of India & Ors., 2017 10 SCC 1

Kant, I. (1956). *Critique of practical reason* (Beck, L. W., Trans.). The University of Chicago Press.

Korsgaard, C. M. (2012). *Kant: Groundwork of the Metaphysics of Morals* (2nd ed.). (Gregor, M., & Timmermann, J., Trans.). Cambridge University Press. DOI: 10.1017/CBO9780511919978

Lyon, D. (2010). Liquid Surveillance: The contribution of Zygmunt Bauman to surveillance studies. *International Political Sociology, 4*(4), 325–338. DOI: 10.1111/j.1749-5687.2010.00109.x

Lyon, D. (2015). *Surveillance after Snowden*. Polity Press. https://site.ebrary.com/id/11115169

Lyon, D. (2017). Digital Citizenship and Surveillancel Surveillance Culture: Engagement, exposure, and ethics in digital modernity. *International Journal of Communication, 11*, 19. https://ijoc.org/index.php/ijoc/article/view/5527

Macnish, K. (2014). Just surveillance? towards a normative theory of surveillance. *Surveillance & Society, 12*(1), 142–153. DOI: 10.24908/ss.v12i1.4515

Mann, S., Nolan, J., & Wellman, B. (2002). Sousveillance: Inventing and using wearable computing devices for data collection in surveillance environments. *Surveillance & Society, 1*(3), 331–355. DOI: 10.24908/ss.v1i3.3344

Mathiesen, T. (2019). The Viewer Society: Michel Foucault's 'Panopticon' revisited (1997). In *Routledge eBooks* (pp. 506–521). DOI: 10.4324/9780367809195-44

Ross, D. (2002). The right and the good. In *Oxford University Press eBooks*. DOI: 10.1093/0199252653.001.0001

Steeves, V. (2009). Reclaiming the social value of privacy. In *Lessons from the Identity Trail: Anonymity* (pp. 191–208). Identity and Privacy in a Networked Society. DOI: 10.1093/oso/9780195372472.003.0011

Walzer, M. (2006). *Just and unjust wars : a moral argument with historical illustrations* (4th ed.). Basic Books.

Chapter 8
The Ethics of Automated Decision-Making in Conflict

Arun Agrawal
https://orcid.org/0000-0001-7233-6660
Institute of Technology and Management, Gwalior, India

Minakshi Shashikant Ghorpade
https://orcid.org/0009-0001-3556-3167
Thakur College of Engineering and Technology, Mumbai, India

Neeta P. Patil
https://orcid.org/0009-0003-1532-3996
Thakur College of Engineering and Technology, Mumbai, India

Pratibha Rohit Prasad
https://orcid.org/0009-0008-3990-9250
Thakur College of Engineering and Technology, Mumbai, India

Purvi Sankhe
Thakur College of Engineering and Technology, Mumbai, India

Deepak Gupta
https://orcid.org/0000-0003-3929-1362
Institute of Technology and Management, Gwalior, India

ABSTRACT

This chapter explains the ethical issues that come with using machines to make decisions during war and conflict. Today, machines are used for tasks like finding threats, choosing targets, and sending aid. These were once done by people. While machines work fast and do not get tired, they cannot feel emotions or understand what is right or wrong. This creates serious problems when machines decide who gets help or who might be harmed. If something goes wrong, it is hard to know who is to blame. The chapter also discusses how unfair data can lead machines to treat some groups badly. Legal systems are not fully ready to deal with these problems. To

DOI: 10.4018/979-8-3373-3611-4.ch008

keep people safe, we need clear rules, careful use, and teamwork between countries. Machines can support people, but they should not replace human care, judgment, or responsibility. Human values must always come first in conflict situations.

1. INTRODUCTION

Technology has changed the way conflicts are managed today. In the past, wars were dominated by human choices. Today, machines and automated systems often play a key role. These systems help spot threats, direct weapons, and even deliver aid. They work quickly and without rest. This makes them very useful in high-risk areas. But it also raises serious concerns. When a system is able to choose actions autonomously, ethical issues become critical.

In modern conflict situations, machines are being given the ability to make rapid decisions. Some of these decisions can even affect the lives of many people (Candrian & Scherer, 2022). These systems are often used to track enemies, find targets, and even decide when to launch an attack. They can also help map crisis areas or manage urgently needed supplies. These roles were once performed by humans. Today, they are often guided by systems based on preset rules and massive data sets.

This shift has made conflict happen faster and sometimes more organized. But it has also created new risks. If a machine acts without consulting humans first, it could make mistakes. It could attack the wrong people. It could send aid to the wrong places. It could miss important information that only humans would notice. These mistakes could cause great harm and lead to a loss of trust. They could also cause long-term damage to the idea of handling conflict fairly and impartially (Köbis, Bonnefon, & Rahwan, 2021).

One of the biggest concerns is the loss of human judgment. Humans are able to feel emotions and understand values such as kindness, justice, and fairness. Machines do not have these emotions (Stark & Hoey, 2021). They only follow orders or learn from old data. If this data is unfair or wrong, the system will repeat the same mistakes. It may unconsciously treat people unfairly. In a war zone, where every choice can affect life and death, this is a serious problem.

Another key question is responsibility. When a system causes harm, who is to blame? Its builders? The people who gave it instructions? Or the machine itself? There is no clear answer. This lack of responsibility can make it more difficult for victims to seek justice and can lead to bad decisions going uncorrected.

People also worry about hidden behaviors. Some systems operate in ways that are difficult to understand. Even the people who use them may not know how they achieve their results. This lack of openness can lead to blind trust. People may accept everything the system says without questioning it. This can create a false sense of security and lead to undesirable outcomes.

For all these reasons, we urgently need to take a hard look at the ethics of using machines in conflict. Ethics means knowing right from wrong and choosing actions that respect life and fairness. As machines play an increasing role in conflict settings, we must ensure that they adhere to these fundamental values (Johnson, 2022).

This chapter will explore this issue from several angles. First, it will explain how machines are being used in conflict zones. Then, it will explore the ethical risks and limitations of autonomous action systems. In addition, it will explore the laws and rules that apply to war and how these laws are affected by automated actions. After that, the chapter will discuss unfair outcomes and the loss of human choice. Finally, it will offer some ideas for using these systems in a fairer and more responsible way.

Machines and automation may thrive in the future. But their power must be wielded with care. By asking tough questions and setting clear rules, we can defend human values even in the toughest times.

2. UNDERSTANDING AI IN CONFLICT ZONES

Modern conflict zones are changing. Machines and automated systems are now being used for many of the tasks once performed by humans (Van Der Aalst, 2021). These systems are fast and work around the clock. They are designed to support soldiers, manage risk, and help civilians. But as this changes, we need to understand what these systems are, how they work, and what problems they can cause.

2.1. What Are Automated Systems in Conflict

An autonomous system is a machine or tool that can complete a task without being told how to do it every time (Sifakis & Harel, 2023). Some systems follow given instructions. Some systems can learn from data and adjust their behavior over time. These systems are being used in war and crisis zones to make decisions, track threats, and process large amounts of information.

Some tools are able to automatically take action when danger is imminent. Others are used to study past data and predict what might happen in the future. These systems don't get tired or scared (Hong, 2022). They are able to process large amounts of data quickly. That's why many organizations have started using them during wars or in areas where people need fast assistance.

2.2. Different Types of Systems Used in Conflict

There is a wide variety of systems currently used in conflict environments. Each system has different goals and methods. Some tools are used on the battlefield, while others are used far away from the war zone but still have a huge impact.

One example is independent weapons systems. These machines can find targets and take action without humans asking them to do so first. They are designed to react quickly, ensuring that no time is wasted (Taddeo & Blanchard, 2023). But they may not always be able to tell if a target is actually a threat. This can lead to wrong actions and harm innocent people.

Another category is conflict prediction tools. These systems study past events, maps and patterns to try to guess where the next fight or danger might occur. They can help groups prepare, or relocate people before a situation gets bad. But these tools can also be wrong if the data they use is unfair or incomplete.

Some systems are used for aid and disaster relief efforts. They help deliver food, water, or shelter to people who need it. These tools work hard to ensure that supplies get to where they are needed most. But sometimes they can overlook details that only those on the front lines can see. This can lead to inequitable or delayed aid.

2.3. From Human Choice to Machine Action

In the past, all choices in conflict were made by people. Leaders, soldiers, and rescuers acted using their own thinking and values. They considered safety, fairness, and humanity. Today, many of these choices are made by machines.

This change isn't always a bad thing. Machines can help reduce errors. They can act faster than humans. They can handle tasks that are difficult or too risky for humans (Kakolu & Faheem, 2023). But they can also make decisions with a lack of caution or understanding. Machines don't feel fear or kindness. They can't understand pain or loss (Boyacı, Canyakmaz, & De Véricourt, 2024). They just follow patterns or past outcomes.

When people allow systems to make critical decisions without scrutiny, there is a risk of harm. Human values may be lost. The system may act in ways that violate fundamental rights. It may treat people as numbers or objects rather than as people.

This shift from human-led to machine-led action requires careful thought. People have to think about who is in control and who is held accountable when things go wrong. It is not enough to simply say that the machine made a mistake. Someone has to be held accountable.

2.4. Why This Shift Matters

The use of machines in conflict is more than a technological issue. It affects how we think about war, security, and life (González, 2022). When decisions are made by systems rather than people, the meaning of right and wrong may change. People may stop asking deep questions. They may forget that every life has value.

There are risks in over-trusting machines. People may come to believe that tools cannot possibly be wrong. This can lead to blind action, undermining the role of human thought and care. In some cases, people may stop checking facts and simply follow the system's instructions.

That's why understanding these tools is so important. It helps us see their power and their limitations. It reminds us that machines are made by people. They must serve humans, not replace them.

3. MORAL AND ETHICAL DILEMMAS

As the use of machines and automated tools in conflict settings increases, new ethical questions arise. These questions concern values such as life, fairness, responsibility, and justice. When machines are allowed to act in ways that affect human lives, the role of ethics becomes critical (Lepri, Oliver, & Pentland, 2021). People must question whether machines are truly capable of making ethical choices. They must also ponder what happens when life-and-death decisions are made by systems that do not think or feel like humans.

3.1. Can Machines Understand Right and Wrong

Machines are designed to follow instructions. Some machines can learn from past data, while others follow fixed steps to perform tasks. But none of them can truly understand what is right and wrong (Bell, 2022). They cannot feel fear, guilt, or kindness. They cannot make moral judgments like humans.

When a soldier is in a war zone, he or she may choose not to shoot. The soldier may think the person in front of him or her is a child or does not pose a threat. This choice is based on feeling, training, and deep thinking. A machine does not have these qualities. It can only recognize a pattern or signal. It may take action without stopping to think whether it should do so.

Some people believe that machines can be designed to follow fair rules. These rules can be added to the design of the machine. But this is different from true ethics. Machines do not understand the meaning behind these rules. They just apply these rules without scruples.

3.2. When Machines Decide Who Lives or Dies

In some cases, machines are given the power to choose when to attack. This is a serious problem. When a system is instructed to find and eliminate a threat, it may use cameras, sensors, and maps. It may decide within seconds what to attack (Sikder, Petracca, Aksu, Jaeger, & Uluagac, 2021). But this decision is not always correct.

If the system gets it wrong, a person who is not participating in the fight may die. A child, a doctor, or a civilian may be harmed. This raises deep ethical questions. Can we allow machines to choose who lives and who dies? Is it right to let a system act without human supervision?

Some tools strike faster than any human can. They are used where time to react is critical. But speed must never come at the expense of safety and truth. Taking a human life is the most serious act. It must be done with caution and forethought. A system cannot bear the weight of such a choice.

3.3. The Effect on Human Dignity and Moral Duty

Every person has value. That value is not based on what they do or where they come from. It is a fundamental right. That value can be lost when machines act without knowing who the other person is. The system may see the other person as a target. This takes the humanity out of the decision.

War already causes great pain. This pain is exacerbated when systems act without emotion or respect. People may feel they are being judged by cold tools. This reduces trust and takes away any sense of fairness from the conflict.

There are also questions of moral responsibility. When a person makes a mistake that harms others, he or she may be called to account. There may be a trial. Steps may be taken to ensure that it does not happen again. But when a system causes harm, who is to blame? Its builders? Its users? Or no one?

This lack of clarity of responsibility is dangerous. If no one takes responsibility, the same mistakes could happen again. Victims could not receive justice. War could become more brutal and less humane.

3.4. The Need for Strong Moral Thinking

Machines are tools, they are not leaders or judges. Their use must always be guided by clear values. Before any system is put into use in a conflict zone, it must be checked for fairness and safety. There must be limits to its capabilities. Someone must always be able to step in and stop wrongdoing.

Ethical thinking must lead the way. If we forget this, we risk losing our humanity. We must not sacrifice speed and control for care and justice. The tools we build must serve human values and must not be used to replace them.

4. KEY AREAS OF CONCERN

4.1 Autonomous Weapons Systems

4.1.1. How These Systems Work

Autonomous weapon systems are machines that can find and attack targets without humans controlling each step. They have built-in sensors and cameras that help them detect movement and heat (Longpre, Storm, & Shah, 2022). The systems are programmed with rules to decide what to attack and when to act. Once activated, they search for targets and launch attacks without approval. Some of these machines move on land, while others fly in the air or fight at sea.

They are used because they can react faster than humans, cover wide areas, and reduce risks to soldiers. This makes them attractive to many armed forces.

4.1.2. Risks of Unintended Harm

These systems are fast, but they are not always accurate. A machine might mistake a civilian for a fighter jet. It might hit a building that was not supposed to be hit. Once an attack is made, it cannot be reversed. These mistakes can lead to innocent casualties.

Such mistakes happen because machines cannot understand emotions. They are not able to perceive the environment like humans. They act based on rules and signals. If these signals are wrong, the consequences can be disastrous.

4.1.3. Questions of Accountability

When a person makes a mistake in war, the law can take action. But when a machine causes harm, it's hard to know who's to blame. The person who wielded the weapon? The one who wrote the program? The one who built the system?

This lack of clarity about responsibility is a serious problem. Without answers, victims may not get justice. That's why all weapons systems must have human control at their core.

4.2 Conflict Prediction and Risk Mapping

4.2.1. Use of Predictive Models

In many conflict zones, systems are used to predict where problems might occur next. These tools study past events, analyzing patterns in news reports, messages, social posts, and satellite imagery to try to spot signs of heightened danger (Okeleke, Ajiga, Folorunsho, & Ezeigweneme, 2024). These systems can issue early warnings to help government aid organizations and security forces prepare in advance. They can also guide where to send aid workers or move people to safety.

These tools work by building models based on data. They search for links between past conflicts and current actions. If a pattern is found, the system issues a warning or indicates a possible risk.

4.2.2. Bias in Data and Decision-Making

Predictive systems, while useful, can also be unfair. Results can also be inaccurate if the data used is old or biased. Some areas may be flagged as high risk based on unfair perceptions of the past. Poor communities or minority groups may be treated with more suspicion. This can lead to wrong actions and deepen mistrust (Dissanayake & Bracewell, 2023).

The system may not understand the full truth behind the data. It may not understand local customs or the causes of conflict. As a result, its recommendations can be misleading or harmful.

4.2.3. Reliability and Transparency Concerns

Many of these tools are not fully accessible to the public. It is often difficult to understand how their results were derived. Even the people who use them may not fully understand how the system works. This lack of transparency can lead to blind trust. If people follow bad advice without questioning it, the results can be dangerous.

To be safe and fair, all predictive tools must be clear and reliable and used in conjunction with human judgment. Systems must support people's decisions, not replace them.

4.3 Automated Humanitarian Aid Allocation

4.3.1. Use of Systems in Distributing Aid

Today, automated systems are being used to manage the distribution of food, water, shelter, and supplies during crises. These systems collect data from multiple sources to analyze the number of people who need help, the type of assistance needed, and the location of each group. Based on this information, the system develops a plan to send aid to where it is most needed (Martin et al., 2023).

In large disaster areas, these systems help make choices quickly. They can find hard-to-reach areas and provide better routes for trucks and rescue teams. This reduces waste and saves time. Aid groups can cover a wider area and reach more people.

4.3.2. Risk of Unequal or Biased Distribution

While useful, these systems are not perfect. If the data fed into the system is wrong or unfair, aid can be distributed in the wrong way. Some groups may receive too much help, while others may receive nothing. This is called allocation bias.

For example, if a system gives more weight to large cities, smaller villages may be overlooked. If it uses past data that ignored certain communities, those people may be overlooked again. These mistakes can lead to anger and mistrust, or they can cause conflict within the groups that need help.

4.3.3. Ethical Questions in Prioritizing Aid

Providing aid is not just a task, but a moral responsibility. When a machine decides who gets aid first, it must follow fair rules. It cannot favor one group over another without reason. People may question how these choices are made.

There must always be human constraints. Aid must be based on need and dignity. Machines can support aid efforts, but humans must lead the final decision.

5. LEGAL AND HUMAN RIGHTS IMPLICATIONS

The use of machines and automated systems in conflict settings raises many legal and human rights issues. When decisions affecting life and safety are made by systems rather than humans, it becomes more difficult to comply with the rules of war. International law is based on human judgment and moral responsibility. These laws were established long before machines were involved in warfare. As a result, today there is a gap between new technologies and old legal systems. This gap creates risks for both civilians and soldiers.

5.1. International Humanitarian Law and Automated Systems

International humanitarian law is a set of rules that govern how wars are conducted. The rules are designed to protect people not taking part in the fighting, including civilians, aid workers and medical personnel. The law also states that force should be used only when necessary and against lawful targets (Jafariandehkordi, 2024).

Adhering to these rules becomes even more difficult when machines are used to find and strike targets. The system may not always be able to identify who is a combatant and who is a civilian. It may not be able to tell whether a building is a hospital or a military base. If it makes a mistake, it could result in casualties. These mistakes could lead to violations of humanitarian law.

For example, a system that attacks a crowd without checking to see if they are armed may violate the principle of distinction. Another system that causes great harm when only a small amount of force is needed may also violate the principle of proportionality. These rules are at the heart of humanitarian law. If machines are to be used in warfare, they must be able to follow them.

5.2. Accountability Under War Crime Frameworks

Accountability means being responsible for actions. In war, this means if someone breaks the law, they must be held accountable. War crimes include intentionally killing civilians, torturing prisoners, or attacking places like schools and hospitals. When a soldier commits such acts, they may be brought to court (Lewis, 2023).

But when machines cause harm, the problem becomes more complicated. If a system kills civilians by mistake, who should be held accountable? The person who sent it? The team that built it? Or no one? Many laws currently don't clearly answer this question.

The lack of clear accountability is dangerous because it can lead to injustice. Victims may not get support. People may start to feel that war crimes caused by machines are not taken seriously. This could undermine trust in the law and the institutions designed to protect people.

We need new legal concepts to handle these cases. The law must ensure that even when machines are used, someone is always responsible. The use of automated tools must never exceed the jurisdiction.

5.3. Civilian Protection and the Loss of Human Oversight

One of the main goals of international law is to protect civilians during war. People not participating in the fighting should not be harmed, including children, the elderly, and families trying to flee conflict (Solf, 2023). Humans are supposed to keep this goal in mind when making decisions on the battlefield. Machines lack this care. They don't feel grief, and they don't stop before causing harm. This care for human life can disappear when humans hand over control to a system. Mistakes made by machines can be swift and deadly. Without a human to oversee or guide the system, harm can spread quickly.

Human oversight means that someone always needs to be involved. It means someone is checking that the system is running. It means someone can stop the machine if something goes wrong. Without this control, the use of automated tools poses a huge risk to civilian lives.

Even the best systems can fail. They can be hacked. They can read the wrong data. They can act too early or too late. When this happens, people can be killed or injured. That's why someone must always be in charge. The law must make this oversight a fundamental rule.

5.4. The Need for Clear and Strong Legal Rules

As machines become more prevalent in warfare, strong legal rules are needed. These rules must be clear, understandable and easy to follow. They must ensure that machines are used in a way that protects human life and complies with the laws of war. They must also ensure that every action is accountable to the right person.

Governments and legal experts must work together to update these rules. They must ensure that justice is not lost in the rush to use new tools. Human rights and human dignity must remain at the heart of all decisions. No system should be allowed to act without clear boundaries.

6. EROSION OF HUMAN AGENCY

As machines and automated tools take on more and more roles in conflict zones, the role of human decision-making is gradually diminishing (Goldfarb & Lindsay, 2021). This change is not just technical, it affects the way people think, act and take responsibility. When machines begin to replace human choices, human autonomy begins to fade. Autonomy refers to the ability to choose, act and take responsibility. When humans lose this control, it can lead to serious problems in war and society.

6.1. Reduced Human Control in War-Related Decisions

In many modern wars, machines help guide weapons, monitor targets, and develop action plans. These machines can quickly process data and give seemingly intelligent and useful results (Aithal, 2023). But in doing so, they may reduce the real choices humans have. People may begin to rely entirely on the results given by the system, and no longer question whether the results are correct or fair.

This shift may lead to lazy thinking. It can cause commanders to act without thinking. They may feel that the system is smarter than they are, so they will follow the system's suggestions without hesitation. This makes the role of humans smaller and weaker. It also means that the system's mistakes may go uncorrected.

When people are excluded from key decision-making processes, problem solving becomes more difficult, and accountability becomes more difficult. Warfare is full of serious choices. These choices must be made carefully. If humans are no longer in control, the entire process of war becomes less humane.

6.2. Delegating Ethical Judgment to Machines

Moral judgment means knowing right from wrong. It also means understanding the value of life, fairness, and justice. In the past, leaders in war had to use reason and emotion to make difficult choices. They had to weigh risks and consider who might be harmed.

Now, many of these choices are handed over to machines. These machines do not understand pain or kindness, and do not feel regret or guilt (Bonnefon, 2021). They just follow rules or patterns in the data. They may be fast and efficient, but they cannot make moral decisions like humans.

Delegating moral judgment to machines is risky. It creates a system where moral questions are replaced by code and formulas. The system might attack a target because it complies with the rules. But the system might not know that the person is innocent, or that the area is a school, or that now is not the best time to act.

When machines make moral choices, the human values that guide warfare begin to fade. This leads to more mistakes and less care, and can also lead to violations of international law and ethical norms. Morality should not be removed from conflict, but strengthened. Only humans can guard this part of war.

6.3. Psychological and Societal Consequences

Losing autonomy doesn't just affect soldiers or commanders, it changes how people in society think and feel. When people trust machines to make all the hard choices, they may feel powerless. They may stop asking questions or expressing concerns. This leads to a passive society where people accept actions without knowing why they happen.

For people working in war zones, using machines can also be stressful. A soldier might carry out an order given by the system, only to later discover that it harmed civilians (Rauch & Ansari, 2022). The soldier might feel guilty, but also confused. Who is responsible? The system gave the order, but it was a human who pulled the trigger. This emotional burden can build over time.

Civilians may also feel fear and mistrust. If they think machines are watching or judging them, they may change the way they live. They may lose trust in aid workers, peacekeepers, and even their own governments. This can weaken the fabric of society and make peace and healing more difficult to achieve.

In the long run, the loss of autonomy can reduce accountability across society. People may think that wrongful behavior is no longer their fault. They may say that the system made the choice. This attitude is dangerous because it allows injustice to flourish unchallenged.

6.4. Keeping Human Agency Alive

To protect human autonomy, humans must remain in control. Systems can assist, but never replace human judgment. There must always be room for human reflection, care, and correction. Training should focus on keeping people alert and engaged. Ethics must be part of every choice.

People must be accountable for their actions, both in war and in peace. Machines can assist them, but never replace their roles. Maintaining autonomy is the only way to ensure conflicts are humane, fair, and accountable.

7. BIAS AND ALGORITHMIC FAILURES

Automated systems are often seen as neutral. People might think they make fair choices based on data alone. But the truth is, these systems are built by humans. They learn from human data. If that data is unfair or biased, the system can become unfair, too. That's called bias. When bias enters a system, it causes harm. It affects real people in real life.

In conflict zones, bias in a system can make things worse. It can exacerbate suffering. It can ignore people who are already at risk (Brosché, 2023). It can even spark more violence. That's why it's so important to understand how bias works and what consequences it can have.

7.1. Examples of Bias in Automated Systems

Bias can enter a system in a number of ways. One common route is through training data. If a system learns from data that primarily shows a certain group, it may not understand other groups. For example, if a system is trained using images of soldiers from a certain region, it may not be able to detect or protect people from another region.

In some cases, facial recognition tools are more likely to fail when identifying images with darker skin tones. This is because most training images have lighter skin tones. In a war setting, this error can lead to incorrect targeting or missed threats.

Another example is conflict prediction tools. These tools try to guess where violence might occur. If they rely on past police records or news reports that overlook certain areas or groups of people, the system might ignore those groups, too. It might flag safe places as dangerous, missing real dangers.

These are not small mistakes. They can spark panic, lead to bad decisions, and potentially put innocent people at risk.

7.2. Impact on Marginalized Groups

Bias hurts everyone differently. It hits already marginalized groups the hardest. These groups may be poor, may speak a different language, may belong to a minority group, or may be refugees. They already suffer more in times of war. When systems are biased, that suffering can be exacerbated.

For example, if a system is used to decide who gets food or shelter, it may miss out on smaller groups. If the system hasn't been trained with data from their region or culture, it may not know how to help them. This can lead to unfair aid and can cause tension between groups.

In areas where people are already facing hatred or violence, a biased system can add fuel to the flames. If the system wrongly labels a group as a threat, that group can be put in even greater danger. This is not just a technical failure, but a moral and social crisis.

These mistakes can undermine trust. People may stop trusting peacekeepers or aid agencies. They may feel the system isn't working for them. This makes healing and rebuilding more difficult.

7.3. Risk of Reinforcing Existing Inequalities

Bias in the system not only causes harm, it can make old problems worse. Many countries already have gaps between the rich and the poor, the powerful and the weak. Automated systems may replicate these gaps, and may even widen them further.

If a system always trusts official data, it may ignore those who live outside the system. This is especially true for people in rural areas or those who are undocumented. Their needs may be ignored again and again. This can lead to further widening of gaps.

Once bias is in a system, it's hard to detect. People may trust a system because it seems smart. They may follow its results without reservation. Over time, this can make the idea of unfairness commonplace. People may stop paying attention to injustice.

And just like that, machine bias becomes part of everyday life. It becomes part of the way wars are fought. It determines who gets helped and who is forgotten.

7.4. Moving Toward Fair Systems

Bias cannot be eliminated in a vacuum; it requires effort and care. Systems must be frequently checked and trained with fair, broad data. People must always keep an eye on who is helped and who is left out.

Human review must be part of the process. Machines should never take full control. Fairness requires human perspective and values. Only then can we build systems that help, not hurt.

Bias in automated tools is not just a flaw. It is a threat to justice. It must be seen, challenged, and fixed at every step.

8. ETHICAL GUIDELINES AND BEST PRACTICES

As technology becomes more prevalent in war zones, so too does the question of how to use it responsibly. Tools once used only in peaceful missions are now used in life-and-death situations. This shift requires strong ethical thinking and action. It is not enough to question whether a system works, we must also ask whether it is right to use it in a certain way.

Ethically using these systems requires clear rules. These rules must guide the design, use, and outcomes of such systems in conflict and crisis. They must protect people and ensure fair treatment every step of the way.

8.1. Principles of Responsible Use

Responsible use begins with core ethical values. These values must guide every aspect of the system's use. First is the value of fairness. Everyone must be treated equally. No group should be favored or ignored.

Second is the value of doing no harm. If a tool can cause harm, it must be tested and improved. Its impact must be studied before it is used in an actual conflict.

Respect for life is another key value. Any system used in conflict must protect life, not take it without cause. Systems must not be used to deprive people of their right to participate in decisions that could lead to death or suffering.

In addition, the system must be able to explain its choices. It should not act in secret. People must know why it does what it does. This helps build trust.

These values are not just good ideas. They are basic rules. They must be built into every part of planning and use.

8.2. Transparency, Accountability, and Human Oversight

Transparency means openness. Everyone affected by a system has the right to understand how it works. This includes what data the system uses, how decisions are made, and who controls it. Hiding this information is not only unfair, but also breeds fear and confusion.

Accountability means someone must be held responsible when something goes wrong. Systems don't run automatically. Behind every tool there is a person or group who created or approved it. If harm occurs, these people must be held accountable. This rule eliminates carelessness and encourages people to think more deeply before acting.

Human oversight means that humans must always be in control. Even with the help of machines, the final choice must be made by humans. Machines should not be the only voice in decisions about war, peace, or life. Humans have wisdom, emotions, and judgment that machines cannot learn.

These three concepts complement each other to ensure that tools are not only useful, but can be used in the right way. They protect both the user and the people affected.

8.3. Need for Global Cooperation and Regulation

Wars are no longer limited by national borders. A system used in one place can affect people far away. That's why no single country can set all the rules. Global tools require global rules.

Countries must come together to develop common laws and programs. These rules must prevent the misuse of technology and ensure that everyone is protected. These laws must also prevent an unfair competition where each country builds more powerful tools without regard to the cost to human lives.

Organizations like the United Nations and the International Red Cross are already working on this. But more needs to be done. Rich countries cannot lead alone. All voices must be heard, including those from smaller regions or those torn by war.

Education and training are also key parts of this effort. Leaders, designers, and users need to understand not only how systems work, but how they affect people. Ethics education should be part of every training program related to technology in conflict.

In the end, rules alone are not enough. What matters is the will to follow them. People must care about doing the right thing. Only then can tools help instead of harm.

9. CONCLUSION

Modern conflicts are no longer limited to human action. Machines are now used in warfare, crisis response, and aid delivery. These changes raise many ethical challenges that we cannot ignore. Tools once controlled by humans now operate with limited human input. This shift raises concerns about fairness, safety, and control. A key issue is the risk of bias. Some systems make unfair decisions that harm certain groups. Others make choices that humans cannot explain. Some systems strip human judgment from life-or-death situations. This reduces trust, diminishes accountability, and increases the likelihood of error. Risks are greater when systems act quickly and without forethought or review. Automated tools used in warfare could cause harm without warning. Aid systems could overlook those who need it most. Decisions once made carefully are now driven by logic and lack emotion. These changes impact human dignity. They also raise urgent ethical questions. We clearly need strong ethical rules. They must guide the design, testing and use of machines. They must protect people in all conflict zones. They must prevent harm. International humanitarian law must cover new systems used in warfare. It must make clear who is responsible when things go wrong. And it must ensure that civilians are protected. These laws cannot be optional. They must transcend borders and all types of conflict. Regulation is not just about stopping misuse, it's also about creating ways to use new tools safely. Every step must be carefully managed. From building a system to using it in a real-world setting, it must be guided by clear standards. These standards must include human judgment and oversight. Countries cannot act alone. Global cooperation is essential. Conflict affects many regions. One country's use of a new system may affect others. Shared rules and joint efforts will help prevent abuse. Open dialogue between governments, civil society, and experts is key to this work. Technology should support human action, not replace human care. In conflict zones, every decision counts. Machines cannot grieve, they cannot understand loss. They follow logic, not empathy. That's why humans must be involved. Even if machines can help speed up aid or improve security, they can never take full control. Human agency must always be at the center. Ethics must guide every step. Tools must serve humans, not rule over them. We face a choice. We can allow systems to develop without rules. Or we can carefully shape how they are used, guided by shared values. This chapter explains why the second path is urgent. Future conflicts may involve machines. But moral responsibility remains human.

REFERENCES

Aithal, P. S. (2023). Super-Intelligent Machines-analysis of developmental challenges and predicted negative consequences. *International Journal of Applied Engineering and Management Letters*, *7*(3), 109–141. DOI: 10.47992/IJAEML.2581.7000.0191

Bell, J. (2022). What is machine learning? *Machine learning and the city: applications in architecture and urban design*, 207-216.

Bonnefon, J. F. (2021). *The car that knew too much: can a machine be moral?* MIT Press.

Boyacı, T., Canyakmaz, C., & De Véricourt, F. (2024). Human and machine: The impact of machine input on decision making under cognitive limitations. *Management Science*, *70*(2), 1258–1275. DOI: 10.1287/mnsc.2023.4744

Brosché, J. (2023). Conflict over the Commons: Government bias and communal conflicts in Darfur and Eastern Sudan. *Ethnopolitics*, *22*(2), 199–221. DOI: 10.1080/17449057.2021.2018221

Candrian, C., & Scherer, A. (2022). Rise of the machines: Delegating decisions to autonomous AI. *Computers in Human Behavior*, *134*, 107308. DOI: 10.1016/j.chb.2022.107308

Dissanayake, H., & Bracewell, P. J. (2023). Bias in Data-Informed Decision Making. In *Encyclopedia of Data Science and Machine Learning* (pp. 1173–1186). IGI Global. DOI: 10.4018/978-1-7998-9220-5.ch068

Goldfarb, A., & Lindsay, J. R. (2021). Prediction and judgment: Why artificial intelligence increases the importance of humans in war. *International Security*, *46*(3), 7–50. DOI: 10.1162/isec_a_00425

González, R. J. (2022). *War virtually: the quest to automate conflict, militarize data, and predict the future*. Univ of California Press.

Hong, S. H. (2022). Predictions without futures. *History and Theory*, *61*(3), 371–390. DOI: 10.1111/hith.12269

Jafariandehkordi, M. (2024). The AI Battlefield: Legal Challenges of Autonomous Weapon Systems under International Humanitarian Law.

Johnson, J. (2022). The AI commander problem: Ethical, political, and psychological dilemmas of human-machine interactions in AI-enabled warfare. *Journal of Military Ethics*, *21*(3-4), 246–271. DOI: 10.1080/15027570.2023.2175887

Kakolu, S., & Faheem, M. A. (2023). Autonomous robotics in field operations: A data-driven approach to optimize performance and safety. *Iconic Research and Engineering Journals*, *7*(4), 565–578.

Köbis, N., Bonnefon, J. F., & Rahwan, I. (2021). Bad machines corrupt good morals. *Nature Human Behaviour*, *5*(6), 679–685. DOI: 10.1038/s41562-021-01128-2 PMID: 34083752

Lepri, B., Oliver, N., & Pentland, A. (2021). Ethical machines: The human-centric use of artificial intelligence. *iScience*, *24*(3), 102249. DOI: 10.1016/j.isci.2021.102249 PMID: 33763636

Lewis, D. A. (2023). War crimes involving autonomous weapons: Responsibility, liability and accountability. *Journal of International Criminal Justice*, *21*(5), 965–980. DOI: 10.1093/jicj/mqad027

Longpre, S., Storm, M., & Shah, R. (2022). Lethal autonomous weapons systems & artificial intelligence: Trends, challenges, and policies. *Edited by Kevin McDermott. MIT Science Policy Review, 3*, 47-56.

Martin, N. M., Sundermeir, S. M., Barnett, D. J., Van Dongen, E. J., Rosman, L., Rosenblum, A. J., & Gittelsohn, J. (2023). Digital strategies to improve food assistance in disasters: A scoping review. *Disaster Medicine and Public Health Preparedness*, *17*, e40. DOI: 10.1017/dmp.2021.281 PMID: 34632974

Okeleke, P. A., Ajiga, D., Folorunsho, S. O., & Ezeigweneme, C. (2024). Predictive analytics for market trends using AI: A study in consumer behavior. *International Journal of Engineering Research Updates*, *7*(1), 36–49. DOI: 10.53430/ijeru.2024.7.1.0032

Rauch, M., & Ansari, S. (2022). Waging war from remote cubicles: How workers cope with technologies that disrupt the meaning and morality of their work. *Organization Science*, *33*(1), 83–104. DOI: 10.1287/orsc.2021.1555

Sifakis, J., & Harel, D. (2023). Trustworthy autonomous system development. *ACM Transactions on Embedded Computing Systems*, *22*(3), 1–24. DOI: 10.1145/3545178

Sikder, A. K., Petracca, G., Aksu, H., Jaeger, T., & Uluagac, A. S. (2021). A survey on sensor-based threats and attacks to smart devices and applications. *IEEE Communications Surveys and Tutorials*, *23*(2), 1125–1159. DOI: 10.1109/COMST.2021.3064507

Solf, W. A. (2023). Protection of civilians against the effects of hostilities under customary international law and under protocol. In *The Conduct of Hostilities in International Humanitarian Law* (Vol. I, pp. 3–21). Routledge. DOI: 10.4324/9781003417255-3

Stark, L., & Hoey, J. (2021, March). The ethics of emotion in artificial intelligence systems. In *Proceedings of the 2021 ACM conference on fairness, accountability, and transparency* (pp. 782-793). DOI: 10.1145/3442188.3445939

Taddeo, M., & Blanchard, A. (2023). A comparative analysis of the definitions of autonomous weapons. In *The 2022 yearbook of the digital governance research group* (pp. 57–79). Springer Nature Switzerland. DOI: 10.1007/978-3-031-28678-0_6

Van Der Aalst, W. M. (2021). Hybrid Intelligence: To automate or not to automate, that is the question. *International Journal of Information Systems and Project Management*, *9*(2), 5–20. DOI: 10.12821/ijispm090201

Chapter 9

Ethical Dilemmas of AI-Driven Warfare and Its Impact on Civilian Health and Medical Neutrality: Collateral Code

Sabina Sehajpal
https://orcid.org/0009-0004-6655-6279
Chandigarh University, India

Menka Sharma
Noida Institute of Engineering and Technology, India

Lalit Singh Dyarakoti
Graphic Era University, India

ABSTRACT

This research explores the ethical, political, and humanitarian implications of AI-driven warfare, focusing on its impact on civilian casualties, healthcare systems, and international governance. By combining qualitative case studies and quantitative data analysis, the study examines conflicts where AI technologies, such as autonomous weapons and drone strikes, have been deployed. It assesses civilian death ratios, misidentifications, and attacks on healthcare facilities, emphasizing the disproportionate toll on non-combatants. The research also evaluates the geopolitical consequences of AI in military operations, highlighting the potential for an AI-driven arms race and shifts in global power dynamics. Through expert interviews and legal analysis, the study explores gaps in international humanitarian law and

DOI: 10.4018/979-8-3373-3611-4.ch009

the need for new regulatory frameworks. Ultimately, it provides insights into the pressing need for global governance to ensure ethical use of AI in warfare while safeguarding civilians and medical neutrality in conflict zones.

INTRODUCTION

The convergence of artificial intelligence (AI) with modern warfare has sparked an unprecedented transformation in military tactics, strategy, and technologies. AI-driven autonomous weapon systems (AWS), machine learning algorithms for intelligence gathering, and predictive analytics in military planning are not merely enhancing the capabilities of armed forces but are also reshaping the very nature of conflict itself (Nocera, 2018). However, this technological revolution, while offering advancements in combat efficiency and precision, introduces an array of ethical dilemmas, particularly when deployed in settings where civilian lives are at risk. The increasing autonomy and decision-making power entrusted to AI systems in warfare raise pressing concerns regarding accountability, the potential for collateral damage, and the erosion of human oversight. These concerns are exacerbated in conflict zones, where the impact of AI warfare intersects with humanitarian law and the principle of medical neutrality, leading to a profound ethical conundrum (Erskine & Miller, 2024).

The ethical dilemmas associated with AI-driven warfare are not confined solely to the battlefield. As warfare increasingly shifts to technologically advanced and automated systems, the collateral consequences extend far beyond military targets, infiltrating civilian spaces, hospitals, and healthcare systems. In regions embroiled in conflict, where medical neutrality—the foundational principle that medical facilities and personnel should remain impartial and uninvolved in hostilities—is already precarious, the introduction of AI into the military apparatus poses a grave threat to the protection of civilian health. The application of AI to autonomous weapons and military decision-making not only raises moral questions about the sanctity of civilian life but also risks undermining the integrity of medical operations, further complicating the already fragile health systems in these regions (Rudolph et al., 2023).

In the context of warfare, AI's potential to inflict harm goes beyond the direct impacts of weaponry. The use of AI-driven systems, such as drone strikes, target recognition algorithms, and surveillance technologies, has the capacity to redefine the nature of warfare by increasing the precision and lethality of military operations (Wallace, 2020). However, this precision is double-edged, as the same technologies that enable surgical strikes in theory often fail to account for the broader context of conflict—namely, the human and infrastructural toll it exerts on the civilian population. The question of whether AI can ever be programmed to adhere to the nuances of international humanitarian law—such as distinguishing between combatants and non-combatants or avoiding the destruction of vital civilian infrastructure—remains an unresolved issue. While these systems operate with increasing autonomy, the lack of human judgment in key decisions about the use of lethal force makes accountability a convoluted issue. Who bears responsibility when AI systems malfunction, or when their decisions result in civilian casualties? Such questions are not easily answered in the context of the principles of war and humanitarian law, and the stakes become even higher when considering the inherent complexity of modern conflict zones (Sticher, 2025a).

Compounding the dilemma is the fact that AI-driven warfare, with its increasing reliance on autonomous decision-making, introduces a new dimension of uncertainty into conflict zones. While military AI systems may be designed to act quickly and efficiently in combat situations, the unpredictable nature of warfare—marked by shifting allegiances, non-state actors, and the blurring of lines between civilian and military spaces—creates fertile ground for miscalculation and erroneous targeting (Regan & Davidovic, 2023). In these environments, AI's capacity for rapid decision-making becomes both an asset and a liability. The ethical ramifications of such mistakes, particularly when they result in civilian harm, are profound. The consequences of an erroneous strike or an AI misidentifying a target can have far-reaching repercussions not only for the individuals involved but for the broader civilian infrastructure, including healthcare facilities, hospitals, and relief efforts that are meant to be protected by international law (Pezzino, 2017).

At the same time, AI in warfare also stands to dramatically impact the delivery of humanitarian aid and medical services in conflict areas. In war-torn regions, where medical neutrality is an essential pillar of international law, the presence of AI technologies on the battlefield further complicates the ability of healthcare providers to operate without interference or fear of becoming targets themselves. Medical facilities, hospitals, and healthcare workers are often caught in the crossfire of conflict, with their activities being scrutinized by military forces that may or may not recognize their protected status (Vykhodets, 2022). The advent of AI in warfare could potentially exacerbate these risks. For instance, AI-powered surveillance systems may inadvertently target medical facilities or personnel, mistaking them for military installations or combatants. Furthermore, AI's role in intelligence gathering and targeting decisions can lead to the destabilization of healthcare systems by depriving civilians of access to critical medical care, either through direct attacks or by disrupting the logistics of healthcare delivery in conflict zones. Such scenarios illustrate the ethical conflict between the military utility of AI and the humanitarian imperative to protect civilian lives and health infrastructure (Lhote, 2015).

The breach of medical neutrality by AI-driven military systems extends beyond the physical realm, into the ethical dimensions of healthcare provision in conflict zones. AI technologies, if not properly governed, could infiltrate and manipulate healthcare resources and decisions in ways that threaten medical impartiality. The integration of AI into medical decision-making processes—such as diagnostic systems or treatment algorithms—has the potential to enhance healthcare delivery in conflict zones. However, this also raises concerns about the potential for manipulation of these systems for military objectives, such as denying medical assistance to certain populations or influencing healthcare outcomes in ways that favor one group over another (Mitgutsch, 2021). The intersection of military AI and healthcare provision in conflict zones raises profound ethical issues about the sanctity of medical care, the protection of vulnerable populations, and the integrity of healthcare systems that operate in fragile environments.

In conclusion, the ethical dilemmas posed by AI-driven warfare and its impact on civilian health and medical neutrality are manifold and far-reaching. As AI technologies continue to evolve and become more integrated into military systems, the risks to civilian health and the sanctity of medical neutrality become increasingly pronounced. The ethical challenge is not only about ensuring that AI systems are designed to minimize harm but also about safeguarding the rights and well-being of civilians, particularly in conflict zones, where the protection of medical infrastructure and personnel is already under siege (Hunter & Bowen, 2024). The need for ethical guidelines and international regulatory frameworks to govern the use of AI in warfare, especially in conflict zones, has never been more urgent. Without careful consideration of these ethical implications, the deployment of AI in warfare could ultimately lead to a world where the balance between technological progress and humanitarian principles is irreparably skewed, resulting in lasting harm to both civilian health and the very foundations of international humanitarian law (Iveković, 2018).

The ethical challenges posed by artificial intelligence (AI) in the domain of warfare and its subsequent impact on civilian health and medical neutrality present a profound intersection of technology, law, and human rights. AI, with its transformative potential, has revolutionized the landscape of modern warfare, offering both opportunities and risks. The ethical dilemmas surrounding AI in warfare, particularly in relation to civilian harm, medical neutrality, and the safeguarding of human rights, are multidimensional. Scholars and practitioners alike have expressed concerns regarding the autonomy of AI-driven military systems, its implications for international humanitarian law, and its capacity to disrupt civilian healthcare systems during armed conflict (Milewski, 2018). In this literature review, the principal themes surrounding the ethical considerations of AI in warfare and healthcare are explored, providing a deeper understanding of the prevailing discourse and identifying critical gaps in the field (Giannotti & Proietti, 2021).

AI-driven warfare, with its autonomous decision-making capacities, fundamentally challenges traditional military ethics and accountability mechanisms. Autonomous weapon systems (AWS), such as drones and robotic combat units, represent a significant departure from conventional methods of warfare. These systems, empowered by machine learning algorithms, are designed to identify, target, and engage adversaries with minimal human intervention. While proponents of these technologies highlight their precision, efficiency, and potential to reduce human casualties on the battlefield, their introduction into combat operations has raised significant ethical concerns (Emery, 2021). The primary ethical dilemma lies in the issue of accountability—who is responsible when an autonomous system makes a decision that leads to civilian harm or violates international law? The delegation of lethal force to machines, without adequate human oversight, generates questions about the potential for errors, misidentifications, and disproportionate harm to non-combatants (Garcia, 2021).

Additionally, the integration of AI into warfare has spurred debates regarding the limits of human control over military decision-making processes. The autonomy of AI systems raises critical concerns about the erosion of human judgment in the use of force. Military ethicists have long upheld the principle that war should be conducted within the boundaries of ethical constraints, such as the distinction between combatants and non-combatants, proportionality in the use of force, and necessity (Black & van Esch, 2021). However, AI's capacity to act independently—based on pre-programmed algorithms or learning from battlefield data—poses a challenge to these traditional principles. Critics argue that AI systems, despite their sophisticated algorithms, cannot fully replicate the nuances of human decision-making in complex combat environments. As such, the deployment of AI in warfare raises a fundamental question: can machines, devoid of human consciousness and empathy, make morally justifiable decisions in the heat of battle? This question lies at the heart of contemporary discussions on the ethics of autonomous weapons and their role in modern conflict (Crews, 2023).

The deployment of AI in warfare does not only affect the dynamics of military operations but also has profound implications for civilian health, particularly in conflict zones. The intersection of AI and healthcare in war-torn regions raises pressing concerns regarding the protection of medical neutrality, an essential tenet of international humanitarian law (Stan, 2020). Medical neutrality dictates that medical facilities and personnel must remain impartial and uninvolved in hostilities, providing care to all individuals, regardless of their affiliation. However, AI technologies, especially those involved in surveillance, intelligence gathering, and targeting, pose a direct threat to this principle. There are instances in which AI-driven military systems have mistakenly targeted civilian infrastructure, including hospitals, healthcare centers, and ambulances. The risk of such errors increases when

AI systems are tasked with distinguishing between legitimate military targets and civilian structures, often relying on imperfect or biased data inputs (Ploumis, 2022).

Moreover, the reliance on AI in warfare can disrupt the already fragile healthcare systems in conflict zones. AI's role in military targeting may inadvertently harm civilian health infrastructure, depriving affected populations of vital medical care (Melnychenko, 2024). The destruction of hospitals, clinics, and supply chains, coupled with the displacement of healthcare workers, exacerbates the humanitarian crisis in conflict zones. In these environments, AI systems could inadvertently target facilities that are supposed to be protected under international law, including those providing essential health services to civilians. These occurrences illustrate the risks associated with AI's deployment in warfare, where the line between military and civilian domains becomes increasingly blurred (Sticher, 2025b).

One of the significant concerns in the literature is the potential for AI systems to perpetuate or exacerbate existing biases, especially in military and healthcare contexts. AI algorithms are only as good as the data on which they are trained, and biased data can lead to biased outcomes. In warfare, this can manifest as discriminatory targeting, where AI systems disproportionately target certain populations based on flawed data inputs, such as racial, ethnic, or geographic biases (Hoffman & D'Amelio, 2024). In the healthcare sector, biased AI algorithms may lead to disparities in treatment, diagnosis, and resource allocation, particularly in conflict zones where healthcare resources are already scarce. Scholars have argued that the risk of algorithmic bias presents a significant challenge to the ethical use of AI in both military and civilian contexts. The need for transparent, accountable, and unbiased AI systems has never been more urgent, particularly as these technologies begin to play an increasingly prominent role in both warfare and healthcare delivery in conflict zones (Jester, 2025).

In the realm of healthcare, AI technologies have the potential to revolutionize patient care, particularly in resource-limited environments. However, the ethical concerns surrounding AI in healthcare are not merely technical but also deeply rooted in issues of trust, privacy, and access (Gellert et al., 2025). AI's potential to provide diagnostic assistance, personalized treatment plans, and predictive analytics can significantly enhance healthcare delivery in conflict zones, where the demand for medical care often exceeds supply. However, the introduction of AI into these environments must be carefully managed to ensure that it does not compromise the privacy and dignity of patients. Ethical issues surrounding data security, informed consent, and the potential for AI to be used as a tool for surveillance are critical in the context of conflict zones, where populations may already be vulnerable to exploitation and harm (García-Huete et al., 2024).

A growing body of literature also discusses the necessity of establishing robust ethical frameworks and international regulations to govern the use of AI in warfare and healthcare. Scholars advocate for global treaties and agreements that address the ethical deployment of AI in military operations, with an emphasis on protecting civilian lives and ensuring accountability for AI-driven actions. Similarly, in healthcare, international regulations that govern the use of AI for patient care are needed to safeguard patient rights and ensure that AI technologies do not undermine the sanctity of medical care. The establishment of ethical guidelines and standards is essential to mitigate the risks posed by AI technologies and ensure their responsible use in both warfare and healthcare contexts (Fauzi et al., 2024).

In conclusion, the literature surrounding AI-driven warfare and its impact on civilian health and medical neutrality reveals a complex and multifaceted ethical landscape. The introduction of AI technologies into warfare and healthcare settings raises critical questions regarding accountability, transparency, bias, and the protection of human rights. While AI holds immense potential for improving both military and healthcare operations, it also presents significant ethical challenges that must be addressed through comprehensive frameworks, international regulations, and rigorous oversight (Huelss, 2024). The ethical dilemmas posed by AI in warfare and healthcare are not merely theoretical but have real-world consequences for the lives of civilians caught in the crossfire of conflict. As AI continues to evolve and play an increasingly prominent role in these domains, it is imperative that the ethical implications of its use are carefully considered and actively addressed.

Through a content analysis of case studies, including the Kosovo War, Iraq invasion, Gaza conflict, and other regional conflicts, the study explores how AI technologies have led to disproportionate civilian casualties, ethical dilemmas in warfare, and breaches of medical neutrality. The review also draws from humanitarian reports and analyses from global organizations like the World Health Organization (WHO) and the United Nations (UN) to assess the effectiveness of current international frameworks in regulating the use of AI in military conflicts.

Furthermore, a comparative case study overview evaluates the geopolitical implications of AI in warfare. This includes examining how AI's role in warfare affects the balance of power, the arms race, and international security, as well as how states' differing access to AI technologies influences diplomatic negotiations and conflict resolution strategies. This comparison looks at the political fallout from AI-driven warfare, particularly in terms of international relations and the challenges of enforcing global governance over such technologies.

Table 1. AI-Driven Targeting & Civilian Casualties

Region / System	Civilians Killed	Civilians Injured	Notes
Gaza (AI "Lavender/Gospel")	~40,732 killed	~92,609 injured	~360,000 buildings destroyed
7 Oct 2023–Apr 2024 Gaza Strip	~48,000 killed (health min.)	15,096 injured	WHO figures
April–Oct 2024 estimate	Likely > 70,000	–	Lancet extrapolation

Table 1 presents data on the impact of AI-driven military targeting in Gaza over different time periods. It highlights the significant civilian casualties, injuries, and destruction of infrastructure caused by AI systems during armed conflicts in the region. This data paints a grim picture of the consequences of AI's involvement in modern warfare, specifically in densely populated areas where civilian life is at high risk.

The first entry in the table refers to the AI systems, "Lavender/Gospel," used in Gaza, which resulted in approximately 40,732 civilian deaths and around 92,609 injuries. The widespread destruction of infrastructure is particularly alarming, with an estimated 360,000 buildings being destroyed. This illustrates the devastating effect of AI-driven warfare on civilian populations, as the AI systems in question likely lacked sufficient safeguards or ethical protocols to distinguish between military targets and civilian areas. The sheer scale of destruction demonstrates how AI, if not carefully controlled, can escalate the human toll of warfare, particularly when deployed in environments where civilians and military targets are intermingled.

The second entry covers the period from October 2023 to April 2024, showing a continuation of the devastating impact on civilian life. According to health ministry data, approximately 48,000 civilians were killed, while over 15,000 others were injured during this period. These figures are corroborated by the World Health Organization (WHO), underlining the reliability of the estimates. The scale of human suffering and loss in this period reflects the broader trend of AI-driven military operations resulting in disproportionate harm to non-combatants. The discrepancy between the numbers of killed and injured further reveals the sheer intensity of the violence and the inability of current AI systems to minimize harm, despite the claims of precision.

The third entry, which provides an estimate for the period from April to October 2024, suggests that the death toll could surpass 70,000 civilians, based on extrapolation from the Lancet. This estimate is indicative of a continuing escalation in casualties and reinforces concerns about the long-term consequences of relying on AI in conflict zones. If the trend continues, the cumulative impact on civilian populations could be catastrophic, with AI systems potentially becoming more destructive as they are refined and further integrated into military strategies.

Overall, the table underscores the profound ethical issues surrounding the use of AI in warfare. The significant number of civilian casualties and injuries, combined with the destruction of infrastructure, highlights the inability of current AI systems to adhere to international humanitarian laws that protect non-combatants. The lack of human oversight, the potential for misidentification, and the disregard for medical neutrality in conflict zones are critical factors contributing to the high civilian toll. Additionally, the estimates provided in the table, especially the projections for 2024, underscore the need for urgent international attention and the development of ethical guidelines and regulations governing the use of AI in warfare. Without such oversight, the deployment of AI in conflict zones risks perpetuating or even exacerbating the human cost of warfare, undermining efforts to protect civilian life, infrastructure, and medical neutrality.

Table 2. Attacks on Healthcare During Conflict

Conflict Zone	Attacks on Healthcare	Health Workers Killed	Workers Injured	Ambulances Hit
Global conflicts (2024)	3,623 incidents (+15%)	927	—	—
Ukraine (to Apr 2024)	1,682 attacks	128 fatalities	288 injuries	—
Gaza & West Bank (to Apr 2024)	906 attacks	—	—	—
Gaza/West Bank to Nov 2023	—	29 killed, 24 injured (first week)	—	—
Lebanon (Oct '23–Nov '24)	137 attacks	226 killed, 199 injured	—	

The data presented in Table 2 offers a disturbing snapshot of the ongoing violence and the direct targeting of healthcare systems and workers during armed conflicts across different regions. The table highlights the number of attacks on healthcare facilities, fatalities and injuries among health workers, and incidents involving ambulances in various global conflict zones in 2024. This data emphasizes the grave implications for civilian health and the functioning of healthcare systems during wartime, underscoring the ethical challenges associated with military operations in conflict areas.

The first row of the table shows the global picture of attacks on healthcare in 2024, with 3,623 incidents recorded, reflecting a 15% increase in such attacks compared to previous years. These incidents involved 927 health workers being killed, with no further details on the number of injuries or attacks on ambulances. The rising frequency of attacks on healthcare facilities points to the growing risks faced by medical professionals and civilians alike in conflict zones. The absence of detailed figures on injuries and ambulances further highlights the scale of the violence targeting the very institutions that are supposed to provide relief during times of war.

Focusing on Ukraine, the data for the period up to April 2024 reports 1,682 attacks on healthcare facilities, resulting in 128 health worker fatalities and 288 injuries. This stark figure underscores the significant toll that the ongoing conflict in Ukraine has had on medical personnel. These attacks have severely hampered the ability of healthcare workers to provide essential care, exacerbating the humanitarian crisis. The absence of data on ambulance hits further complicates the situation, suggesting that medical transport may also be increasingly vulnerable to attack, preventing timely medical intervention and exacerbating the suffering of wounded civilians.

In Gaza and the West Bank, 906 attacks on healthcare were reported up to April 2024, though there is no data provided for health workers killed or injured, or for ambulances targeted. These attacks on healthcare infrastructure in Gaza and the West Bank contribute to an already dire humanitarian situation. The lack of data for fatalities or injuries of healthcare workers in this case suggests the difficulty in tracking such incidents amid the chaos and the destruction in these regions. It also reflects the challenges in reporting accurate figures when healthcare systems are overwhelmed, and medical professionals are operating under constant threat.

The data from Gaza and the West Bank for the first week of November 2023 reveals 29 health workers killed and 24 injured, but again, no information is provided regarding attacks on ambulances. This specific snapshot indicates the immediate risks faced by healthcare professionals in the early stages of conflict. The loss of such a significant number of health workers within the first week underscores the extreme dangers they face when providing care in conflict zones. It is clear that the ability to deliver medical care is severely compromised when healthcare workers are directly targeted, and when medical facilities are destroyed or rendered inoperative.

Lastly, in Lebanon, during the period between October 2023 and November 2024, 137 attacks on healthcare facilities were reported, resulting in 226 health workers killed and 199 injured. While this row provides a more complete picture of the scale of violence, it again fails to include information on ambulance attacks. The high number of fatalities and injuries in Lebanon indicates the extent to which healthcare workers are becoming victims of conflict, further hindering medical efforts and worsening the public health crisis. The sheer number of deaths and injuries among medical staff emphasizes the devastating consequences of conflict for those who are striving to alleviate suffering and provide essential services.

In conclusion, Table 2 reveals the widespread and escalating nature of attacks on healthcare facilities and workers during global conflicts, as well as the growing risk to healthcare infrastructure in conflict zones. These attacks not only directly harm medical personnel but also undermine the overall healthcare system, creating long-term consequences for public health in affected regions. The absence of specific data on ambulances and injuries in some instances further highlights the complexity and scale of this issue, suggesting that the full extent of damage is difficult to quantify in real-time. The trends indicated by this table point to the urgent need for international intervention to protect healthcare workers and ensure that medical neutrality is upheld in conflict zones.

Table 3. AI Accuracy & Misidentification

AI System / Conflict	Estimated Error Rate	Human Oversight	Civilian Impact
"Lavender" in Gaza	~10% misidentification	Minimal (~20 sec)	Civilian deaths from false targeting
AI-guided strikes ratio setting	Up to 30 civilians per low-rank militant	—	High civil damage

Table 3 presents critical insights into the performance and consequences of AI-driven targeting systems in warfare, highlighting the significant errors and civilian impacts associated with AI-guided military operations. This data underscores the risks of misidentification, the role of human oversight, and the resulting harm to civilian populations in conflict zones.

The first row of the table addresses the use of the "Lavender" AI system in Gaza, which has an estimated error rate of approximately 10% in misidentifying targets. This error rate is not insignificant, as it translates into a substantial number of incorrect targeting decisions, with potential deadly consequences for civilians. The system is noted to have minimal human oversight, with an intervention time of only about 20 seconds. This brief window of human oversight raises serious concerns about the ability of military personnel to adequately correct or intervene in targeting decisions before irreversible harm is done. Such minimal oversight increases the likelihood that errors in AI judgment will go unchecked, leading to civilian casualties. In this case, the primary civilian impact is the tragic loss of life due to false targeting, where civilians are killed because the AI system erroneously identifies them as combatants or military targets. This scenario illustrates a major ethical issue in the use of AI in warfare: the inability of AI systems to always distinguish between combatants and non-combatants, particularly in complex urban environments where military and civilian spaces are often intermingled.

The second entry in the table describes AI-guided strike ratio settings, where the error rate could result in up to 30 civilian deaths for every low-ranking militant targeted. This figure points to the significant civilian harm caused by AI-driven targeting systems, where the use of algorithms designed to prioritize military targets often leads to disproportionately high civilian casualties. The absence of detailed human oversight in this context amplifies the potential for collateral damage, as these systems may lack the capacity to assess the broader context of a given strike, such as the presence of nearby civilians or the surrounding environment. The civilian impact here is categorized as "high civil damage," underscoring the extensive harm caused by such misidentifications. In such instances, AI systems can cause widespread destruction, further compounding the human toll of conflict by failing to adequately discriminate between military and civilian targets.

Together, the data from Table 3 illustrates the inherent risks and ethical dilemmas posed by the increasing reliance on AI in military operations. The errors in targeting, compounded by limited human oversight, contribute to civilian deaths and destruction, raising fundamental questions about the accountability of military forces using these technologies. The minimal human intervention allowed in the "Lavender" system and the unquantified risk of civilian casualties in AI-guided strikes suggest that the deployment of AI in warfare requires more stringent oversight mechanisms to ensure that its use adheres to international humanitarian law and ethical principles. The data calls for a reevaluation of the safeguards surrounding AI-driven targeting systems, advocating for more robust human involvement and more refined error-detection algorithms to prevent unnecessary civilian harm. This highlights the pressing need for ethical frameworks that balance the efficiency and precision of AI with the imperative to protect civilian lives in conflict zones.

Table 4. Drone Attacks on Health Facilities

Conflict	Context / Weapon	Health Facility Impact
Sudan, Jan 2025	Drone strike on hospital	~70 killed, 19–100 injured
Gaza & West Bank, July 2024	Explosive/drones	464 facilities hit; 727 workers killed; 933 injured; 113 ambulances lost
Lebanon conflict (Oct '23–Nov '24)	Airstrikes on hospitals	~50% attacks fatal; multi casualties

Table 4 highlights the devastating impact of drone strikes and airstrikes on healthcare infrastructure and personnel in conflict zones. The table presents data from several regions, including Sudan, Gaza & the West Bank, and Lebanon, illustrating the immense toll these attacks have on health facilities, workers, and patients. The findings underscore the vulnerability of healthcare systems during armed conflicts and the ethical implications of targeting medical facilities in violation of international humanitarian law.

The first row of the table reports a drone strike on a hospital in Sudan in January 2025. This attack resulted in approximately 70 deaths and between 19 and 100 injuries, reflecting the severe consequences of using drones to target healthcare infrastructure. The specific targeting of hospitals raises significant ethical concerns, as medical facilities are supposed to be protected under international law, particularly the Geneva Conventions, which guarantee the sanctity of medical care during armed conflict. The number of casualties from this single strike demonstrates the devastating power of drones, which, despite their precision, still result in significant harm to civilians and healthcare workers when misdirected or used irresponsibly.

The second entry in the table focuses on the Gaza and West Bank regions in July 2024, where explosive drones were used in attacks on healthcare facilities. In this instance, 464 health facilities were hit, resulting in the deaths of 727 healthcare workers and injuring 933 others. Additionally, 113 ambulances were lost. This data paints a grim picture of the scale of destruction in Gaza and the West Bank, where healthcare infrastructure was deliberately targeted during the conflict. The numbers highlight the systematic nature of these attacks, leading to severe disruptions in the ability of medical personnel to provide care to those in need. The targeting of ambulances, which are critical for transporting the injured, further exacerbates the crisis, depriving civilians of essential healthcare services. The extent of the destruction underscores the profound consequences of using drones in warfare, particularly in urban settings where military and civilian structures are often interwoven.

The third entry in the table discusses the Lebanon conflict from October 2023 to November 2024, where airstrikes targeted hospitals, with approximately 50% of these attacks resulting in fatalities and multiple casualties. The high fatality rate of these attacks further emphasizes the lethal nature of airstrikes and drone operations in conflict zones. The targeting of hospitals, which are often operating at full capacity during conflict, leads to catastrophic consequences for both healthcare workers and the civilian population. The multiple casualties reported in this entry highlight the challenges healthcare providers face when they are themselves at risk of becoming targets.

In summary, Table 4 underscores the alarming frequency and severity of drone attacks on healthcare facilities in conflict zones. These attacks not only result in the direct loss of life but also cripple healthcare systems, depriving vulnerable populations of essential care. The targeting of health workers, ambulances, and hospitals violates the principle of medical neutrality, further compounding the humanitarian crises in these regions. The data presented calls for a reevaluation of the use of drones in warfare, advocating for stronger international protections for healthcare facilities and personnel to ensure that medical care remains impartial and accessible even in times of conflict.

Table 5. Global Civilian vs Combatant Casualty Ratios

Conflict / War	Combatant Deaths	Civilian Deaths	Civilian %
Kosovo War (1998–99)	2,500–5,000	~13,548	73–84%
Iraq 2003 invasion	~6,000	~4,000	~40%
Russo-Georgian War (2008)	~350	~400	~53%
Donbass conflict	~10,000	~3,300	~25%
ISIL intervention (Iraq/Syria)	~140,000	~54,000	~28%

Table 5 presents a comparative analysis of civilian and combatant deaths during various conflicts around the world. The table reveals the disproportionate toll on civilians in these wars and provides insight into the severity of collateral damage in modern warfare. The data highlights the stark contrast between military casualties and civilian deaths, emphasizing the ethical and humanitarian concerns surrounding contemporary conflict dynamics.

The first row of the table focuses on the Kosovo War, which took place between 1998 and 1999. In this conflict, the total number of combatant deaths ranged from 2,500 to 5,000, while civilian deaths were estimated to be around 13,548, accounting for 73% to 84% of the total casualties. This strikingly high percentage of civilian deaths demonstrates the devastating impact of the war on the civilian population. The Kosovo War, which involved NATO-led airstrikes, is a prime example of how modern warfare, particularly air campaigns, can result in a disproportionate number of civilian casualties. The civilian deaths in this conflict were largely attributed to indiscriminate bombing and the breakdown of law and order, which left civilians vulnerable to violence. The high percentage of civilian casualties relative to combatant deaths raises important ethical questions about the conduct of war, particularly with regard to the principles of proportionality and distinction, which are central to international humanitarian law.

The second entry in the table concerns the Iraq 2003 invasion, which led to approximately 6,000 combatant deaths and around 4,000 civilian deaths, with civilians making up roughly 40% of the total fatalities. The invasion, led by the United States and its allies, was marked by a combination of airstrikes, ground operations, and urban warfare. The relatively lower percentage of civilian casualties in this conflict, compared to the Kosovo War, may reflect the different nature of the warfare tactics employed, including the use of precision-guided munitions and a focus on minimizing collateral damage. However, even with these technological advancements, the Iraq invasion still resulted in significant harm to the civilian population. The 40% civilian death toll underscores the difficulty of protecting non-combatants in urban warfare, where military operations often take place in close proximity to civilian populations.

In the Russo-Georgian War of 2008, which lasted for a brief five days, the civilian death toll was relatively high, with 400 civilian deaths compared to 350 combatant deaths. This meant that civilians accounted for 53% of the total fatalities. The conflict, which involved Russian military intervention in Georgia, was marked by heavy artillery bombardments and airstrikes that targeted both military and civilian infrastructure. The high proportion of civilian deaths in this war reflects the indiscriminate nature of the fighting, particularly in the areas where civilians lived. The Russo-Georgian War serves as a reminder that even short, intense conflicts can result in significant civilian casualties, especially when military tactics fail to adequately distinguish between combatant and non-combatant targets.

The Donbass conflict in Ukraine, which has been ongoing since 2014, saw approximately 10,000 combatant deaths and 3,300 civilian deaths, with civilians making up 25% of the total casualties. The Donbass conflict is marked by a combination of conventional military engagements and hybrid warfare tactics, including the use of artillery, missiles, and drones. The relatively lower percentage of civilian deaths compared to the previous conflicts can be attributed to the nature of the conflict, which involved more front-line military engagements and less widespread targeting of civilian infrastructure. However, the ongoing violence, displacement of civilians, and destruction of infrastructure continue to take a heavy toll on the population, even if the overall casualty ratio is lower.

The final entry in the table discusses the ISIL intervention in Iraq and Syria, where the combatant death toll reached approximately 140,000, while civilian deaths were around 54,000, representing 28% of the total fatalities. The ISIL intervention, which spanned several years, was characterized by widespread violence, including bombings, massacres, and the targeting of civilian populations by extremist groups. The relatively low percentage of civilian casualties in this conflict can be attributed to the large-scale military operations against ISIL fighters, which were primarily aimed at combatants rather than civilians. However, the absolute number of civilian deaths remains alarming, reflecting the brutal nature of the conflict and the extensive damage inflicted on civilian populations caught in the crossfire between opposing forces.

In summary, Table 5 presents a sobering look at the civilian toll during various conflicts, demonstrating that civilians often bear the brunt of modern warfare. While military casualties are often the focus of traditional war reporting, the civilian death toll is frequently disproportionate, as seen in the Kosovo War and the Russo-Georgian War, where civilians accounted for the majority of the fatalities. Even in conflicts where efforts were made to minimize collateral damage, such as in the Iraq 2003 invasion, civilian deaths remain a significant concern. The data emphasizes the ethical dilemmas of warfare, particularly regarding the protection of non-combatants and the challenges of adhering to international humanitarian law. The civilian casualty rates in these conflicts underscore the urgent need for international efforts to strengthen the protection of civilians in conflict zones, ensure accountability for violations of humanitarian law, and promote strategies that minimize harm to non-combatants.

POLITICAL IMPLICATIONS

The intersection of artificial intelligence (AI) with warfare, healthcare, and civilian protection presents a complex web of political implications, which must be viewed through both a technological and humanitarian lens. As AI continues to redefine military tactics, the political ramifications are profound, impacting both the strategic calculus of state actors and the international governance mechanisms intended to safeguard human rights and preserve the sanctity of medical neutrality. The increasing reliance on AI-driven autonomous weapons systems (AWS) has created a new paradigm in military conflict, where ethical considerations must now be juxtaposed with the evolving capabilities of technology. At the heart of this transformation lies the question of accountability: who bears responsibility when an AI system makes a lethal decision? The legal, moral, and geopolitical dimensions of this dilemma are far-reaching, suggesting that contemporary warfare, with its increasing automation, may fundamentally alter international relations and the structure of global governance.

The first political implication arises from the evolving nature of warfare itself, driven by AI technologies. As evidenced in conflicts like the Kosovo War, Iraq, and Gaza, the use of AI in military operations has exacerbated the scale of civilian casualties, particularly as autonomous systems fail to distinguish between combatants and non-combatants. The political consequences of such failures are profound, as governments and international organizations are increasingly confronted with the moral and legal ramifications of AI-driven warfare. In the case of AI systems like "Lavender" in Gaza, where a 10% misidentification rate leads to civilian deaths, the political fallout is not limited to the direct humanitarian crisis but extends to the legitimacy of state actions in conflict. Nations deploying these technologies must navigate the delicate balance between military necessity and international law, particularly the Geneva Conventions, which call for the protection of civilians. The legal ambiguity surrounding the use of AI in warfare threatens to erode the trust between states and their citizens, as well as between states and international bodies tasked with regulating armed conflict. The political consequences of misidentified targets and civilian casualties thus cannot be understated, as they influence diplomatic relations, humanitarian interventions, and international conflict resolution strategies.

Furthermore, the development and deployment of AI in military operations introduce an entirely new set of power dynamics into international relations. States that develop and control AI technologies gain a strategic advantage on the battlefield, which may inadvertently lead to an arms race in AI-driven warfare. This technological asymmetry can exacerbate existing geopolitical tensions, as nations scramble to either acquire or counteract AI technologies in military systems. For example, in regions like the Middle East and Eastern Europe, where geopolitical fault lines have already been drawn, the use of AI in warfare could increase the volatility of conflicts by enabling state and non-state actors to execute more precise, yet devastating, attacks. The power to deploy AI-driven autonomous weapons systems, which can operate with minimal human oversight, could tilt the balance of power, leading to new forms of warfare where traditional military strength is no longer the sole determinant of success. As AI becomes an integral part of military strategy, it further complicates diplomatic efforts to prevent conflict and preserve peace, as nations may perceive an imbalance in technological capabilities as a threat to their national security.

The political implications extend beyond the battlefield, particularly in the realm of humanitarian law and medical neutrality. The ongoing attacks on healthcare facilities and workers in conflict zones, as shown in Table 4, illustrate the devastating consequences of warfare on civilian infrastructure. AI-driven targeting systems have shown an alarming tendency to misidentify civilian targets, as evidenced in the drone attacks on hospitals and ambulances in Gaza and Sudan. The systematic nature of these attacks raises critical questions about the ability of international institutions to uphold medical neutrality in conflict zones. If AI technologies are increasingly used to target health facilities, then the principle of medical neutrality—which mandates the protection of medical infrastructure and personnel—becomes increasingly difficult to enforce. The political ramifications of this are profound, as international bodies such as the World Health Organization (WHO) and the United Nations (UN) are left struggling to hold states accountable for violations of international law. In the absence of strict regulations governing the use of AI in warfare, medical facilities, and humanitarian organizations face an existential threat, leading to calls for a new framework of international governance that specifically addresses the intersection of AI, warfare, and humanitarian protection.

The civilian casualty rates documented in Table 5 further highlight the political fallout from the use of AI in modern warfare. The disproportionate number of civilian deaths in conflicts such as the Kosovo War, Iraq, and the Russo-Georgian War underscores the failure of military operations to safeguard non-combatants, particularly in urban warfare settings. The high civilian death tolls in these conflicts, which can reach upwards of 70% in some instances, serve as a stark reminder that the current rules of engagement are inadequate in preventing mass casualties. The political implications are far-reaching: governments involved in these conflicts are increasingly facing scrutiny from international human rights organizations and the global public, who demand greater accountability for the protection of civilians. The use of AI in warfare exacerbates this issue, as the increasing reliance on autonomous decision-making systems without sufficient human oversight contributes to misidentification and civilian deaths. As the political pressure mounts, states may be forced to reevaluate the ethical and legal frameworks that govern the use of AI in military operations, potentially leading to the development of new international treaties or norms aimed at regulating the deployment of such technologies.

The final political consequence concerns the broader implications for global governance in the face of AI-driven warfare. As AI technologies continue to evolve, existing international laws and institutions are struggling to keep pace with the rapid advancements in military technology. The United Nations, in particular, has been slow to establish clear frameworks for regulating AI in warfare, and as a result, the responsibility for the ethical use of AI falls to individual nations and military organizations. This lack of a cohesive international regulatory framework opens the door for an increased reliance on AI in military operations, raising the stakes for the future of global security. The growing gap between technological capabilities and international regulations has the potential to destabilize the current international order, as states with superior AI technologies may be able to act with impunity in conflict zones, while others may be unable to counter these capabilities. This technological divide could lead to new forms of geopolitical competition, where AI technologies become central to the balance of power and influence in global politics.

The political implications of AI in warfare are both profound and far-reaching. From the ethical and legal challenges posed by AI-driven targeting systems to the growing concerns over medical neutrality and civilian protection, the deployment of AI technologies in conflict zones has the potential to reshape the future of warfare and international relations. As AI continues to redefine the landscape of military conflict, global governance structures must evolve to address these new challenges, ensuring that the use of such technologies aligns with international humanitarian law and ethical principles. The political dynamics surrounding AI in warfare will play a critical role in determining the future of global peace, security, and diplomacy in the 21st century.

In conclusion, the integration of artificial intelligence (AI) into warfare and its impact on global political, ethical, and humanitarian landscapes raises a host of critical concerns that extend far beyond technological advancements. The data and insights presented throughout the discussion, including the use of AI in military targeting, attacks on healthcare facilities, civilian and combatant casualty ratios, and the resulting political and humanitarian ramifications, underscore the profound implications of AI's role in modern conflicts. AI-driven warfare, exemplified by systems like "Lavender" in Gaza, autonomous weapon systems, and drone strikes, has fundamentally transformed the nature of warfare, making it more precise but also exponentially more dangerous for non-combatants. The use of such technologies, while promising military efficiency and strategic superiority, raises urgent ethical questions about accountability, the protection of civilians, and the sanctity of medical neutrality.

The stark statistics on civilian casualties, as seen in conflicts like the Kosovo War, Iraq invasion, Gaza conflict, and others, illustrate the disproportionate impact on non-combatants, who often bear the brunt of AI-driven warfare. With systems misidentifying targets at alarming rates, the political consequences are severe. Misidentification can lead to unnecessary deaths, undermining international trust, and escalating global tensions. The ethical challenge lies in the inability of AI systems to fully replicate the nuances of human decision-making, particularly in complex combat situations where military and civilian spaces overlap. The data points to the need for more stringent human oversight and robust international frameworks to ensure that these technologies adhere to international humanitarian laws and principles such as the protection of civilian life and medical infrastructure.

The consequences of these AI-driven conflicts extend beyond battlefield casualties, impacting healthcare systems in conflict zones. The targeting of healthcare facilities, workers, and ambulances, as demonstrated in Gaza, Sudan, and Lebanon, undermines medical neutrality, a cornerstone of international law. As AI technologies continue to evolve, the targeting of health infrastructure becomes a more frequent occurrence, leaving vulnerable populations without access to life-saving medical care. This direct assault on healthcare deepens the humanitarian crisis in conflict zones, placing additional strain on international bodies tasked with delivering aid and ensuring compliance with international law. The increasing vulnerability of healthcare systems due to AI-driven warfare emphasizes the urgency for international legal frameworks that specifically address the protection of healthcare in conflict zones.

The political implications are further compounded by the geopolitical ramifications of AI in warfare. The development and deployment of AI technologies in military systems have created a new arms race, where technological superiority determines strategic advantage. This technological asymmetry threatens to destabilize international relations, as states with superior AI capabilities gain unprecedented military power. Nations without access to these technologies are left at a strategic disadvantage, potentially leading to new global tensions and an imbalance of power. Furthermore, the growing reliance on AI in military operations complicates diplomatic efforts to prevent conflicts, as nations may be hesitant to engage in dialogue or negotiate under the shadow of AI-enhanced military strategies. The use of AI also raises questions about the future of warfare itself, where the role of human soldiers may be diminished, and the unpredictability of autonomous systems creates new forms of risk and instability.

The ethical challenges posed by AI-driven warfare, such as accountability for misidentifications and the protection of civilians, also extend to broader issues of global governance. As AI continues to evolve, current international laws and governance structures struggle to keep pace with the rapid development of these technologies. The lack of a cohesive international regulatory framework for AI in warfare leaves room for misuse and the potential for unchecked military actions by states and non-state actors. The absence of clear global guidelines for the ethical deployment of AI in military operations opens the door for greater risks, where unchecked technological advancements could override human rights and international law, leading to a future where warfare becomes more automated and less constrained by moral and legal norms.

Ultimately, the conclusion drawn from the discussion is clear: while AI holds immense potential to revolutionize military operations, its deployment in warfare must be carefully managed to avoid catastrophic humanitarian consequences. The rapid advancement of AI technologies necessitates a coordinated global effort to establish ethical guidelines, enforce international humanitarian law, and ensure that AI systems in warfare are subjected to stringent oversight. Without such measures, the continued integration of AI into warfare may exacerbate the suffering of civilians, destabilize international relations, and undermine global efforts to protect human rights and preserve peace. As AI-driven warfare becomes more prevalent, the international community must rise to the challenge of regulating these technologies to prevent the misuse of AI and mitigate the devastating impact on non-combatants and global stability.

REFERENCES

Black, J. S., & van Esch, P. (2021). AI-enabled recruiting in the war for talent. *Business Horizons*, *64*(4), 513–524. DOI: 10.1016/j.bushor.2021.02.015

Crews, C. (2023). AI, Land Wars in Asia, and the Classic Blunders of Foresight. *Research Technology Management*, *66*(4), 48–50. DOI: 10.1080/08956308.2023.2208487

Emery, J. R. (2021). Algorithms, AI, and Ethics of War. *Peace Review*, *33*(2), 205–212. DOI: 10.1080/10402659.2021.1998749

Erskine, T., & Miller, S. E. (2024). AI and the decision to go to war: Future risks and opportunities. *Australian Journal of International Affairs*, *78*(2), 135–147. DOI: 10.1080/10357718.2024.2349598

Fauzi, M., Jhoni, M., Mohammad, M., Mabruroh, F., & Oviyanti, F. (2024). Implementing the Power of Blended Learning in the Era of AI War in Indonesia; [Implementación del poder del Blended Learning en la era de la guerra de la IA en Indonesia]. *Pixel-Bit. Revista de Medios y Educacion*, *70*, 77–95. DOI: 10.12795/pixelbit.103035

Garcia, D. (2021). Stop the emerging AI cold war. *Nature*, *593*(7858), 169. DOI: 10.1038/d41586-021-01244-z

García-Huete, E., Ignacio-Cerrato, S., Pacios, D., Vázquez-Poletti, J. L., Pérez-Serrano, M. J., Donofrio, A., Cesarano, C., Schetakis, N., & Di Iorio, A. (2024). Evaluating the role of generative AI and color patterns in the dissemination of war imagery and disinformation on social media. *Frontiers in Artificial Intelligence*, *7*, 1457247. Advance online publication. DOI: 10.3389/frai.2024.1457247

Gellert, G. A., Kuszczyński, K., Gellert, G. L., Kabat-Karabon, A., Nowicka, A., & Price, T. (2025). AI-Based Virtual Triage and Telemedical Health Care for Ukrainian War Refugees and Displaced Persons. *JAMA Network Open*, *8*(5), e258839. Advance online publication. DOI: 10.1001/jamanetworkopen.2025.8839

Giannotti, A., & Proietti, G. (2021). Law of Thasos concerning honors for the war dead and their families [Legge di taso sugli onori ai caduti in guerra e alle loro famiglie]. *Axon (Italy)*, *5*(1), 123–154. DOI: 10.30687/Axon/2532-6848/2021/01/005

Hoffman, F., & D'Amelio, A. (2024). AI's impact on war's enduring nature. *Orbis*, *68*(1), 72–91. DOI: 10.1016/j.orbis.2023.11.006

Huelss, H. (2024). Transcending the fog of war? US military "AI", vision, and the emergent post-scopic regime. *European Journal of International Security*. DOI: 10.1017/eis.2024.21

Hunter, C., & Bowen, B. E. (2024). We'll never have a model of an AI major-general: Artificial Intelligence, command decisions, and kitsch visions of war. *The Journal of Strategic Studies*, *47*(1), 116–146. DOI: 10.1080/01402390.2023.2241648

Iveković, R. (2018). Enough with Europe's war against migrants [Smetterla con la guerra dell'Europa ai migranti]. *Lectora*, *24*, 13–26. DOI: 10.1344/Lectora2018.24.2

Jester, N. (2025). Encountering Virtual Veterans: AI chatbots, martial ontologies, and memories of war. *Critical Military Studies*, *11*(1), 104–108. DOI: 10.1080/23337486.2024.2417622

Lhote, F. (2015). The war of Algeria today, between "commemorative period" and fiction: Where I Left My Soul (2010) by Jerome Ferrari [Laguerre d'algérie aujourd'hui, entre 'temps commémoratif' et fiction: où j'ai laissé mon âme (2010) de jérôme ferrari]. *French Studies Bulletin*, *36*(137), 83–86. DOI: 10.1093/frebul/ktv022

Melnychenko, O. (2024). Utilising AI Models to Analyse the Relationship between Battlefield Developments in the Russian-Ukrainian War and Fluctuations in Stock Market Values. *Forum Scientiae Oeconomia*, *12*(4), 83–98. DOI: 10.23762/FSO_VOL12_NO4_5

Milewski, D. (2018). Military contacts of the polish-lithuanian commonwealth and the duchy of prussia in the first years of the livonian war (1600-1602) [Contacts militaires de l'union polonaise-lituanienne et du duché de prusse pendant les premières années de la guerre de livonie (1600-1602).]; [Contactele militare ale uniunii statale polono-lituaniene cu ducatul prusiei în primii ani ai războiului livonian (1600-1602)]. *Codrul Cosminului*, *24*(2), 323–340.

Mitgutsch, I. (2021). The war crime of attacking buildings dedicated to religion in light of the trial of Ahmad Al Faqi Al Mahdi [Das Kriegsverbrechen des Angriffs auf der Religion gewidmete Gebäude im Lichte des Verfahrens gegen Ahmad AI Faqi AI Mahdi]. *Osterreichisches Archiv Fur Recht Und Religion*, *68*(1), 15–32.

Nocera, R. (2018). Italy, Latin America, Chile: From the second world war to the early cold war [Italia, America latina, Cile: Dalla Seconda guerra Mondiale ai primi anni della guerra Fredda]. *Acta Histriae*, *26*(3), 673–690. DOI: 10.19233/AH.2018.27

Pezzino, P. (2017). Resistance, civil resistance, war to civilians, divided memories: Notes in the margin of Mario Mirri's essay [Resistenza, resistenza civile, guerra ai civili, memorie divise: Note in margine al saggio di Mario Mirri]. *Societa e Storia, 2017*(158), 693–704. DOI: 10.3280/SS2017-158007

Ploumis, M. (2022). AI weapon systems in future war operations; strategy, operations and tactics. *Comparative Strategy, 41*(1), 1–18. DOI: 10.1080/01495933.2021.2017739

Regan, M., & Davidovic, J. (2023). Just preparation for war and AI-enabled weapons. *Frontiers in Big Data, 6*, 1020107. Advance online publication. DOI: 10.3389/fdata.2023.1020107

Rudolph, J., Tan, S., & Tan, S. (2023). War of the chatbots: Bard, Bing Chat, ChatGPT, Ernie and beyond. The new AI gold rush and its impact on higher education. *Journal of Applied Learning and Teaching, 6*(1), 364–389. DOI: 10.37074/jalt.2023.6.1.23

Stan, A. (2020). Genres of realism across the former cold war divide. Neoliberal novels and self-fiction [genuri ale realismului la cei doi fo ti poli ai războiului rece. Romanul neoliberal i autofic iunea]. *Dacoromania Litteraria, 7*, 116–125. DOI: 10.33993/drl.2020.7.116.125

Sticher, V. (2025a). War and peace in the age of AI. *British Journal of Politics and International Relations, 27*(2), 542–550. DOI: 10.1177/13691481241293066

Sticher, V. (2025b). War and peace in the age of AI. *British Journal of Politics and International Relations, 27*(2), 542–550. DOI: 10.1177/13691481241293066

Vykhodets, R. S. (2022). Large AI Spaces and Russia's Strategy in the Context of the "Sanctions War." *Vestnik RUDN. International Relations, 22*(2), 256–270. DOI: 10.22363/2313-0660-2022-22-2-256-270

Wallace, R. (2020). Cognitive instabilities under contention, friction, and the fog-of-war challenge the AI revolution. *Connection Science, 32*(3), 264–279. DOI: 10.1080/09540091.2019.1684441

Compilation of References

Adewopo, V. (2021). *Exploring open source intelligence for cyber threat prediction*. University of Cincinnati.

Aggarwal, C. C. (2018). *Neural networks and deep learning*. Springer. DOI: 10.1007/978-3-319-94463-0

Agrawal, N., & Saxena, A. (2024). Artificial intelligence (AI) equipped edge internet of things (IoT) devices in security. In *Advanced IoT Technologies and Applications in the Industry 4.0 Digital Economy* (pp. 296–308). CRC Press. DOI: 10.1201/9781003434269-16

Ahern, D. (2025). The new anticipatory governance culture for innovation: Regulatory foresight, regulatory experimentation and regulatory learning. *European Business Organization Law Review*, *26*(2), 241–283. DOI: 10.1007/s40804-025-00348-7

Ahmed, U., Nazir, M., Sarwar, A., Ali, T., Aggoune, E.-H. M., Shahzad, T., & Khan, M. A. (2025). Signature-based intrusion detection using machine learning and deep learning approaches empowered with fuzzy clustering. *Scientific Reports*, *15*(1), 1726. DOI: 10.1038/s41598-025-85866-7

Aithal, P. S. (2023). Super-Intelligent Machines-analysis of developmental challenges and predicted negative consequences. *International Journal of Applied Engineering and Management Letters*, *7*(3), 109–141. DOI: 10.47992/IJAEML.2581.7000.0191

Al Kurdi, B., Alquqa, E. K., Nuseir, M. T., Alzoubi, H. M., Alshurideh, M. T., & AlHamad, A. (2024). Impact of cyber security and risk management on green operations: Empirical evidence from security companies in the UAE. In *Cyber security impact on digitalization and business intelligence: Big cyber security for information management: Opportunities and challenges* (pp. 151–167). Springer International Publishing. DOI: 10.1007/978-3-031-31801-6_9

Allen, G., & Chan, T. (2017). *Artificial Intelligence and National Security*. Belfer Center for Science and International Affairs, Harvard Kennedy School. https://www.belfercenter.org/publication/artificial-intelligence-and-national-security

Allen, G., & Chan, T. (2017). *Artificial Intelligence and National Security*. Harvard Belfer Center.

Allmer, T. (2012). *Towards a Critical Theory of Surveillance in Informational Capitalism*. Peter Lang Verlag., DOI: 10.3726/978-3-653-01459-4

Alotaibi, A., & Rassam, M. A. (2023). Adversarial machine learning attacks against intrusion detection systems: A survey on strategies and defense. *Future Internet*, *15*(2), 62. DOI: 10.3390/fi15020062

Apolo, Y., & Michael, K. (2024). Beyond a reasonable doubt? Audiovisual evidence, AI manipulation, deepfakes, and the law. *IEEE Transactions on Technology and Society*, *5*(2), 156–168. DOI: 10.1109/TTS.2024.3427816

Arif, A. (2024). An overview of cyber threats generated by AI. *International Journal of Multidisciplinary Sciences and Arts*, *3*(4), 67–76. DOI: 10.47709/ijmdsa.v3i4.4753

Arifin, M. M. (2024). A survey on the application of generative adversarial networks in cybersecurity: prospective, direction and open research scopes. arXiv preprint arXiv:2407.08839.

Aristotle, , & Crisp, R. (2014). *Nicomachean ethics*. Cambridge University Press. DOI: 10.1017/CBO9781139600514

Arunthavanathan, R., Sajid, Z., Khan, F., & Pistikopoulos, E. (2024). Artificial intelligence–Human intelligence conflict and its impact on process system safety. *Digital Chemical Engineering*, *11*, 100151. DOI: 10.1016/j.dche.2024.100151

Bacalu, F. (2021). Digital Policing Tools as Social Control Technologies: Data-driven Predictive Algorithms, Automated Facial Recognition Surveillance, and Law Enforcement Biometrics. *Analysis and Metaphysics*, *20*(0), 74. Advance online publication. DOI: 10.22381/AM2020215

Badada, B., Delina, G., Krishnaraj, R., & Thiruthuvanathan, M. M. (2024, April). Application of XAI in Integrating Democratic and Servant Leadership to Enhance the Performance of Manufacturing Industries in Ethiopia. In *International Conference on Innovations in Computational Intelligence and Computer Vision* (pp. 123-138). Singapore: Springer Nature Singapore. DOI: 10.1007/978-981-97-6995-7_10

Badada, B., Delina, G., Krishnaraj, R., & Thiruthuvanathan, M. M. (2025). Charting the Course of Leadership Through the Digital Era: A Synergy of Leadership Styles, Technology Integration, and Deep Learning. In *Leadership Paradigms and the Impact of Technology* (pp. 119-156). IGI Global Scientific Publishing.

Bala, B., & Behal, S. (2024). AI techniques for IoT-based DDoS attack detection: Taxonomies, comprehensive review and research challenges. *Computer Science Review*, *52*, 100631. DOI: 10.1016/j.cosrev.2024.100631

Baresi, U. (2025). Neo-colonial intelligence: How AI risks reinforcing spatial injustices in a digitally divided world. *Cities (London, England)*, *166*, 106232. DOI: 10.1016/j.cities.2025.106232

Baumgardt, D. (1952). *Bentham and the ethics of today*. Princeton University Press.

Bell, J. (2022). What is machine learning? *Machine learning and the city: applications in architecture and urban design*, 207-216.

Benbouzid, B. (2019). Values and consequences in predictive machine evaluation. A sociology of predictive policing1. *Science & Technology Studies*, *32*(4). Advance online publication. DOI: 10.23987/sts.66156

Bennett, C. J. (2011). In defence of privacy: The concept and the regime. *Surveillance & Society*, *8*(4), 485–496. DOI: 10.24908/ss.v8i4.4184

Bentham, J. (1843). *The Works of Jeremy Bentham* (Vol. 1). William Tait.

Berk, R. A. (2021). Artificial Intelligence, Predictive Policing, and Risk Assessment for Law Enforcement. In *Annual Review of Criminology* (Vol. 4, Issue 1). DOI: 10.1146/annurev-criminol-051520-012342

Bhambri & Bajdor (2024). AI-Powered Predictive Analysis for Proactive Cyber Defense. Handbook of AI-Driven Threat Detection and Prevention. CRC Press.

Binnendijk, H., & Libicki, M. C. (2020). *Cybersecurity and Cyberwar: What Everyone Needs to Know*. Oxford University Press.

Bistron, M., & Piotrowski, Z. (2021). Artificial intelligence applications in military systems and their influence on sense of security of citizens. *Electronics (Basel)*, *10*(7), 871. DOI: 10.3390/electronics10070871

Black, J. S., & van Esch, P. (2021). AI-enabled recruiting in the war for talent. *Business Horizons*, *64*(4), 513–524. DOI: 10.1016/j.bushor.2021.02.015

Blanchard, A., & Taddeo, M. (2024). Autonomous weapon systems and jus ad bellum. *AI & Society*, *39*(2), 705–711. DOI: 10.1007/s00146-022-01425-y

Bonfanti, M. E. (2022). Artificial intelligence and the offence-defence balance in cyber security. In *Cyber Security: Socio-Technological Uncertainty and Political Fragmentation* (pp. 64–79). Routledge. DOI: 10.4324/9781003110224-6

Bonnefon, J. F. (2021). *The car that knew too much: can a machine be moral?* MIT Press.

Boulanin, V., & Verbruggen, M. (2017). *Mapping the development of autonomy in weapon systems*. Stockholm International Peace Research Institute (SIPRI). https://www.sipri.org/sites/default/files/2017-11/siprireport_mapping_the_development_of_autonomy_in_weapon_systems_1117_1.pdf

Boulanin, V., Goussac, N., & Wareham, M. (2020). *Limits on autonomous weapon systems: Identifying practical elements of human control*. Stockholm International Peace Research Institute (SIPRI). https://www.sipri.org

Boyacı, T., Canyakmaz, C., & De Véricourt, F. (2024). Human and machine: The impact of machine input on decision making under cognitive limitations. *Management Science*, *70*(2), 1258–1275. DOI: 10.1287/mnsc.2023.4744

Boyson, S. (2019). AI and the end-to-end supply chain: A new era of digital logistics. *Supply Chain Management Review*, *23*(5), 26–33.

Brambilla, M., Ferrante, E., Birattari, M., & Dorigo, M. (2013). Swarm robotics: A review from the swarm engineering perspective. *Swarm Intelligence*, *7*(1), 1–41. DOI: 10.1007/s11721-012-0075-2

Brooks, C. (2024). *Inside Cyber: How AI, 5G, IoT, and Quantum Computing Will Transform Privacy and Our Security*. John Wiley & Sons. DOI: 10.1002/9781394310562

Brosché, J. (2023). Conflict over the Commons: Government bias and communal conflicts in Darfur and Eastern Sudan. *Ethnopolitics*, *22*(2), 199–221. DOI: 10.1080/17449057.2021.2018221

Brundage, M., et al. (2018). *The Malicious Use of Artificial Intelligence: Forecasting, Prevention, and Mitigation*. Future of Humanity Institute.

Buchanan, B. (2020). *The Hacker and the State: Cyber Attacks and the New Normal of Geopolitics*. Harvard University Press.

Burdette, Z. (2025). *The Risks of Preventive Attack in the Race for Advanced Artificial Intelligence*. Center for Open Science.

Burkhardt, A. (2025). Infrastructural Perspectives on Artificial Intelligence—on the Implications of AI Infrastructures for Global. In *Justice. In Transnational Infrastructures and the Transformation of Global Orders* (pp. 81–96). Springer Nature Switzerland. DOI: 10.1007/978-3-031-74846-2_6

Burns, J. H., Rosen, F., & Schofield, P. (1968). *The Collected works of Jeremy Bentham* (Vol. 4). Oxford University Press.

Caluya, G. (2010). The post-panoptic society? Reassessing Foucault in surveillance studies. *Social Identities*, *16*(5), 621–633. DOI: 10.1080/13504630.2010.509565

Candrian, C., & Scherer, A. (2022). Rise of the machines: Delegating decisions to autonomous AI. *Computers in Human Behavior*, *134*, 107308. DOI: 10.1016/j.chb.2022.107308

Charfeddine, M., Kammoun, H. M., Hamdaoui, B., & Guizani, M. (2024). Chatgpt's security risks and benefits: Offensive and defensive use-cases, mitigation measures, and future implications. *IEEE Access : Practical Innovations, Open Solutions*, *12*, 30263–30310. DOI: 10.1109/ACCESS.2024.3367792

Chen, Y., Du, Z., & Yang, G. (2020). Computer vision-based logistics warehouse monitoring. *Journal of Intelligent Manufacturing*, *31*(2), 285–296. DOI: 10.1007/s10845-019-01468-5

Chien, S., Tran, D., Rabideau, G., & Davies, A. (2020). *Predictive maintenance in military systems using AI: Reducing mission downtime. IEEE Aerospace Conference Proceedings*, 1–12. DOI: 10.1109/AERO47225.2020.9172301

Christie, E. H., Ertan, A., Adomaitis, L., & Klaus, M. (2024). Regulating lethal autonomous weapon systems: Exploring the challenges of explainability and traceability. *AI and Ethics*, *4*(2), 229–245. DOI: 10.1007/s43681-023-00261-0

Cihon, P. (2019). Standards for AI governance: International standards to enable global coordination in AI research & development. *Future of Humanity Institute. University of Oxford*, *40*(3), 340–342.

Ciolacu, M. I., Marghescu, C., Mihailescu, B., & Svasta, P. (2024, May). Does Industry 5.0 need an engineering Education 5.0? Exploring potentials and challenges in the age of generative AI. In *2024 IEEE global engineering education conference (EDUCON)* (pp. 1-10). IEEE.

Coates, A. J. (1997). *The ethics of war*. Manchester University Press.

Crespo-Pereira, D., López-Cedrún, J., García-Álvarez, M. T., & López-Carreiro, I. (2021). AI and satellite-based logistics: A vision for global operations. *Journal of Space Policy and Logistics*, *3*(2), 45–58.

Crews, C. (2023). AI, Land Wars in Asia, and the Classic Blunders of Foresight. *Research Technology Management*, *66*(4), 48–50. DOI: 10.1080/08956308.2023.2208487

Csernatoni, R., Broeders, D., Andersen, L. H., Hoijtink, M., Bode, I., Lindsay, J. R., & Schwarz, E. (2025). Myth, Power, and Agency: Rethinking Artificial Intelligence, Geopolitics and War. *Minds and Machines*, *35*(3), 37. DOI: 10.1007/s11023-025-09741-0

Cummings, M. L. (2019). Artificial Intelligence and the Ethics of Cyber Warfare. *International Journal of Military Ethics*, *18*(2), 123–140.

Da Veiga, A. (2025). Encouraging Creativity and Innovation in the Cybersecurity Culture of the Organisation for Sustainable Value and Growth. In *Diversity, AI, and Sustainability for Financial Growth* (pp. 1-28). IGI Global Scientific Publishing. DOI: 10.4018/979-8-3693-6011-8.ch001

Danks, D., & London, A. J. (2017). Algorithmic Bias in Autonomous Systems. *Proceedings of the 26th International Joint Conference on Artificial Intelligence*, 4691–4697.

Defense Innovation Board. (2021). *AI principles: Recommendations on the ethical use of AI by the Department of Defense*. U.S. Department of Defense. https://innovation.defense.gov

Defense Science Board. (2019). *AI and the Future of Defense Logistics*. U.S. Department of Defense.

Deleuze, G. (2009). 9 'Postscript on the societies of Control.' In *Media studies.* (pp. 89–93). DOI: 10.1515/9781474473231-011

Dencik, L., & Cable, J. (2017). The Advent of Surveillance Realism: Public Opinion and Activist Responses to the Snowden Leaks. *International Journal of Communication, 11*. http://orca.cf.ac.uk/97855/

Di Nucci, E. (2020). *The control paradox: From AI to populism*. Rowman & Littlefield. DOI: 10.5040/9798881816193

Digmelashvili & Lagvilava. (2023). Cyber Deterrence Strategies in the 21st Century. Future Human Image, 20.

Dissanayake, H., & Bracewell, P. J. (2023). Bias in Data-Informed Decision Making. In *Encyclopedia of Data Science and Machine Learning* (pp. 1173–1186). IGI Global. DOI: 10.4018/978-1-7998-9220-5.ch068

Drašar, M. (2023). The Road Towards Autonomous Cybersecurity Agents: Remedies for Simulation Environments. *European Symposium on Research in Computer Security*, Springer.

Drucker, S. J., & Gumpert, G. (2000). CyberCrime and punishment. *Critical Studies in Media Communication*, *17*(2), 133–158. DOI: 10.1080/15295030009388387

Dsouza, D. S. (2024). Deepfakes in Social Engineering Attacks. Space Law Principles and Sustainable Measures. Springer. DOI: 10.1007/978-3-031-64045-2_8

Dugo, D., Kant, S., & Alemu, Z. K. (2025). Servant Leadership Influence on Organizational Citizenship Behavior with the Mediation Role of Emotional Intelligence: A Case of Public Universities in Ethiopia. In *Generation Alpha and Next Generation Leadership for Greener Futures* (pp. 269-292). IGI Global Scientific Publishing. DOI: 10.4018/979-8-3693-9281-2.ch014

el Rahwan, A. (2022). Artificial Intelligence and Interoperability for Solving Challenges of OSINT and Cross-Border Investigations. Eur. L. Enf't Rsch. Bull., 6(179).

Emery, J. R. (2021). Algorithms, AI, and Ethics of War. *Peace Review*, *33*(2), 205–212. DOI: 10.1080/10402659.2021.1998749

Enemark, C. (2025). Loyal Wingmen, Artificial Intelligence, and Cognitive Enhancement: A Warning Against Cyborg-Drone Warfare. *Journal of Military Ethics*, *24*(1), 1–17. DOI: 10.1080/15027570.2025.2507458

Erendor, M. E. (2024). *Cyber Security in the Age of Artificial Intelligence and Autonomous Weapons*. CRC Press. DOI: 10.1201/9781003441700

Eriksen, R. (2005). Transforming military logistics: A necessary revolution. *Joint Forces Quarterly*, (39), 57–65.

Erskine, T. (2024). Before algorithmic Armageddon: Anticipating immediate risks to restraint when AI infiltrates decisions to wage war. *Australian Journal of International Affairs*, *78*(2), 175–190. DOI: 10.1080/10357718.2024.2345636

Erskine, T., & Miller, S. E. (2024). AI and the decision to go to war: Future risks and opportunities. *Australian Journal of International Affairs*, *78*(2), 135–147. DOI: 10.1080/10357718.2024.2349598

Esteban, J. (2022). *Simulating Network Lateral Movements through the CyberBattleSim Web Platform*. Massachusetts Institute of Technology.

European Union Agency for Cybersecurity (ENISA). (2020). *Threat Landscape for Artificial Intelligence*.

Fakhouri, H. N. (2024). Ai-driven solutions for social engineering attacks: Detection, prevention, and response. 2024 2nd International Conference on Cyber Resilience (ICCR), IEEE.

Falade, P. V. (2023). Decoding the threat landscape: Chatgpt, fraudgpt, and wormgpt in social engineering attacks. arXiv preprint arXiv:2310.05595.

Fan, W. Q., Ismail, A. S., Mohammed, F., & Mukred, M. (2025). AI-Driven Smart City Security and Surveillance System: A Bibliometric Analysis. In *Current and Future Trends on AI Applications: Volume 1* (pp. 305–328). Springer. DOI: 10.1007/978-3-031-75091-5_17

Fauzi, M., Jhoni, M., Mohammad, M., Mabruroh, F., & Oviyanti, F. (2024). Implementing the Power of Blended Learning in the Era of AI War in Indonesia; [Implementación del poder del Blended Learning en la era de la guerra de la IA en Indonesia]. *Pixel-Bit. Revista de Medios y Educacion*, *70*, 77–95. DOI: 10.12795/pixelbit.103035

Fisher, K. (2022). The role of gender in providing expert advice on cyber conflict and artificial intelligence for military personnel. *Frontiers in Big Data*, *5*, 992620. DOI: 10.3389/fdata.2022.992620

Fitzgerald, R., & Jenkins, L. (2020). AI in Cybersecurity: Opportunities and Threats in Warfare. *International Conference on AI and Security*, 103–117.

Focarelli, C. (2021). Self-defence in cyberspace. Research handbook on international law and cyberspace. Edward Elgar Publishing. DOI: 10.4337/9781789904253.00026

Fontes, C., Hohma, E., Corrigan, C. C., & Lütge, C. (2022). AI-powered public surveillance systems: Why we (might) need them and how we want them. *Technology in Society*, *71*, 102137. Advance online publication. DOI: 10.1016/j.techsoc.2022.102137

Fuchs, C. (2011). How to define surveillance? *Matrizes*, *5*(1), 109. DOI: 10.11606/issn.1982-8160.v5i1p109-136

Galič, M., Timan, T., & Koops, B. (2016). Bentham, Deleuze and Beyond: An Overview of Surveillance Theories from the Panopticon to Participation. *Philosophy & Technology*, *30*(1), 9–37. DOI: 10.1007/s13347-016-0219-1

Gansler, J. S., & Lucyshyn, W. (2020). Transforming logistics through AI: Enabling agile defense support. *Journal of Defense Analytics and Logistics*, *4*(1), 45–58.

Garcia, D. (2021). Stop the emerging AI cold war. *Nature*, *593*(7858), 169. DOI: 10.1038/d41586-021-01244-z

Garcia, D. (2024). Algorithms and decision-making in military artificial intelligence. *Global Society*, *38*(1), 24–33. DOI: 10.1080/13600826.2023.2273484

García-Huete, E., Ignacio-Cerrato, S., Pacios, D., Vázquez-Poletti, J. L., Pérez-Serrano, M. J., Donofrio, A., Cesarano, C., Schetakis, N., & Di Iorio, A. (2024). Evaluating the role of generative AI and color patterns in the dissemination of war imagery and disinformation on social media. *Frontiers in Artificial Intelligence*, *7*, 1457247. Advance online publication. DOI: 10.3389/frai.2024.1457247

Garza, V. R., (2020). Machine Learning Techniques for Identifying Anomalous Network Traffic. Academic Press.

Gebrehans, G., Ilyas, N., Eledlebi, K., Lunardi, W. T., Andreoni, M., Yeun, C. Y., & Damiani, E. (2025). Generative Adversarial Networks for Dynamic Malware Behavior: A Comprehensive Review, Categorization, and Analysis. *IEEE Transactions on Artificial Intelligence*, *6*(8), 1955–1976. DOI: 10.1109/TAI.2025.3537966

Gellert, G. A., Kuszczyński, K., Gellert, G. L., Kabat-Karabon, A., Nowicka, A., & Price, T. (2025). AI-Based Virtual Triage and Telemedical Health Care for Ukrainian War Refugees and Displaced Persons. *JAMA Network Open*, *8*(5), e258839. Advance online publication. DOI: 10.1001/jamanetworkopen.2025.8839

Ghaleb, M. M. S., & Pardaev, J. (2025). Controlling Cyber Crime through Information Security Compliance Behavior: Role of Cybersecurity Awareness, Organizational Culture and Trust in Management. *International Journal of Cyber Criminology*, *19*(1), 1–26.

Ghosh, A., Chakraborty, D., & Law, A. (2018). Artificial intelligence in Internet of things. *CAAI Transactions on Intelligence Technology*, *3*(4), 208–218. DOI: 10.1049/trit.2018.1008

Giannotti, A., & Proietti, G. (2021). Law of Thasos concerning honors for the war dead and their families [Legge di taso sugli onori ai caduti in guerra e alle loro famiglie]. *Axon (Italy)*, *5*(1), 123–154. DOI: 10.30687/Axon/2532-6848/2021/01/005

Gil de Zúñiga, H., Goyanes, M., & Durotoye, T. (2024). A scholarly definition of artificial intelligence (AI): Advancing AI as a conceptual framework in communication research. *Political Communication*, *41*(2), 317–334. DOI: 10.1080/10584609.2023.2290497

Gilbert, C., & Gilbert, M. A. (2024). The security implications of artificial intelligence (AI)-powered autonomous weapons: Policy recommendations for international regulation. *International Research Journal of Advanced Engineering and Science, 9*(4), 205–219.

Gill, A. S. (2020). The changing role of multilateral forums in regulating armed conflict in the digital age. *International Review of the Red Cross, 102*(913), 261–285. DOI: 10.1017/S1816383121000059

Gioti, A. (2024). *Advancements in Open Source Intelligence (OSINT) Techniques and the role of artificial intelligence in Cyber Threat Intelligence (CTI).* Πανεπιστήμιο Πειραιώς.

Glaessgen, E. H., & Stargel, D. S. (2012). The digital twin paradigm for future NASA and U.S. Air Force vehicles. *53rd AIAA/ASME/ASCE/AHS/ASC Structures, Structural Dynamics and Materials Conference*, 1–14. DOI: 10.2514/6.2012-1818

Goel, A., Goel, A. K., & Kumar, A. (2023). The role of artificial neural network and machine learning in utilizing spatial information. In *Spatial Information Research* (Vol. 31, Issue 3). DOI: 10.1007/s41324-022-00494-x

Goldfarb, A., & Lindsay, J. R. (2021). Prediction and judgment: Why artificial intelligence increases the importance of humans in war. *International Security, 46*(3), 7–50. DOI: 10.1162/isec_a_00425

Gonzalez-Feliu, J., & Morana, J. (2014). *Sustainable urban logistics: Concepts, methods and information systems*. Springer. DOI: 10.1007/978-3-642-31788-0

Gonzalez, M., & Shukla, R. (2022). Predictive maintenance using AI in military equipment logistics. *Defence Science Journal, 72*(1), 34–42. DOI: 10.14429/dsj.72.17042

González, R. J. (2022). *War virtually: the quest to automate conflict, militarize data, and predict the future*. Univ of California Press.

Gordon, C., Coleman, S., & Tavassoli, A. (2021). Cybersecurity in military logistics: The growing role of AI and blockchain. *Military Cyber Affairs, 6*(1), 1–17.

Gunzinger, M., & Dougherty, C. (2020). *Resilient logistics: The key to winning future high-end wars*. Center for Strategic and Budgetary Assessments (CSBA). https://csbaonline.org/research/publications/resilient-logistics

Gururaj, H. (2024). *Social Engineering in Cybersecurity: Threats and Defenses.* CRC Press.

Gustetic, J., Rose, D., & Linick, J. (2021). Trust in human-machine teams: A multi-dimensional perspective. *Journal of Cognitive Engineering and Decision Making*, *15*(1), 3–17. DOI: 10.1177/1555343420959863

Hadjimatheou, K. (2013). The relative moral risks of untargeted and targeted surveillance. *Ethical Theory and Moral Practice*, *17*(2), 187–207. DOI: 10.1007/s10677-013-9428-1

Haggerty, K. D. (2006). Tear down the walls: on demolishing the panopticon 1 2. In *Theorizing surveillance* (pp. 23–45). Willan.

Haggerty, K. D., & Ericson, R. V. (2000). The surveillant assemblage. *The British Journal of Sociology*, *51*(4), 605–622. DOI: 10.1080/00071310020015280 PMID: 11140886

Hall, S. W., Sakzad, A., & Choo, K. R. (2022). Explainable artificial intelligence for digital forensics. *WIREs Forensic Science*, *4*(2), e1434. Advance online publication. DOI: 10.1002/wfs2.1434

Hamilton, M. (2021). Predictive policing through risk assessment. In *Predictive policing and artificial intelligence* (pp. 58–78). Routledge. DOI: 10.4324/9780429265365-4

Haque, S. (2025). Empowering Ethiopia's digital citizenship in early-career health-care leadership. *PLOS Digital Health*, *4*(5), e0000845. DOI: 10.1371/journal.pdig.0000845 PMID: 40333784

Heath, J. (2019). *The Ethics of Cyberwarfare*. Oxford University Press.

Henrico, I. (2025). Modern approaches in military geoscience: Leveraging advanced geospatial technologies for strategic advantage. *Geology Today*, *41*(4), 166–175. DOI: 10.1111/gto.12522

Hoffman, F., & D'Amelio, A. (2024). AI's impact on war's enduring nature. *Orbis*, *68*(1), 72–91. DOI: 10.1016/j.orbis.2023.11.006

Hong, S. H. (2022). Predictions without futures. *History and Theory*, *61*(3), 371–390. DOI: 10.1111/hith.12269

Hong, Y., Chen, T., & Zhang, Y. (2025). Individual intellectual capital, creative process engagement and information security policy compliance. *Journal of Intellectual Capital*, *26*(6), 1–24. DOI: 10.1108/JIC-04-2025-0141

Hosmer, L. T. (1994). Strategic planning as if ethics mattered. *Strategic Management Journal*, *15*(S2), 17–34. DOI: 10.1002/smj.4250151003

Hossain, M. T., Afrin, R., & Biswas, M. A.-A. (2024). A Review on Attacks against Artificial Intelligence (AI) and Their Defence Image Recognition and Generation Machine Learning, Artificial Intelligence. *Control Systems and Optimization Letters*, *2*(1), 52–59. DOI: 10.59247/csol.v2i1.73

Huelss, H. (2024). Transcending the fog of war? US military "AI", vision, and the emergent post-scopic regime. *European Journal of International Security*. DOI: 10.1017/eis.2024.21

Hunter, C., & Bowen, B. E. (2024). We'll never have a model of an AI major-general: Artificial Intelligence, command decisions, and kitsch visions of war. *The Journal of Strategic Studies*, *47*(1), 116–146. DOI: 10.1080/01402390.2023.2241648

Hussain, A., Khan, S. U., Khan, N., Shabaz, M., & Baik, S. W. (2024). AI-driven behavior biometrics framework for robust human activity recognition in surveillance systems. *Engineering Applications of Artificial Intelligence*, *127*, 107218. Advance online publication. DOI: 10.1016/j.engappai.2023.107218

Huston, J. A. (1966). *The Sinews of War: Army Logistics, 1775–1953*. U.S. Army Center of Military History.

Hutchens, J. (2023). *The Language of Deception: Weaponizing Next Generation AI*. John Wiley & Sons.

Hynek, N., & Solovyeva, A. (2021). Operations of power in autonomous weapon systems: Ethical conditions and socio-political prospects. *AI & Society*, *36*(1), 79–99. DOI: 10.1007/s00146-020-01048-1

Ibragimov, I., & Kadagidze, L. (2025). Leadership and Its Correlation with Employee Affective Commitment: A Focus on LMX and OCB in Digital Transformation. *International Journal of Business and Social Science*, *16*, 78–89. DOI: 10.30845/ijbss.v16p6

International Committee of the Red Cross (ICRC). (2021). *Autonomous Weapon Systems: Implications of Increasing Autonomy in the Critical Functions of Weapons*.

Inuwa, M. M., & Das, R. (2024). A comparative analysis of various machine learning methods for anomaly detection in cyber attacks on IoT networks. *Internet of Things : Engineering Cyber Physical Human Systems*, *26*, 101162. DOI: 10.1016/j.iot.2024.101162

Iveković, R. (2018). Enough with Europe's war against migrants [Smetterla con la guerra dell'Europa ai migranti]. *Lectora*, *24*, 13–26. DOI: 10.1344/Lectora2018.24.2

Jafariandehkordi, M. (2024). The AI Battlefield: Legal Challenges of Autonomous Weapon Systems under International Humanitarian Law.

Jafariandehkordi, M. (2024). The AI Battlefield: Legal Challenges of Autonomous Weapon Systems under International Humanitarian Law. Academic Press.

Jeffrey, N., Tan, Q., & Villar, J. R. (2023). A review of anomaly detection strategies to detect threats to cyber-physical systems. *Electronics (Basel)*, *12*(15), 3283. DOI: 10.3390/electronics12153283

Jester, N. (2025). Encountering Virtual Veterans: AI chatbots, martial ontologies, and memories of war. *Critical Military Studies*, *11*(1), 104–108. DOI: 10.1080/23337486.2024.2417622

Jimmy, F. (2021). Emerging threats: The latest cybersecurity risks and the role of artificial intelligence in enhancing cybersecurity defenses. *Valley International Journal Digital Library*, *1*(2), 564–574. DOI: 10.18535/ijsrm/v9i2.ec01

Jio, W., Kant, S., & Lemi, K. (2025). Ethical Leadership: Effect on Future of Organizational Citizenship Behavior by Mediation of Organizational Culture in Ethiopia. In *Generation Alpha and Next Generation Leadership for Greener Futures* (pp. 41-62). IGI Global Scientific Publishing.

Jio, W., Kant, S., & Lemi, K. (2025). The influence of ethical leadership on organizational citizenship behavior by the mediating role of organizational commitment in ethiopia. In *Humanizing the Hyperconnected Workplace* (pp. 221–248). IGI Global Scientific Publishing. DOI: 10.4018/979-8-3693-8171-7.ch008

Johnson, A. F. (2020). Communications, Cyber Resilience, and the Future of the US Electric Power System: *Proceedings of a Workshop*, National Academies Press.

Johnson, J. (2022). The AI commander problem: Ethical, political, and psychological dilemmas of human-machine interactions in AI-enabled warfare. *Journal of Military Ethics*, *21*(3-4), 246–271. DOI: 10.1080/15027570.2023.2175887

Joseph, J., & Pandey, A. (2025). Human-AI Collaborative Intelligence: Ethical and Legal Considerations. In *Humans and Generative AI Tools for Collaborative Intelligence* (pp. 403-422). IGI Global Scientific Publishing.

Justice K.S. Puttaswamy (Retd.) & Anr. vs. Union of India & Ors., 2017 10 SCC 1

Kais, S. (2021). *Quantum Information and Computation for Chemistry*. Wiley.

Kakolu, S., & Faheem, M. A. (2023). Autonomous robotics in field operations: A data-driven approach to optimize performance and safety. *Iconic Research and Engineering Journals*, *7*(4), 565–578.

Kaloudi, N., & Li, J. (2020). The ai-based cyber threat landscape: A survey. *ACM Computing Surveys*, *53*(1), 1–34. DOI: 10.1145/3372823

Kania, E. B. (2018). *Battlefield singularity: Artificial intelligence, military revolution, and China's future military power*. Center for a New American Security. https://www.cnas.org

Kania, E. B. (2022). Artificial intelligence in China's revolution in military affairs. In *Defence Innovation and the 4th Industrial Revolution* (pp. 65–92). Routledge. DOI: 10.4324/9781003268215-4

Kant, S., Adula, M., & Badi, S. (2025). Leading With Wisdom: The Role of Wise Leaders in Ethiopia. In *Harnessing Happiness and Wisdom for Organizational Well-Being* (pp. 361-390). IGI Global Scientific Publishing.

Kant, S., Adula, M., Niguse, T., & Terefe, A. (2025). Future of AI on Job Markets by Mediation of Ethical Considerations in the Horn of Africa. In *Exploring AI Implications on Law, Governance, and Industry* (pp. 293-318). IGI Global Scientific Publishing. DOI: 10.4018/979-8-3373-3384-7.ch012

Kant, I. (1956). *Critique of practical reason* (Beck, L. W., Trans.). The University of Chicago Press.

Kar, S., Yadav, M., & Panda, T. K. (2025). Inclusive organizational behaviour–the dynamic rules of building new workplaces. *VINE Journal of Information and Knowledge Management Systems*, *55*(2), 492–510. DOI: 10.1108/VJIKMS-05-2022-0155

Kebede, D. A., Werke, S. Z., & Kebede, T. A. (2024). Strategic leadership practices in emerging economies: A systematic review and empirical investigation. *Cogent Business & Management*, *11*(1), 2418425. DOI: 10.1080/23311975.2024.2418425

Khan, A. (2025). Future Trends and Challenges in Cybersecurity and Generative AI. Reshaping CyberSecurity With Generative AI Techniques, 491-522.

Khan, F. A., Li, G., Khan, A. N., Khan, Q. W., Hadjouni, M., & Elmannai, H. (2023). AI-Driven Counter-Terrorism: Enhancing Global Security Through Advanced Predictive Analytics. *IEEE Access : Practical Innovations, Open Solutions*, *11*, 135864–135879. Advance online publication. DOI: 10.1109/ACCESS.2023.3336811

Khan, K., Khurshid, A., & Cifuentes-Faura, J. (2024). Is artificial intelligence a new battleground for cybersecurity? *Internet of Things : Engineering Cyber Physical Human Systems*, *28*, 101428. DOI: 10.1016/j.iot.2024.101428

Khan, M. I. (2024). AI's Revolutionary Role in Cyber Defense and Social Engineering. *International Journal of Multidisciplinary Sciences and Arts*, *3*(4), 57–66. DOI: 10.47709/ijmdsa.v3i4.4752

Khoei, T. T., & Singh, A. (2024). A survey of Emotional Artificial Intelligence and crimes: Detection, prediction, challenges and future direction. *Journal of Computational Social Science*, *7*(3), 2359–2402. DOI: 10.1007/s42001-024-00313-3

Kim, S. (2022). The Inter-network Politics of Cyber Security and Middle Power Diplomacy: A Korean Perspective. Korea's Middle Power Diplomacy: Between Power and Network. Springer.

Köbis, N., Bonnefon, J. F., & Rahwan, I. (2021). Bad machines corrupt good morals. *Nature Human Behaviour*, *5*(6), 679–685. DOI: 10.1038/s41562-021-01128-2 PMID: 34083752

Koch, W. (2021). On digital ethics for artificial intelligence and information fusion in the defense domain. *IEEE Aerospace and Electronic Systems Magazine*, *36*(7), 94–111. DOI: 10.1109/MAES.2021.3066841

Kolluri, V. (2024). Revolutionary research on the ai sentry: An approach to overcome social engineering attacks using machine intelligence. *International Journal of Advanced Research and Interdisciplinary Scientific Endeavours*, *1*(1), 53–60.

Kolosnjaji, B. (2024). *Artificial Intelligence for Cybersecurity: Develop AI approaches to solve cybersecurity problems in your organization*. Packt Publishing Ltd.

Konert, A., & Balcerzak, T. (2021). Military autonomous drones (UAVs)-from fantasy to reality. Legal and Ethical implications. *Transportation Research Procedia*, *59*, 292–299. DOI: 10.1016/j.trpro.2021.11.121

Koormala, H., Reddy, C. K. K., Balusa, V. S., Jillapalli, N., & Hanafiah, M. M. (2025). Enhancing urban safety: AI-driven security solutions for smart cities. In *Information Security Governance using Artificial Intelligence of Things in Smart Environments* (pp. 146–163). CRC Press. DOI: 10.1201/9781003606307-7

Korkmaz, S. C. (2024). Emerging Technologies and Power Asymmetry in International System: An Analysis over Artificial Intelligence. *Artificial Intelligence*, 84–99.

Korsgaard, C. M. (2012). *Kant: Groundwork of the Metaphysics of Morals* (2nd ed.). (Gregor, M., & Timmermann, J., Trans.). Cambridge University Press. DOI: 10.1017/CBO9780511919978

Kostka, G., Steinacker, L., & Meckel, M. (2021). Between security and convenience: Facial recognition technology in the eyes of citizens in China, Germany, the United Kingdom, and the United States. *Public Understanding of Science (Bristol, England), 30*(6), 671–690. Advance online publication. DOI: 10.1177/09636625211001555 PMID: 33769157

Kott, A., & Arnold, R. (2017). The Promises and Perils of Artificial Intelligence in National Security. *The Cyber Defense Review, 2*(2), 79–93.

Kott, A., & Perconti, P. (2018). Long-term challenges for autonomous systems. *Computer, 51*(5), 70–75. DOI: 10.1109/MC.2018.2381130

Kuwar, V., Sonavaney, V., Shankar, U., Yadav, A., Radhakrishnan, V., Upreti, K., & Jain, R. (2025). Workforce transformation and value creation in the era of Industry 4.0, 5.0 and 6.0: Challenges and enablers. *Int. J. Basic Appl. Sci, 14*(1), 314–324. DOI: 10.14419/r61ag136

Lavi & Jabotinsky (2025). Seeing is Believing? Deepfakes in Financial Markets. Deepfakes in Financial Markets, 44.

Lazaro, C., & Rizzi, M. (2023). Predictive analytics and governance: A new socio-technical imaginary for uncertain futures. *International Journal of Law in Context, 19*(1), 70–90. DOI: 10.1017/S1744552322000477

Lele, A., & Goswami, P. (2020). Predictive maintenance using AI for military vehicles. *Defence Science Journal, 70*(3), 256–263. DOI: 10.14429/dsj.70.15367

Lepri, B., Oliver, N., & Pentland, A. (2021). Ethical machines: The human-centric use of artificial intelligence. *iScience, 24*(3), 102249. DOI: 10.1016/j.isci.2021.102249 PMID: 33763636

Lewis, D. A. (2023). War crimes involving autonomous weapons: Responsibility, liability and accountability. *Journal of International Criminal Justice, 21*(5), 965–980. DOI: 10.1093/jicj/mqad027

Lhote, F. (2015). The war of Algeria today, between "commemorative period" and fiction: Where I Left My Soul (2010) by Jerome Ferrari [Laguerre d'algérie aujourd'hui, entre 'temps commémoratif' et fiction: où j'ai laissé mon âme (2010) de jérôme ferrari]. *French Studies Bulletin, 36*(137), 83–86. DOI: 10.1093/frebul/ktv022

Lin, Z. (2025). Adaptive Cyber Defense Against APT28: A Comparative Evaluation of Reinforcement Learning-Based Policies in an Emulated Network Environment.

Lin, H. (2016). Attribution of Malicious Cyber Incidents. *Journal of National Security Law & Policy, 6*(1), 1–22.

Longabaugh, E. E. (2020). *Signaling for coercion in cyberspace*. Naval Postgraduate School.

Longpre, S., Storm, M., & Shah, R. (2022). Lethal autonomous weapons systems & artificial intelligence: Trends, challenges, and policies. *Edited by Kevin McDermott. MIT Science Policy Review, 3*, 47-56.

Lucarelli, S. (2021). *NATO decision-making in the age of big data and artificial intelligence*. NATO.

Luttwak, E. N. (2001). *The Grand Strategy of the Roman Empire: From the First Century A.D. to the Third*. Johns Hopkins University Press.

Lyon, D. (2015). *Surveillance after Snowden*. Polity Press. https://site.ebrary.com/id/11115169

Lyon, D. (2010). Liquid Surveillance: The contribution of Zygmunt Bauman to surveillance studies. *International Political Sociology, 4*(4), 325–338. DOI: 10.1111/j.1749-5687.2010.00109.x

Lyon, D. (2017). Digital Citizenship and Surveillancel Surveillance Culture: Engagement, exposure, and ethics in digital modernity. *International Journal of Communication, 11*, 19. https://ijoc.org/index.php/ijoc/article/view/5527

Lysaght, T. (2022). Anticipatory governance and foresight in regulating for uncertainty. *The American Journal of Bioethics, 22*(1), 51–53. DOI: 10.1080/15265161.2021.2001111

Mačák, K. (2017). From cyber norms to cyber rules: Re-engaging states as law-makers. *Leiden Journal of International Law, 30*(4), 877–899. DOI: 10.1017/S0922156517000358

Macnish, K. (2014). Just surveillance? towards a normative theory of surveillance. *Surveillance & Society, 12*(1), 142–153. DOI: 10.24908/ss.v12i1.4515

Mahor, V., Bijrothiya, S., Rawat, R., Kumar, A., Garg, B., & Pachlasiya, K. (2022). IoT and Artificial Intelligence Techniques for Public Safety and Security. In *Smart Urban Computing Applications*. DOI: 10.1201/9781003373247-5

Malatji, M., & Tolah, A. (2024). Artificial intelligence (AI) cybersecurity dimensions: A comprehensive framework for understanding adversarial and offensive AI. *AI and Ethics*, 1–28.

Mann, S., Nolan, J., & Wellman, B. (2002). Sousveillance: Inventing and using wearable computing devices for data collection in surveillance environments. *Surveillance & Society, 1*(3), 331–355. DOI: 10.24908/ss.v1i3.3344

Marrow, A. A. (2025). *Quantum Computing: Evaluating the Threat Landscape and Risk Management Strategies*. Capitol Technology University.

Martin, N. M., Sundermeir, S. M., Barnett, D. J., Van Dongen, E. J., Rosman, L., Rosenblum, A. J., & Gittelsohn, J. (2023). Digital strategies to improve food assistance in disasters: A scoping review. *Disaster Medicine and Public Health Preparedness*, *17*, e40. DOI: 10.1017/dmp.2021.281 PMID: 34632974

Mathiesen, T. (2019). The Viewer Society: Michel Foucault's 'Panopticon' revisited (1997). In *Routledge eBooks* (pp. 506–521). DOI: 10.4324/9780367809195-44

McGinnis, J. O. (2018). Accelerating AI. Research handbook on the law of artificial intelligence. Edward Elgar Publishing.

McGowan, J. (2025). How Thiel, Musk & Omidyar Turned UFO Hype Into A Security Risk. *SSRN*. DOI: 10.2139/ssrn.5261806

McKinsey & Company. (2017). *The future of military logistics: Rethinking supply chain agility and resilience*. https://www.mckinsey.com/industries/public-and-social-sector/our-insights/the-future-of-military-logistics

Meddeb, H., Abdellaoui, Z., & Houaidi, F. (2023). Development of surveillance robot based on face recognition using Raspberry-PI and IOT. *Microprocessors and Microsystems*, *96*, 104728. Advance online publication. DOI: 10.1016/j.micpro.2022.104728

Medvidovic, N., & Edwards, G. (2010). Software architecture and mobility: A roadmap. *Journal of Systems and Software*, *83*(6), 885–898. DOI: 10.1016/j.jss.2009.11.004

Melnychenko, O. (2024). Utilising AI Models to Analyse the Relationship between Battlefield Developments in the Russian-Ukrainian War and Fluctuations in Stock Market Values. *Forum Scientiae Oeconomia*, *12*(4), 83–98. DOI: 10.23762/FSO_VOL12_NO4_5

Mengesha, G. H., Belay, E. G., & Adams, R. (2024). Social justice considerations in developing and deploying AI in Africa. *Data & Policy*, *6*, e65. DOI: 10.1017/dap.2024.73

Meyer, P. (2020). Norms of responsible state behaviour in cyberspace. The ethics of cybersecurity, 347-360.

Milewski, D. (2018). Military contacts of the polish-lithuanian commonwealth and the duchy of prussia in the first years of the livonian war (1600-1602) [Contacts militaires de l'union polonaise-lituanienne et du duché de prusse pendant les premières années de la guerre de livonie (1600-1602).]; [Contactele militare ale uniunii statale polono-lituaniene cu ducatul prusiei în primii ani ai războiului livonian (1600-1602)]. *Codrul Cosminului*, *24*(2), 323–340.

Miller, B. W., & Frazier, A. W. (2021). Machine learning for logistics demand forecasting in military operations. *Military Operations Research*, *26*(1), 19–35. DOI: 10.5711/1082598326115

Minhaj, S. M. U. H. (2023). Study of artificial intelligence in cyber security and the emerging threat of AI-driven cyber attacks and challenge. Available at *SSRN* 4652028.

Mishra, A. K., Tyagi, A. K., Dananjayan, S., Rajavat, A., Rawat, H., & Rawat, A. (2024). Revolutionizing Government Operations. In *Conversational Artificial Intelligence*. DOI: 10.1002/9781394200801.ch34

Mishra, N., Habtemariam, G. M., Esseynew, S., Nayak, R. K., Tripathy, R., & Padhi, B. K. (2024). The Transnational ICT Leadership Assessment Based on the Available Infrastructure in the Governmental Organizations: A Case Study of the Ethiopian Northern Shewa Zone. In *Developments and Future Trends in Transnational Higher Education Leadership* (pp. 301-322). IGI Global. DOI: 10.4018/979-8-3693-2857-6.ch017

Mišić, J. (2021). Ethics and governance in the digital age. *European View*, *20*(2), 175–181. DOI: 10.1177/17816858211061793

Mitgutsch, I. (2021). The war crime of attacking buildings dedicated to religion in light of the trial of Ahmad Al Faqi Al Mahdi [Das Kriegsverbrechen des Angriffs auf der Religion gewidmete Gebäude im Lichte des Verfahrens gegen Ahmad AI Faqi AI Mahdi]. *Osterreichisches Archiv Fur Recht Und Religion*, *68*(1), 15–32.

Monika, E., & Kumar, T. R. (2024). Advancements in AI-based Crime Detection and Prediction. *2024 8th International Conference on Electronics, Communication and Aerospace Technology (ICECA)*, 1557–1562.

Montasari, R. (2023). The Application of Big Data Predictive Analytics and Surveillance Technologies in the Field of Policing. In *Advances in Information Security* (Vol. 101). DOI: 10.1007/978-3-031-21920-7_5

Montasari, R. (2024). *National security in the Artificial Intelligence era: Challenges and implications of advanced technologies*. Cardiff Metropolitan University.

Moriuchi, E. (2021). An empirical study of consumers' intention to use biometric facial recognition as a payment method. *Psychology and Marketing*, *38*(10), 1741–1765. Advance online publication. DOI: 10.1002/mar.21495

Mugari, I., & Obioha, E. E. (2021). Predictive Policing and Crime Control in The United States of America and Europe: Trends in a Decade of Research and the Future of Predictive Policing. *Social Sciences (Basel, Switzerland)*, *10*(6), 234. Advance online publication. DOI: 10.3390/socsci10060234

National Academies of Sciences. (2024). AI for Scientific Discovery. *Proceedings of a Workshop*.

National Institute of Standards and Technology (NIST). (2018). *Framework for Improving Critical Infrastructure Cybersecurity* (Version 1.1). U.S. Department of Commerce.

NATO. (2020). *Science & Technology Trends 2020–2040*. NATO Science and Technology Organization. https://www.nato.int/science/reports/2020-trends

NATO. (2023). *Climate Change and Security Impact Assessment*. NATO Headquarters. https://www.nato.int/cps/en/natohq/topics_91048.htm

Negeri, D. D., Kant, S., & Huluka, A. T. (2025). Knowledge Management Effect on Customer Experience by Mediation of Strategic Leadership in Private Banks in Ethiopia. In *Demystifying Emotion AI, Robotics AI, and Sentiment Analysis in Customer Relationship Management* (pp. 105-128). IGI Global Scientific Publishing. DOI: 10.4018/979-8-3373-1867-7.ch006

Nissenbaum, H., & van den Hoven, J. (2020). Ethical Challenges in Cyber Warfare: The Role of AI and Autonomous Systems. *Ethics and Information Technology*, *22*(1), 17–34.

Nocera, R. (2018). Italy, Latin America, Chile: From the second world war to the early cold war [Italia, America latina, Cile: Dalla Seconda guerra Mondiale ai primi anni della guerra Fredda]. *Acta Histriae*, *26*(3), 673–690. DOI: 10.19233/AH.2018.27

Nye, J. S.Jr. (2016). Deterrence and dissuasion in cyberspace. *International Security*, *41*(3), 44–71. DOI: 10.1162/ISEC_a_00266

O'Meara, A., & Kania, E. (2020). AI and future warfare: Implications for international security. *The Journal of Strategic Studies*, *43*(2), 145–170. DOI: 10.1080/01402390.2020.1773524

O'Regan, J. P., & Ferri, G. (2025). Artificial intelligence and depth ontology: Implications for intercultural ethics. *Applied Linguistics Review*, *16*(2), 797–807. DOI: 10.1515/applirev-2024-0189

Obioha Val, O. (2025). Cyber Espionage in the Age of Artificial Intelligence: A Comparative Study of State-Sponsored Campaign. Cyber Espionage in the Age of Artificial Intelligence: A Comparative Study of State-Sponsored Campaign.

Okeleke, P. A., Ajiga, D., Folorunsho, S. O., & Ezeigweneme, C. (2024). Predictive analytics for market trends using AI: A study in consumer behavior. *International Journal of Engineering Research Updates*, *7*(1), 36–49. DOI: 10.53430/ijeru.2024.7.1.0032

Oniani, D., Hilsman, J., Peng, Y., Poropatich, R. K., Pamplin, J. C., Legault, G. L., & Wang, Y. (2023). Adopting and expanding ethical principles for generative artificial intelligence from military to healthcare. *NPJ Digital Medicine*, *6*(1), 225. DOI: 10.1038/s41746-023-00965-x

Pagallo, U. (2017). *The laws of robots: Crimes, contracts, and torts*. Springer.

Pandey, A. (2026). Harnessing Artificial Intelligence for Sustainable Innovation and Policy: The Eco-Intelligence. In *Leveraging AI for Inclusive and Equitable Development* (pp. 159-178). IGI Global Scientific Publishing.

Pandey, A., & Joseph, J. (2025). Sustainable Service Marketing: The Ethics of Corporate Social Responsibility. In *Strategic Workforce Reskilling in Service Marketing* (pp. 295-314). IGI Global Scientific Publishing.

Pandey, A., & Joseph, J. (2025a). Emerging Trends in Usage of Drone Technology: Exploring the Ethico-Legal Frontiers. *Innovations and Developments in Unmanned Aerial Vehicles*, 171-196.

Payne, B. K., Oesteraas, I., & May, D. C. (2025). Cybersecurity Students' Interest in Government Careers: Impact of Demographic Characteristics and Job Dynamics. *Journal of Applied Security Research*, *20*(1), 1–23. DOI: 10.1080/19361610.2023.2277513

Pezzino, P. (2017). Resistance, civil resistance, war to civilians, divided memories: Notes in the margin of Mario Mirri's essay [Resistenza, resistenza civile, guerra ai civili, memorie divise: Note in margine al saggio di Mario Mirri]. *Societa e Storia*, *2017*(158), 693–704. DOI: 10.3280/SS2017-158007

Pinney, J., Bentotahewa, V., & Tomlinson, M. (2024). Exploring Applications and Implications of Big Data Predictive Analytics in Policing Cyberspace. In *Navigating the Intersection of Artificial Intelligence, Security, and Ethical Governance: Sentinels of Cyberspace* (pp. 1–18). Springer.

Plantinga, P., Shilongo, K., Mudongo, O., Umubyeyi, A., Gastrow, M., & Razzano, G. (2024). Responsible artificial intelligence in Africa: Towards policy learning. *Data & Policy*, *6*, e72. DOI: 10.1017/dap.2024.60

Ploumis, M. (2022). AI weapon systems in future war operations; strategy, operations and tactics. *Comparative Strategy*, *41*(1), 1–18. DOI: 10.1080/01495933.2021.2017739

Pöhler, J. (2025). Keeping the human in the loop: are autonomous decisions inevitable? i-com, 24(1), 9-25.

Poria, S., Cambria, E., Hazarika, D., & Vij, P. (2021). Natural language processing in military communications: Advances and challenges. *IEEE Intelligent Systems*, *36*(2), 72–80. DOI: 10.1109/MIS.2021.3054259

Por, L. Y. (2024). A systematic literature review on the methods and challenges in detecting zero-day attacks: Insights from the recent crowdstrike incident. *IEEE Access : Practical Innovations, Open Solutions*.

Prieto, I., & Blakely, B. (2023). Proposed uses of generative AI in a cybersecurity-focused soar agent. *Proceedings of the AAAI Symposium Series*.

Rahman, A. (2025). *Reinforcement Learning for Cyber Operations: Applications of Artificial Intelligence for Penetration Testing*. John Wiley & Sons. DOI: 10.1002/9781394206483

Raji, I. D., Smart, A., White, R., Mitchell, M., Gebru, T., Hutchinson, B., & Barnes, P. (2020). Closing the AI accountability gap: Defining an end-to-end framework for internal algorithmic auditing. *Conference on Fairness, Accountability, and Transparency (FAT)*. DOI: 10.1145/3351095.3372873

RAND Corporation. (2020). *Leveraging Artificial Intelligence to Improve Army Sustainment*. https://www.rand.org/pubs/research_reports/RR4292.html

Rashid, A. B., Kausik, A. K., Al Hassan Sunny, A., & Bappy, M. H. (2023). Artificial intelligence in the military: An overview of the capabilities, applications, and challenges. *International Journal of Intelligent Systems*, *2023*(1), 8676366. DOI: 10.1155/2023/8676366

Rauch, M., & Ansari, S. (2022). Waging war from remote cubicles: How workers cope with technologies that disrupt the meaning and morality of their work. *Organization Science*, *33*(1), 83–104. DOI: 10.1287/orsc.2021.1555

Razmak, J., Refae, G. A. E., & Farhan, W. (2025). The role of AI applications in production and operations management: Complementing or replacing human labour. *International Journal of Economics and Business Research, 29*(13), 1–28. DOI: 10.1504/IJEBR.2025.146325

Rebala, G. (2019). Machine learning definition and basics. An introduction to machine learning, 1-17.

Regan, M., & Davidovic, J. (2023). Just preparation for war and AI-enabled weapons. *Frontiers in Big Data, 6*, 1020107. Advance online publication. DOI: 10.3389/fdata.2023.1020107

Rickli, J. M., & Mantellassi, F. (2023). Artificial intelligence in warfare: military uses of AI and their international security implications. In *The AI wave in defence innovation* (pp. 12–36). Routledge. DOI: 10.4324/9781003218326-2

Riesen, E. (2022). The moral case for the development and use of autonomous weapon systems. *Journal of Military Ethics, 21*(2), 132–150. DOI: 10.1080/15027570.2022.2124022

Rodriguez, M. (2025). A framework for evaluating emerging cyberattack capabilities of ai. arXiv preprint arXiv:2503.11917.

Ross, D. (2002). The right and the good. In *Oxford University Press eBooks*. DOI: 10.1093/0199252653.001.0001

Roy, K. (2024). *Artificial intelligence, ethics and the future of warfare: Global perspectives*. Taylor & Francis. DOI: 10.4324/9781003421849

Rudolph, J., Tan, S., & Tan, S. (2023). War of the chatbots: Bard, Bing Chat, ChatGPT, Ernie and beyond. The new AI gold rush and its impact on higher education. *Journal of Applied Learning and Teaching, 6*(1), 364–389. DOI: 10.37074/jalt.2023.6.1.23

Ruppert, L. (2024). Geopolitics of technological futures: Warfare technologies and future battlefields in German security debates. *Geopolitics, 29*(2), 581–606. DOI: 10.1080/14650045.2023.2174431

Saharan, S. (2024). Cyber Forensics: A Boon to Cybersecurity. Digital Technologies in Modeling and Management: Insights in Education and Industry. IGI Global.

Saharan, S. (2024). The future of Cyber-Crimes and cyber war in the metaverse. Forecasting cyber crimes in the age of the metaverse. IGI Global Scientific Publishing.

Saharan, S. (2025). Human-AI Collaboration in Moderating AI-Generated Harmful Content. Content Moderation in the Age of AI. IGI Global Scientific Publishing.

Saharan, S. (2025). Role of Drones in Climate Change Mitigation and Adaptation. Artificial General Intelligence-Based Drones for Climate Change. IGI Global Scientific Publishing. DOI: 10.4018/979-8-3693-6457-4.ch003

Saharan, S., & Yadav, B. (2022). Digital and cyber forensics: A contemporary evolution in forensic sciences. Crime Scene Management within Forensic Science: Forensic Techniques for Criminal Investigations. Springer.

Sahebi, S., & Formosa, P. (2024). Artificial Intelligence (AI) and Global Justice. *Minds and Machines*, *35*(1), 4. DOI: 10.1007/s11023-024-09708-7

Sakr, G., & Hakme, O. (2025). The Impact of Artificial Intelligence on Military and Security in the MENA. In *AI in the Middle East for Growth and Business: A Transformative Force* (pp. 363–383). Springer Nature Switzerland. DOI: 10.1007/978-3-031-75589-7_21

Saniuk, S. (2024). *Smart Organizations in Industry 5.0: A Human-centric Approach*. Taylor & Francis.

Sanjeewani, P., Neuber, G., Fitzgerald, J., Chandrasena, N., Potums, S., Alavi, A., & Lane, C. (2024). Real-time personal protective equipment non-compliance recognition on AI edge cameras. *Electronics (Basel)*, *13*(15), 2990. DOI: 10.3390/electronics13152990

Sarker, I. H. (2024). *AI-driven cybersecurity and threat intelligence: cyber automation, intelligent decision-making and explainability*. Springer Nature. DOI: 10.1007/978-3-031-54497-2

Schmid, S., Lambach, D., Diehl, C., & Reuter, C. (2025). Arms race or innovation race? Geopolitical AI development. *Geopolitics*, *30*(4), 1–30. DOI: 10.1080/14650045.2025.2456019

Schmitt, M. N. (2020). Autonomous weapon systems and international humanitarian law: A reply to the critics. *Harvard National Security Journal*, *4*(1), 1–37.

Science, C. (2025). The Age of AI in the Life Sciences: Benefits and Biosecurity Considerations. Academic Press.

Shandilya, S. K. (2023). GPT Based Malware: Unveiling Vulnerabilities and Creating a Way Forward in Digital Space. *2023 International Conference on Data Security and Privacy Protection (DSPP)*, IEEE. DOI: 10.1109/DSPP58763.2023.10404552

Sharkey, N. (2019). Autonomous weapons systems, killer robots and human dignity. *Ethics and Information Technology*, *21*(2), 75–87. DOI: 10.1007/s10676-018-9494-0

Sharma, A., Kumar, P., & Singh, M. (2021). AI-based route optimization in dynamic logistics environments: Military applications and challenges. *Defense Transportation Journal*, *77*(3), 22–31.

Sharma, D. (2025). *Artificial Intelligence for Cyber Security and Industry 4.0*. CRC Press. DOI: 10.1201/9781032657264

Sifakis, J., & Harel, D. (2023). Trustworthy autonomous system development. *ACM Transactions on Embedded Computing Systems*, *22*(3), 1–24. DOI: 10.1145/3545178

Sigfrids, A., Nieminen, M., Leikas, J., & Pikkuaho, P. (2022). How should public administrations foster the ethical development and use of artificial intelligence? A review of proposals for developing governance of AI. *Frontiers in Human Dynamics*, *4*, 858108. DOI: 10.3389/fhumd.2022.858108

Sikder, A. K., Petracca, G., Aksu, H., Jaeger, T., & Uluagac, A. S. (2021). A survey on sensor-based threats and attacks to smart devices and applications. *IEEE Communications Surveys and Tutorials*, *23*(2), 1125–1159. DOI: 10.1109/COMST.2021.3064507

Singh, T. (2024). *Artificial Intelligence and Ethics: A Field Guide for Stakeholders*. CRC Press. DOI: 10.1201/9781003502708

Solf, W. A. (2023). Protection of civilians against the effects of hostilities under customary international law and under protocol. In *The Conduct of Hostilities in International Humanitarian Law* (Vol. I, pp. 3–21). Routledge. DOI: 10.4324/9781003417255-3

Sołtysik, M., Gawłowska, M., Śnieżyński, B., & Gunia, A. (Eds.). (2024). *Artificial Intelligence, Management and Trust*. Routledge.

Stan, A. (2020). Genres of realism across the former cold war divide. Neoliberal novels and self-fiction [genuri ale realismului la cei doi fo ti poli ai războiului rece. Romanul neoliberal i autofic iunea]. *Dacoromania Litteraria*, *7*, 116–125. DOI: 10.33993/drl.2020.7.116.125

Stark, L., & Hoey, J. (2021, March). The ethics of emotion in artificial intelligence systems. In *Proceedings of the 2021 ACM conference on fairness, accountability, and transparency* (pp. 782-793). DOI: 10.1145/3442188.3445939

Steeves, V. (2009). Reclaiming the social value of privacy. In *Lessons from the Identity Trail: Anonymity* (pp. 191–208). Identity and Privacy in a Networked Society. DOI: 10.1093/oso/9780195372472.003.0011

Sticher, V. (2025a). War and peace in the age of AI. *British Journal of Politics and International Relations*, *27*(2), 542–550. DOI: 10.1177/13691481241293066

Strikwerda, L. (2021). Predictive policing: The risks associated with risk assessment. *The Police Journal*, *94*(3), 422–436. Advance online publication. DOI: 10.1177/0032258X20947749

Syllaidopoulos, I., Ntalianis, K., & Salmon, I. (2025). A Comprehensive Survey on AI in Counter-Terrorism and Cybersecurity: Challenges and Ethical Dimensions. *IEEE Access : Practical Innovations, Open Solutions*, *13*, 91740–91764. DOI: 10.1109/ACCESS.2025.3572348

Szabadföldi, I. (2021). Artificial intelligence in military application–opportunities and challenges. *Land Forces Academy Review*, *26*(2), 157–165. DOI: 10.2478/raft-2021-0022

Tabassi, E., Burns, K. J., Hadjimichael, M., Molina-Markham, A. D., & Sexton, J. T. (2019). A taxonomy and terminology of adversarial machine learning. *NIST IR*, *2019*, 1–29. DOI: 10.6028/NIST.IR.8269-draft

Taddeo, M., & Floridi, L. (2019). "The Ethics of Cyberwarfare." *In Ethics in the Age of Technology*, Springer, 143-160.

Taddeo, M., & Floridi, L. (2021). Regulate artificial intelligence to avert cyber arms race. Ethics, Governance, and Policies in Artificial Intelligence. Springer. DOI: 10.1007/978-3-030-81907-1_14

Taddeo, M. (2024). *The Ethics of Artificial Intelligence in Defence*. Oxford University Press. DOI: 10.1093/oso/9780197745441.001.0001

Taddeo, M., & Blanchard, A. (2023). A comparative analysis of the definitions of autonomous weapons. In *The 2022 yearbook of the digital governance research group* (pp. 57–79). Springer Nature Switzerland. DOI: 10.1007/978-3-031-28678-0_6

Taddeo, M., & Floridi, L. (2018). Regulate Artificial Intelligence to Avert Cyber Arms Races. *Nature*, *556*(7701), 296–298. DOI: 10.1038/d41586-018-04602-6 PMID: 29662138

Tanikonda, A. (2022). Advanced AI-Driven Cybersecurity Solutions for Proactive Threat Detection and Response in Complex Ecosystems. *Journal of Science and Technology*, *3*(1).

Tan, K. H., Lim, C. P., & Platts, K. (2019). Real-time logistics systems and the Internet of Military Things: Towards autonomous battlefield resupply. *International Journal of Production Research*, *57*(9), 2760–2773. DOI: 10.1080/00207543.2018.1511535

Tanti, R. (2024). Study of Phishing Attack and their Prevention Techniques. International journal of scientific research in engineering and management, 10(8), 1-8.

Tapscott, B. (2024). *Trivergence: Accelerating Innovation with AI, Blockchain, and the Internet of Things*. John Wiley & Sons.

Tapscott, D., & Tapscott, A. (2016). *Blockchain revolution: How the technology behind bitcoin is changing money, business, and the world*. Penguin.

Tayyab, M. (2025). AI-Powered Threat Detection in Business Environments: Strategies and Best Practices. Generative AI for Web Engineering Models. IGI Global.

Thakur, N., Nagrath, P., Jain, R., Saini, D., Sharma, N., & Hemanth, D. J. (2021). Artificial Intelligence Techniques in Smart Cities Surveillance Using UAVs: A Survey. In *Studies in Computational Intelligence* (Vol. 971). DOI: 10.1007/978-3-030-72065-0_18

Thealla, P., Nadda, V., Dadwal, S., Oztosun, L., & Cantafio, G. (Eds.). (2024). *Corporate Cybersecurity in the Aviation, Tourism, and Hospitality Sector*. IGI Global. DOI: 10.4018/979-8-3693-2715-9

Tolk, A., Diallo, S. Y., & Turnitsa, C. D. (2020). *Modeling and Simulation Support for System of Systems Engineering Applications*. Wiley.

Tranter, R., & Earley, B. (2022). Automated diagnostics in combat zones: The role of AI in technical maintenance. *Defense Technology Review*, *9*(2), 30–39.

Tufa, G., Kinde, Z., & Kant, S. (2025). Strategic Leadership: Effect on Employee Performance With Mediation of Dynamic Capabilities in Case of Ethiopian Public Organizations. In *Generation Alpha and Next Generation Leadership for Greener Futures* (pp. 115-138). IGI Global Scientific Publishing.

U.S. Department of Defense. (2021). *Artificial Intelligence and Military Modernization Report*. https://media.defense.gov/2021/Mar/01/AI-logistics-report

Umbrello, S., Bernstein, M. J., Vermaas, P. E., Resseguier, A., Gonzalez, G., Porcari, A., Grinbaum, A., & Adomaitis, L. (2023). From speculation to reality: Enhancing anticipatory ethics for emerging technologies (ATE) in practice. *Technology in Society*, *74*, 102325. DOI: 10.1016/j.techsoc.2023.102325

United Nations Group of Governmental Experts (UN GGE). (2021). *Norms of Responsible State Behavior in Cyberspace*. United Nations Office for Disarmament Affairs.

Urueña, S. (2021). Responsibility through anticipation? The 'future talk'and the quest for plausibility in the governance of emerging technologies. *NanoEthics*, *15*(3), 271–302. DOI: 10.1007/s11569-021-00408-5

Usama, M., Ullah, U., & Sajid, A. (2024). Cyber attacks against intelligent transportation systems. In *Cyber Security for Next-Generation Computing Technologies* (pp. 190–230). CRC Press.

Van Creveld, M. (1977). *Supplying War: Logistics from Wallenstein to Patton*. Cambridge University Press.

Van Der Aalst, W. M. (2021). Hybrid Intelligence: To automate or not to automate, that is the question. *International Journal of Information Systems and Project Management*, *9*(2), 5–20. DOI: 10.12821/ijispm090201

Vargas-Hernandez, J. G., & González-Ávila, F. J. (2025). Organizational citizenship behavior: enhancing workplace dynamics. *Evolving Strategies for Organizational Management and Performance Evaluation*, 445-462.

Vykhodets, R. S. (2022). Large AI Spaces and Russia's Strategy in the Context of the "Sanctions War." *Vestnik RUDN. International Relations*, *22*(2), 256–270. DOI: 10.22363/2313-0660-2022-22-2-256-270

Waizel, G. (2024). Bridging the AI divide: The evolving arms race between AI-driven cyber attacks and AI-powered cybersecurity defenses. International Conference on Machine Intelligence & Security for Smart Cities (TRUST) Proceedings.

Wallace, R. (2020). Cognitive instabilities under contention, friction, and the fog-of-war challenge the AI revolution. *Connection Science*, *32*(3), 264–279. DOI: 10.1080/09540091.2019.1684441

Walzer, M. (2006). *Just and unjust wars : a moral argument with historical illustrations* (4th ed.). Basic Books.

Wang, H., Li, J., & Zhang, Y. (2023). Digital twin-based logistics optimization in military operations. *Journal of Defense Modeling and Simulation*, *20*(2), 118–131. DOI: 10.1177/15485129221110932

West, P. (2023). "The Generative AI paradox": What it can create, it may not understand. arXiv preprint arXiv:2311.00059.

Wood, N. G. (2024). Explainable AI in the military domain. *Ethics and Information Technology*, *26*(2), 29. DOI: 10.1007/s10676-024-09762-w

Xue, Y., Fang, C., & Dong, Y. (2021). The impact of new relationship learning on artificial intelligence technology innovation. *International Journal of Innovation Studies*, *5*(1), 2–8. DOI: 10.1016/j.ijis.2020.11.001

Yao, M., Yang, L., & Shen, H. (2023). AI in battlefield healthcare logistics: Trends, technologies, and ethics. *Military Medicine*, *188*(3-4), e701–e710. DOI: 10.1093/milmed/usac255

Yaseen, A. (2022). Accelerating the SOC: Achieve greater efficiency with AI-driven automation. *International Journal of Responsible Artificial Intelligence*, *12*(1), 1–19.

Yu, J. (2024). The Shadow of Fraud: The Emerging Danger of AI-powered Social Engineering and its Possible Cure. arXiv preprint arXiv:2407.15912.

Yun, M. H., Rhiu, I., Kim, W., Lee, Y., & Kim, Y. M. (2022). AI in human behavior analysis. In *Human-Centered Artificial Intelligence* (pp. 191–204). Elsevier. DOI: 10.1016/B978-0-323-85648-5.00010-4

Zhang, J., Wu, P., London, J., & Tenney, D. (2025). Benchmarking and Evaluating Large Language Models in Phishing Detection for Small and Midsize Enterprises: A Comprehensive Analysis. *IEEE Access : Practical Innovations, Open Solutions*, *13*, 28335–28352. DOI: 10.1109/ACCESS.2025.3540075

Zhao, Y., Meng, M. Q. H., & Hu, X. (2022). Autonomous systems for military transport logistics. *Robotics and Autonomous Systems*, *147*, 103903. DOI: 10.1016/j.robot.2021.103903

Zhong, Y., Oh, S., & Moon, H. C. (2021). Service transformation under industry 4.0: Investigating acceptance of facial recognition payment through an extended technology acceptance model. *Technology in Society*, *64*, 101515. Advance online publication. DOI: 10.1016/j.techsoc.2020.101515

Zhou, R., & Miao, X. (2021). Emergency logistics coordination in complex terrains using AI and UAVs. *Journal of Humanitarian Logistics and Supply Chain Management*, *11*(2), 145–160.

Zhou, X., & Kim, J. (2021). “AI and Cyber Defense: From Deterrence to Active Defense.” *Proceedings of the 13th International Conference on Artificial Intelligence and Cybersecurity*, 42–53.

About the Contributors

Latif Oztosun is a seasoned educator and industry professional specializing in Tourism, Hospitality, and Event Management. With a strong background in both academia and the tourism sector, Latif serves as a Lecturer at the University of Sunderland in London and is a Programme Coordinator with over a decade of teaching experience. He holds a Master's degree in International Tourism and Hospitality Management from the University of Greenwich and a Diploma in Education and Training from Canterbury Christ Church University. As a Senior Fellow of Advance HE and a certified Microsoft Educator, Latif demonstrates a commitment to innovative teaching practices, particularly in digital learning technologies. His research focuses on sustainable and responsible planning practices in tourism and the transformative role of digital learning technologies. Currently pursuing a PhD, his thesis explores the impact of vocational education in prisons on reintegration and reducing recidivism. Beyond academia, Latif is actively involved in his community as a Local Parish Councillor and Chair of Planning. Latif's published works include studies on enhancing learning experiences through digital strategies and the societal impacts of tourism development. His passion for fostering student success and advancing the tourism field underscores his professional endeavours.

* * *

Munir Ahmad is a seasoned professional in the realm of Spatial Data Infrastructure (SDI), Geo-Information Productions, Information Systems, and Information Governance, boasting over 25 years of dedicated experience in the field. With a PhD in Computer Science, Dr. Ahmad's expertise spans Spatial Data Production, Management, Processing, Analysis, Visualization, and Quality Control. Throughout his career, Dr. Ahmad has been deeply involved in the development and deployment of SDI systems specially in the context of Pakistan, leveraging his proficiency in Spatial Database Design, Web, Mobile & Desktop GIS, and Geo Web

Services Architecture. His contributions to Volunteered Geographic Information (VGI) and Open Source Geoportal & Metadata Portal have significantly enriched the geospatial community. As a trainer and researcher, Dr. Ahmad has authored over 50 publications, advancing the industry's knowledge base and fostering innovation in Geo-Tech, Data Governance, and Information Infrastructure, and Emerging Technologies. His commitment to Research and Development (R&D) is evident in his role as a dedicated educator and mentor in the field.

Rajarshi Chakraborty is an Assistant Professor with an MPhil and PhD in International Studies from Jawaharlal Nehru University (JNU), New Delhi. His research interests include migration studies, foreign policy, and peacebuilding. He has presented papers at various national and international conferences, appeared on foreign media to discuss global issues, and has published articles in both Indian and international newspapers.

Shampa Dev is a Professor of Law at the School of Law, CHRIST University.

Minakshi Shashikant Ghorpade is pursuing her PhD in Information Technology from Mumbai University. She has earned her Bachelor's degree in Computer Science and Engineering from Shivaji University, Kolhapur & Master's degree in Computer Engineering from University of Mumbai. Currently she is working as an Assistant Professor in the Department of Information Technology, Thakur College of Engineering & Technology. Her area of interest is Software Engineering & Data Mining. She has more than 11 years' experience in the teaching field.

S. Ida Evangeline is presently working as an Assistant Professor in the Department of Electrical and Electronics Engineering at the Government College of Engineering, Tirunelveli, Tamilnadu, India. She obtained her Bachelor's in Electrical and Electronics Engineering from Manonmaniam Sundaranar University in 2003, and Master's in Power Systems Engineering from Anna University, Chennai, Tamilnadu, India in 2005. She completed her PhD degree in 2023 at Anna University, Chennai, Tamilnadu, India. She has published six research papers in international journals. Her current research interests include optimal power flow, renewable energy, soft computing, machine learning, and deep learning.

Barno Matchanova is working at Department of National Idea and Philosophy, Urgench State Pedagogical Institute, Uzbekistan.

Neeta P. is an Associate Professor in the Department of Information Technology at Thakur College of Engineering and Technology. She holds a Master's in

Engineering and a Ph.D. in Technology from the University of Mumbai. Dr. Patil has authored over 21 research papers in esteemed national and international journals and has actively participated in numerous conferences at both levels. As a reviewer for reputed international journals, she contributes significantly to the academic community. With more than 19 years of experience teaching undergraduate and postgraduate students, she has excelled in various academic and administrative roles, showcasing remarkable expertise and leadership in the field of education.

Ananya Pandey is a Research Scholar in School of Law at Christ University, Bangalore. She has her research interests in the field of Constitutional Law, Environment Law, Human Rights, Food Security, Intellectual Property Law and Jurisprudence.

Pratibha R. Prasad is an Assistant Professor of Information Technology at Thakur College of Engg. and Technology, Mumbai, with an M.Tech in Computer Science and Engineering from Shivaji University. She teaches core subjects including Database Management Systems, Cloud Computing, Advanced Java, Python, and Software Testing, and is known for her student-centric teaching and strong technical proficiency. With prior experience as a Assistant Professor at TCET College and she continues to contribute to academic growth through effective teaching, research interest, and active participation in institutional activities.

Sameer Saharan is a dedicated researcher in Forensic Science, specializing in fingerprint analysis, cyber forensics, and DNA fingerprinting. He holds a Ph.D. in Forensic Science from Amity University, Haryana, and has authored several research papers and book chapters. With a passion for continuous learning, Dr. Saharan actively contributes to the advancement of forensic science through his expertise and knowledge. He is committed to nurturing the next generation of forensic scientists and making a positive impact in the field.

Purvi Sankhe is currently pursuing a Ph.D. in Computer Science and Engineering. She holds a Master's degree in Computer Engineering. Her areas of specialization include Software Engineering, Human–Computer Interaction (HCI), and Artificial Intelligence & Machine Learning (AI/ML). With a strong passion for research and innovation, she has published over 55 + research papers in reputed national and international journals and conferences. She is also the author of two published books, contributing to the advancement of knowledge in the field of computing and technology.

Sandeep Sharda is an assistant professor at SIOM, Nashik. He is an Engineering graduate with PhD in spare parts inventory management in 2022. PhD was based on wider spectrum perspective to petroleum and fertilizer industries across India and Gulf. He has double MBA in H.R.M., Materials and Finance in 2009 and 2015 respectively. He was faculty member in management department with Rajasthan Technical University since 2007 prior to join SIOM. Published three Copyrights on Inventory Management (analytical and qualitative models), Book chapter with CRC Press, T & F, Book chapters on Project Management (MBA Course) with Vardhman University, Presented paper at IIM Indore, a Scopus paper with few more published in international journal of repute. In the past, he has worked for 16 years with industries in companies like Reliance industries, Chambal Fertilizers and abroad with SABIC Kingdom of Saudi Arabia. Dr. Sharda has been a faculty in Operations, Project Management, SCM, SAP-MM, Analytics with an expertise of planning and scheduling software like MSP, Primavera. He has developed and conducted many unique modules of MDP's. pertaining to Project management, inventory management, SCM, advance procurement management and reliability centered maintenance.

Mridu Sharma is an Assistant Professor of Forensic Science at Mody University of Science and Technology, Rajasthan. She holds a Ph.D. in Forensic Sciences from Amity University, Noida. Her research interests include fingerprint analysis, questioned documents, cyber forensics, and forensic chemistry. Dr. Sharma has authored several research papers and book chapters with publishers such as Taylor & Francis, IGI Global, and Scrivener Publishing.

Index

M

N

O

P

Q

R

S

T

www.ingramcontent.com/pod-product-compliance
Lightning Source LLC
LaVergne TN
LVHW081521300926
849161LV00006B/1250